BEYOND YOUR
WILDEST DREAMS . . .

I believe life is an eternal spiritual journey. By constructively meeting your daily obstacles you develop talents and achieve growth, thus fulfilling your eternal mandate. Dreams are a monitoring system that stems from the soul. They are a tool to help you deal with the concrete, here-and-now part of this eternal journey of the spirit.

Have you ever dreamed of making love to a relative and wondered what it meant? How would you like dreams to help you lose weight or to help you stop smoking? How would you like a regular health report from the one who is most familiar with your body—your own psyche? How would you like an accurate, educated guess as to how a decision will turn out? Would you like to stabilize and enhance your growth as a human being, as a friend, and as a soul? Would you like to expand your present talents and discover new ones? If you would like any of these things, then you have a reason to use your dreams!

THE BEDSIDE GUIDE TO DREAMS

Stase Michaels, M.A.

FAWCETT CREST • NEW YORK

A Fawcett Crest Book
Published by Ballantine Books
Copyright © 1995 by Stase Michaels

Library of Congress Catalog Card Number: 95-90664

ISBN 0-449-22384-1

Printed in Canada

First Edition: January 1996

10 9 8 7

Dedicated to You

You have a sword. You may not know it, but you have a sword of excellence, a talent that is so powerful that when you use it, others become quiet with wonder and feel amazingly loved. It may be a mother's smile that leaves others feeling safe and special. It may be the gleam of truth in a teacher's eye that inspires a reluctant student to step forward and dare to become all he can be. It may be a businessman's ability to put forth a superior product, and at a fair price no less. Such acts quietly but brilliantly transform the world. This book is dedicated to that sword in you. If you already know the talent that most expresses you and you use it, then God bless you; go ahead and use it with even more brilliance after reading this book. If you have not yet discovered your special self to express to the world, go ahead and find the tools that will empower you to discover that self.

There are many ways to put yourself in touch with who you really are and your ability to express it. One of my once-in-a-while-all-time-favorites is the Landmark Education Seminar (see Appendix for further information). If something leaves you stuck or unable to express yourself or you are unhappy and don't even know why, take their Three-Day Seminar and be miraculously transformed as I was and thousands of others have been, yes, in only three days. My personal-all-time-favorite-everyday tools are meditation and, of course, dreams, which is why I wrote this book. If this book puts you in touch with yourself through your dreams and furthers you in your efforts to bring your talents into the world, then my sword has flashed successfully. If this book leaves you feeling empowered as you go about your regular business, then it has done its work. This book is an expression of my love for you and my knowledge that your unique talent is a gift the world is waiting for. Find your gift and share it loudly and clearly. This book is dedicated to you, a fellow explorer on this Journey of Light.

> I am a part of all that I have met;
> Yet all experience is an arch wherethru'
> Gleams that untravelled road whose margin fades
> For ever and for ever when I move . . .
> How dull it is to pause, to make an end,
> To rust unburnished, not to shine in use!
> As though to breathe were life! Life piled on life
> Were all too little, and of one to me
> Little remains; but every hour is saved
> From that eternal silence, something more,
> A bringer of new things; and vile it were
> For some three suns to store and hoard myself,
> And this gray spirit yearning in desire
> To follow knowledge like a sinking star
> Beyond the utmost bound of human thought.
> —*Tennyson's Ulysses,*
> *as he begins another journey*

Contents

SECTION I

SECTION II
The 27 Dream Types

SECTION I

◊

SECTION 1

The Dream Adventure:
A Terrific Gift to Give
Yourself

AN INITIATION

Here she was, a sensitive but daring nineteen-year-old college student, climbing the narrow staircase leading to the attic of a dark, old creaky house—the kind you see in haunted-house movies! There was a heavy wooden door at the top of the stairs. She knew a very old woman stood behind the door holding a huge ax in her hand, intent on killing her if she entered. In semi-shock she continues because, aside from the dangerous old lady, the attic contains a secret that can change her life! She reaches the top and, taking a deep breath, opens the door, freezing in her tracks as the ax in the old woman's hand strikes down toward her skull.

I shot straight up in my bed and woke up terrified. This was my initiation into the study of dreams. As a psychology student in my junior year of college, I had just read psychologist Carl Jung's book *Memories, Dreams, and Reflections*, in which he gives an account of exploring his life via dreams. I decided to do the same. I was intensely excited at the prospect of discovering my true self through dreams, as Jung had done, and I could hardly wait to begin my dream journey. I fell into a happy sleep on that first night, and could hardly wait to see what my dream would be. What a shock it was to meet the old woman's murderous threat!

At the time I didn't know what the dream meant. I went back to sleep feeling quite sober, but I somehow knew that something good had happened. Now, years later, I know the old woman represented a part of myself, the part carrying hidden fears of getting to know myself. I didn't know that by deciding to use my dreams for personal growth, I was knocking on the doors of my unconscious for the very first time, and I felt a bit like an intruder. This was like an ancient knight riding his noble steed through a deep, dark forest to rescue a princess, unaware of what lurks within.

The old woman was a convenient symbol of my fears since, as a child, I would collapse into terrified tears if I saw anyone who was gray and wrinkled. She represented the "old self" I was now ready to do away with. Climbing the stairs was an image that paralleled my decision to continue to explore my dreams despite my fears; the upward direction implied that I was trying to reach the higher awareness in myself that was at stake, that was the prize at the end of my fear. As the ax fell, the doors of my unconscious opened. What died was my old self, a fearful, limited, child part of me that would have held me back from growing.

As I fell back to sleep, I knew at some mystical level that I had just cut some psychological apron string and was entering a new era of my life as an adventurous adult. Those instincts were correct, because the dream journey turned out to be the best inner adventure I could have hoped to encounter, a kaleidoscope that's not only useful, but also enchanting.

That first dream I had was an initiation dream. Such initiation dreams give you the opportunity to make a decision and the chance to ask yourself: "Do I really want to get to know myself?" If the answer is yes, then you go forward in the dream no matter what the obstacle, just as I did. In case you should meet such an initiation dream, you'll be glad to know that I haven't had another one like it and I don't expect to. My experience of working with dream groups, traveling across the country giving seminars, and using dreams in counseling has taught me that the doors of the unconscious are always friendly ones. And just in case you don't remember too many of your dreams to begin with, don't worry about it. Like a trickle that becomes a stream and turns into a refreshing lake, a desire to use your dreams will quickly stimulate your recall. So if you are interested, hang in there.

WHAT USE ARE YOUR DREAMS?

I believe life is an eternal spiritual journey. By constructively meeting your daily obstacles, you develop talents and achieve growth, thus fulfilling your eternal mandate. Dreams are a monitoring system that stems from the soul. They are a tool to help you deal with the concrete here-and-now part of this eternal journey of the spirit.

Have you ever dreamed of making love with a relative and wondered what it meant? How would you like dreams to help you lose weight or to help you stop smoking? How would you like a regular health report from the one who is most familiar with your body—your own psyche? How would you like an accurate, educated guess as to how a decision will turn out? Would you like to stabilize and enhance your growth as a human being, as a friend, and as a soul? Would you like to expand your present talents and discover new ones? If you would like any of these things, then you have a reason to use your dreams.

SIGNPOSTS ALONG THE ROAD

In Section II of this book you will discover twenty-seven different kinds of dreams. Each dream type comes to you with a different mission and brings you a special type of message. For each dream type, you will share stories of how real people used their dreams. These stories will illustrate how dreams translate into help for real-life situations. Names have been changed, but every shared dream episode is a true story of how someone used practical insights from his dreams to help him live a full life. In order to distinguish each dream type, at the end of every chapter you will find a summary of unique features of that dream type that will help you recognize it in your own dream landscape. As you share others' stories and explore your own dreams, you will see that your dreams have the power to put you directly in touch with who you really are. Know that your dreams are a natural tool that anyone can learn to use. Just like the car you drive, dreams take you only where you want to go, as far as you want to go, and at your own speed. You can rush headlong into exploring your dreams, or you can take twenty years to explore every fascinating twist and turn in the dream pathway, savoring the landscape every step along the way, as I did. Happy trails to you. . . .

An Introduction to Dreams

MODERN PERSPECTIVES ON DREAMS

Sigmund Freud

Freud, this century's most famous psychoanalyst and psychologist, was not the first to study dreams. Distinguished predecessors such as Scottish physician Robert McNish (1802–1837) noticed that "a man wearing a damp nightshirt" dreamed of being dragged through a stream. This brought up the question of whether sensations of the body produce dreams. By the time Freud came onto the scene, research on how physical stimuli affect dreams was quite the rage. Recent research disproves this notion; instead, it confirms that outside factors such as cold or noise can affect the small details of a dream, but do not change a dream's overall story.

Freud was the first, though, to identify the subconscious as the part of the mind that stores all our memories and desires. In the area of dreams, the identification of the unconscious became a major contribution that enabled us to understand how dreams are linked to daily activities and motives. Discovery of the unconscious was a way to show that dreams act as a mirror of the psyche's contents. Freud thus revived and explained an idea readily accepted by the ancients, namely, that dream content is linked to our waking life.

Freud left many brilliant observations that opened up our understanding of the mind and psyche. Nevertheless,

he also left us some distortions about dreams. One of the
most pronounced of his distortions was to link dream content too often to sexual themes, a perspective no longer
held in modern times. Freud's biographers described his
struggle with his own sexuality, which may explain how
sexual questions in the psyche came to strike him as a major area of study. He thought that perhaps because it applied to him, it applied to everyone in the same way. And
he lived during the aftermath of the Victorian Age. Sex
was a hidden but still hot topic. All things considered,
Freud's brilliant legacies in understanding ourselves will
always be gratefully acknowledged.

Carl Jung

Jung was a young contemporary of Freud who led us further into the understanding of dreams. He provided the
amazing insight that dreams are a focal point and a tool for
growing into one's full potential, and not just a mirror of
our memories and associations. Jung restored balance to
Freud's perspective by adding the dimensions of spirituality,
self-awareness, and growth as major aspects of the potential
of dream use.

Dream Laboratories

The next major breakthrough in our understanding of
dreams and sleep came with the research work of Nathaniel
Kleitman, a physiologist at the University of Chicago who
set up a "sleep laboratory" in order to understand better the
physiology of sleep. Working well into the night one night
in 1952, he and a colleague returned to his home to unwind. As he checked in on his infant child, who was sleeping peacefully, he noticed that his son's eyes, though
closed, were moving back and forth as though watching a
tennis match. Kleitman wondered whether this was what
happened when a dream was taking place. To find out, in
the weeks that followed he attached electrodes (tiny metal

plates that record an electrical impulse or a movement) to the eyes of sleeping adults in a sleep lab and woke them whenever their eyes moved back and forth. Kleitman and his associates were astonished that each time they woke someone up, the person reported that they had been dreaming. They named this phenomenon rapid eye movement sleep, or REM sleep, for short.

Using this technique of attaching electrodes to the eyes of a sleeping person, scientists were able to discover a great deal more about dreams and sleep. Everyone dreams each night, whether or not they remember their dreams. In fact, we dream like clockwork every ninety minutes or so for a total of twenty percent of our sleep time. Such research showed us that a dream can last from ten to thirty minutes and tends to be the longest and clearest just before waking.

Next, dream researchers William Dement and Charles Fisher of New York's Mount Sinai Hospital were the first to show that the dream, or REM portion, of sleep is important for psychological well-being and is not related to the physical rest of the body. In their dream deprivation experiments, people were awakened whenever a dream began, and they were not allowed to finish any dream. In fact, they were not allowed to dream at all for up to six nights, nor to nap during the day. These dream-deprived subjects became more and more anxious and irritable, and their decisions became poorer and less in accord with choices they would normally make. For example, they drank more, smoked more, and showed increasingly more and more hostility and resentment, as compared to their normal state.

Thus, these scientists suggested that lack of dreams rather than lack of sleep was related to this strange behavior, since they had kept a second control group of people awake during the same nights. They were awake for equal amounts of time, but only during nondreaming time of sleep; in effect, they were equally sleep deprived, but not dream deprived. This second group who were merely sleep deprived rather than dream deprived showed little change in personality or behavior. Such research brought to our attention the fact that dreams are critical to our psychological welfare.

Dream Content

As scientists began to ask the question "What does this dream mean?" they were looking at the content of dreams. This led to two crucial observations. First, they noticed that dreams are stories linked to waking scenarios revolving around our daily problems and activities. Secondly, these story lines, or themes, in a dream make a significant, relevant statement about the direction our waking lives are taking. This is true even for what appear to be mere snatches of a dream.

Conclusions

The early researchers on dreams went on to conclude that dreams are worthy of serious consideration. This substantiates the ancient words from many traditions such as the well-known Hebrew text found in the Talmud that states that dreams are "a letter unopened from a friend." It is time for us to become adept at opening these letters.

MY PERSONAL PERSPECTIVES ON DREAMS

I believe life is an eternal spiritual journey. By constructively meeting daily obstacles and challenges and by developing our talents, we attain "wholeness." Because we are on such a journey, I believe there are spiritual and universal laws by which we need to live, laws of unseen processes that are as real as the more observable physical processes. Dreams are one of these unseen, untouchable items that follow lawful processes, and that are a tool given to us for attaining spiritual, emotional, and psychological wholeness. Dreams provide a way to help us through the concrete here-and-now part of this journey. You don't need to subscribe to spiritual beliefs to benefit from dreams, but this perspective is shared by many, including psychologist Carl Jung, my first dream mentor.

Like Jung, I think each of us is as unique as a snowflake. We unfold a pattern of talents and purposes that no one else can fill quite as well. Like notes in a symphony, we express our uniqueness, yet participate as a single instrument, adding to the music of the whole show. Working with your dreams helps you to find this true self and shows you how to express it for your own happiness, and also to gain the world's applause.

The Five-Step Method of Dream Analysis: A New Approach

Make no mistake about it. If you are interested in discovering what your dreams mean, you can learn to do it, and with ease. It is not difficult or time-consuming once you get the knack. In this section I'm going to describe one of the easiest and most effective techniques you can use to gain insight from your dreams. It is called the five-step method. If you practice it for just a few weeks, it will become second nature to you. Whether you are new to dream analysis or have been working with your dreams for a long time, try this technique if it is new to you. Even experienced dreamers have come back and thanked me for it. Although it's not difficult, it does take a little practice. But first, here are some general hints on how to begin to work with and interact with your dreams.

BEGIN BY BEGINNING

Learning to analyze your dreams is like learning to ride a bicycle. Someone can tell you about different types of bicycles and what riding one feels like, but it is only when you sit on a bike and actually ride it that you get a sense of what bike-riding is all about. You sit on the bike, pedal, and find your own balance point. The same thing happens in regard to working with dreams. The theory doesn't make sense at all until you try it out for yourself and note your own perceptions of your own dreams. Only by recording your dreams and trying out techniques do you begin to understand them. Thus your own experience is your most valuable tool in learning to understand your dreams. At the same time, there are helpful ground rules to observe. This section shows you how to begin to ride, and points out traffic and road rules, while this book gives you a glimpse into the territory you will ride through.

YOUR PSYCHE'S CAR

Dreams are a tool your psyche has that can help you live in a more meaningful and joyful way. We have physical tools such as cars and arms. Dreams are an invisible tool of your psyche, but your psyche is a very real part of you nonetheless. It is the emotional, spiritual, and psychological part of yourself that needs as much attention as your body does. Dreams are a tool for understanding yourself, to help you grow and fulfill your potential. Just as anyone can learn to drive a car, so can most people learn to use dreams to "get around" more easily and comfortably in life.

We now have enough knowledge about our psyche and enough experience with dreams for them to become useful to almost anyone. Because we live in a very complex and stressful world, using dreams as a self-help, self-guidance, and self-therapy tool becomes increasingly valuable.

Like any tool, dreams require some upkeep, some application in a practical way, and should be used with discrimination. And just as a car can take you to a shopping center or on a cross-country trip, so you can use your dreams merely a little now and then to explore yourself, or you can use your dreams extensively to get to know yourself quite thoroughly.

DREAM HORIZONS AND PERSPECTIVES

Dreams are not a way to bypass struggles and challenges, but they can make it easier to meet them, gently or head-on. They help you define problems more clearly by pointing out their source and by suggesting ways to handle them constructively. In the end, it is your responsibility both to gain insight from a dream and to apply it in a practical and consistent way. For example, if you feel the pinch financially, dreams won't give you the number of a winning lottery ticket as a way to solve your problem. But they can point out talents and skills, both new or forgotten, which you can use to increase your earnings. Or earnings may be hampered by personality traits; for example, a bad temper can keep you from getting along with colleagues and therefore can block a promotion. Dreams quickly pinpoint traits that create roadblocks and show how to turn them into stepping-stones. The psyche knows, as do psychologists, that behind every negative trait lies energy that can be used positively. For example, temper can denote a strong will and insight that can be turned into enthusiastic leadership; this would be a step toward promotion and higher earnings. By the same token, dreams don't tell you how to change a boss, a spouse, or an in-law who is a thorn in your side. Instead, they help you work on yourself and your own perceptions. As you change your own attitudes and grow, your relationships improve.

An important ground rule, then, is that dreams first aim to bring out the best in you. Once you achieve inner balance and relative wholeness, dreams can then give you insight and help for others too. And, like a tuning-fork effect, if you become more effective and happier, those around you automatically begin to change for the better. So take the time to nurture yourself by using your dreams. What you do for yourself helps everyone in the long run. At an advanced level, dreams help you to develop new talents and skills, unfold creativity and ideas, and can be a source of help for others. Working with your dreams consistently can make the difference between getting by in life reasonably well and reaching your full potential.

HOW TO GET STARTED

Get a Notebook

Writing dreams down is a good first step to analyzing your dreams. You will soon notice that even the words you pick to record the dream often give you interesting insights. Writing dreams down also allows you to review them at a later time, which helps you see large patterns in your dream life and make sense out of dreams that you did not initially understand.

Some people suggest keeping a notebook beside your bed so that if you wake up during the night, you can record a dream. I do this, but with a slight difference. I give myself the suggestion to remember my dream just before waking, unless it's an important dream that won't be repeated later. If I don't give myself this kind of instruction, I can wake up often throughout the night and get too little sleep. Because dream story lines are generally repeated in later dreams, like rough drafts that are later turned into polished prose, it's okay to simply plug into the last batch of dreams you have just before waking. With this set of "programmed" instructions, I manage to get my sleep and have my dreams, too.

However, if you have trouble with recall, you need to prime your unconscious pump, and in that case, waking up occasionally for a few minutes during the night in order to record a dream may be the path to take, at least initially. Use the method that works best for you. To some extent, your psyche is like a computer and can be programmed and interacted with as suits you best.

Relax and Unwind

Before going to sleep at night, take a few minutes to unwind, and get in touch with the quiet, relaxed part of yourself. Remember that you lead two lives: the outer, role-oriented one that includes your family, friends, and career, and a second, inner life that consists only of feelings, thoughts, and reactions, all of which are very private and happen very quickly throughout the day. Every day, as we carry out our outer roles, we also engage in private thoughts, feelings, reactions, and perceptions, and these two lives combined make up the content of your dreams. By taking a few moments to relax before you go to sleep, you make room for your psyche to shift gears from your outer roles to your inner life. This allows your psyche to more easily review all your new daily input, to consolidate your two lives, and to prepare you to meet your unconscious psyche and your dreams.

Look at What's on Your Mind

As you doze off, notice what thoughts, ideas, feelings, hopes, and questions are going through your mind. Dreams deal with whatever your attention is focusing on during waking hours, which your pre-sleep random thoughts reflect. Thus, if you notice what is going on in your mind and in your feelings as you fall asleep, you are also noticing what topics your dreams will cover that night. As a result, when you wake up in the morning, you can be halfway to figuring out what your dreams mean, because the first thing you need to determine is which area of your life they apply to. As you begin to feel a rapport with your psyche, you can begin to ask yourself a question and you can expect your psyche to provide an answer. This technique is called dream incubation. Your dreams will always answer a question because the psyche is naturally set up to dialogue with you, especially through your dreams.

Give Yourself a Suggestion

By telling yourself "I will remember my dreams tonight," you establish a mind-set, or "attention cue," that any activity requires in order to get started. At this point, because of my philosophy that life is a spiritual journey, I also say a prayer asking for guidance to come through where I need it most, in a dream form that I will understand and remember clearly. This is all part of my own self-suggestion package; it is like setting an oven to cook something according to your needs, or setting a temperature control unit to create the heat or coolness that you want. In the same way, by giving yourself some suggestions, you give your psyche guidelines regarding what you want and need on a particular night or period of your life. Afterward, I put myself in the hands of the Almighty for the night, and gratefully lay my head down on the pillow to embrace the comfort of sleep.

Wake Up Comfortably

It's important to get sufficient sleep. During times when you get less sleep than you need, your dream recall can temporarily disappear or be reduced. This is normal, and is nothing to worry about. Most people need an average of seven to eight hours sleep per night. Although there are times when loss of sleep is unavoidable, getting too little sleep or too much sleep over prolonged periods of time can lead to temporary imbalances in personality and in being in touch with your inner self.

Also, in order to wake up comfortably, use an alarm clock with a sound that is not too loud or too jarring. Loud noises tend to throw you out of your unconscious mind and into your conscious mind too abruptly, thus severing the line to your dreams. Once that contact is broken, you can't remember a dream even if you knew you were dreaming. So wake up gently if possible.

Before I began to use my dreams on a regular basis,

waking up was a chore and I walked around in a half-daze for the first hour or two of the morning. I would feel grumpy and sip coffee very slowly, until some sort of humanity descended upon me. Now that I have been using my dreams regularly to get to know who I am and to bring happiness and insight into my life, I am more in tune with myself, so I usually wake up with zest or calmness, glad to be alive and raring to get started on the day's agenda. And since becoming a regular dream user, I no longer need to set my alarm clock. It seems as though my psyche always knows what time it is, and no matter what time I set my alarm for, I wake up five to ten minutes before it rings. So I tend to awaken gracefully most of the time, feeling in touch with my true self.

Don't Jump Out of Bed

Experience shows that sudden movements or sudden activity and *jumps* into the conscious waking life can interfere with dream recall. So, as you awaken, take a few minutes to just lie still and get your bearings. While you were asleep, you were deeply immersed in the unconscious part of yourself. As you awaken, you edge closer to the conscious part of yourself once again. It's a journey from the language of imagery that the unconscious uses, back to the language of words and symbols that the conscious mind uses. The journey from the unconscious back to the conscious is a very quick one, and yet also a long one, and if not taken gently and properly, you lose not only your recall of dreams but also that sense of being in touch with yourself. Those few minutes between sleep and waking are called the hypnopompic state, the in-between stage between the conscious and the unconscious mind. There is another reason to savor these few moments of time: your most creative thoughts and ideas tend to come through then, so you want to pay attention.

Even if you don't remember a dream, notice how you feel and what's on your mind. As you do so, a dream segment may pass through your thoughts unexpectedly. In a relaxed way, savor what you remember. As you do so, you may suddenly remember other scenes and snatches, or even whole dreams. Go back over these once again too. Once a dream is remembered comfortably, there's no point in lazing around any longer. It is time to get up and, of course, it is time to write down the dream. I generally record dreams in the first half hour of waking. If you don't have time to record the entire dream, jot down the story line, but get into the habit of writing out the whole dream sometime later in the day. Otherwise, the details will tend to evaporate. Now, if you've come this far, you are ready for the real thing—the basics of interpretation and the five-step method of dream interpretation. And away we go. . . .

THE METHOD

The main feature of the five-step method is the technique of finding the theme of a dream. I did not invent this technique*, but I did adapt and streamline it into an easy-to-use approach. Each step is important in the overall process. Initially, you may want to write out the steps for the first dozen or so dreams just to make the steps concrete for yourself. Soon the steps come with ease and you quickly flow into the meaning of a dream without writing anything down. In the end, you will not need to put aside any special time to work on your dreams, because you can do it in your head. You can analyze your dreams as you walk, take a coffee break, wash dishes, or whatever. By doing dream analysis regularly, you will understand your dreams as naturally as you make up a shopping list.

*As best as I can trace, the idea came from Montague Ullman, M.D., a psychiatrist who, over the last forty years, has pioneered the use of dreams for the general public.

Here are the five steps:

Step 1: Emotions

The first question you need to ask about a dream is: "How did I feel during the dream, and what was I feeling as I woke up?" Is it a feeling you often have, or one you could use more of? Does it reflect something new, or something from your past? Is it shaking you up? Or is it bringing out feelings you didn't realize you could have? Feelings in a dream and your reaction to the dream as you awaken are the first clue toward a dream's meaning. So even if you don't yet understand the dream, pause and note your feelings.

Step 2: Finding the Theme or Story Line

The second step to analyzing your dream is to decide on a "dream theme" which is the story line of the dream. A theme allows you to step back and look at the dream from a wider perspective. This step is often one of the most fruitful pieces of the puzzle, and adopting a "playful" attitude toward finding a theme can be helpful. Finding a dream theme means that you summarize the *actions* going on and only the actions, without interpreting anything yet.

Instead of actually naming the objects or people in the dream, use words like "someone" or "something" to refer to them, and summarize the actions going on into a basic, one-sentence story line. Think of yourself as a movie director trying to describe what the movie is really all about—in one sentence. A successful theme is a very general statement, but it brings out what is really important. Here are some examples of actual dreams and their themes.

DREAM 1:

> There is a small flowerpot on the windowsill with a new, small plant growing. It has one major stem, just a few inches tall, and two or three small offshoots with a few leaves on each. The plant is vibrant and healthy

and each leaf is a shiny, dark green color. It's very beautiful. Then, as I look more closely, I see a bug on one of the leaves eating up the leaf, and I know it can destroy the whole plant. I'm startled and disappointed. I know if I act quickly I can remove the bug, but don't know if I can do it in time. I wake up feeling very hurt and on guard, not wanting to see something that is beautiful and precious to me destroyed.

THEME:

Someone sees something beautiful, but in order to keep it so, has to act quickly to put a stop to something.

REVISED THEME:

After several attempts to reword the story line, it might become:

Someone has to nip something in the bud in order to keep it healthy and beautiful.

Notice that nothing was mentioned about the actual details of the dream such as the plant, its leaves, the bug, or the actual fears. Instead, the theme extracts only the action in the dream in summary form (someone has to nip something in the bud). Let's try another example:

DREAM 2:

I see a young Asian boy who was very much looking forward to passing a test. But when I ask him about it, he's totally silent, so I know he failed. I wait, then I passionately tell him he needs to keep trying. I outline a whole series of steps he could take to keep himself going with it, and then what he could do to eventually reapply for the test and pass it.

THEME:

Someone sees someone who feels he has failed and strongly encourages him to keep trying.

Notice that from the theme, you wouldn't know that it was an Asian boy, or what it was that he failed at. As usual, you obscure and block out the actual details. You do so by using words like "someone" and "something" to replace characters and objects, and then describing the actions and reaction of the dream in words different from what actually happens in the dream. For each story line, you're trying to get not only a summary of actions and reactions, but also a summary of "meaning" that gets to the heart of the matter of the dream's major concern or thrust.

FINAL NOTES ON THE THEME

By using words such as "someone" and "something" to replace the actual details in a dream, you cut to the action, and begin to get a feeling for the large picture. This is a way to prevent yourself from jumping into an interpretation too quickly, which is the most common mistake people tend to make. We use a theme to deliberately slow ourselves down. Themes are a way to keep from jumping to conclusions, enabling you to scout the territory before deciding which path you want to take.

A long dream can actually be two dreams that feel like one, or it can be one dream containing two or three parts. In that case, it is a good idea to give each part a separate theme. Then, as you read the themes all in a row, they often add up to a larger, related picture. This step, that of translating a theme into its action equivalent, is the single most important technique you can practice in order to gain a quick understanding of a dream.

Step 3: Matching the Theme or Story Line to an Area of Life

Once you find a theme or story line that describes all the important actions and overall thrust of the dream, it becomes a very useful tool for interpretation. The question then becomes: "If the theme were a reflection of an area of my life or a part of me, which area would it be?" That is to say, you do not ask "What does this dream mean?" Instead, the real question is "To what area of my life or to what part of me does the dream refer?"

If you correctly found the theme, you will be surprised that you can quite easily match the theme to an area of your life. Once you get the theme-to-life match done, getting the message or point of the dream happens quickly. This matching process is a significant leap toward understanding the dream. Let's look at how the dreams we found themes for in step 2 piece together with actual life situations. To refresh your memory, this was the first dream for which we found a theme:

DREAM 1:
There is a small flowerpot on the windowsill with a new, small plant growing. It has one major stem, just a few inches tall, and two or three small offshoots with a few leaves on each. The plant is vibrant and healthy and each leaf is a shiny, dark green color. It's very beautiful. Then, as I look more closely, I see a bug on one of the leaves eating up the leaf, and I know it can destroy the whole plant. I'm startled and disappointed. I know if I act quickly I can remove the bug, but don't know if I can do it in time. I wake up feeling very hurt and on guard, not wanting to see something that is beautiful and precious to me destroyed.

AND THIS WAS THE THEME:
Someone has to nip something in the bud in order to keep it healthy and beautiful.

MATCH OF THEME TO AN AREA OF LIFE

In order to determine what area of your life matches the theme, ask yourself what questions the theme brings up for you. For example:
(a) What in my life has been showing new directions or

"growth"? Is there something negative brewing about this new direction which I have to "nip in the bud" or put a stop to?

Or stated in another way:

(b) What has been working well recently that may be related to something new in myself or my life? Has something developed that could threaten the positive direction this has been taking?

THEME-TO-LIFE MATCH

The dreamer recognized that the theme related to her attitude toward her boss at work. For a while she had been very negative toward him and her attitude had created problems between them. Then she decided to forgive their past disputes and become friendly and cooperative, and this new attitude had genuinely improved their relationship and made her work environment much more pleasant. At the time of this dream, however, some old grievances had resurfaced, souring her attitude. Keeping in mind that dreams can exaggerate in order to make a point (although sometimes they do not exaggerate), this dream suggested: "Nip this sour attitude of yours that is reemerging in the bud, or all your recent efforts to create a good atmosphere at work will come to naught." Fortunately, this advice from her inner self came in time to help the situation.

DREAM 2:

I see a young Asian boy who was very much looking forward to passing a test. But when I ask him about it, he's totally silent, so I know he failed. I wait, then I passionately tell him he needs to keep trying. I outline a whole series of steps he could take to keep himself going with it, and then what he could do to eventually reapply for the test and pass it.

AND THIS WAS THE THEME:

Someone sees someone who feels they have not succeeded, and strongly encourages them to keep trying.

MATCH OF THEME TO AN AREA OF LIFE

To determine the area of life that matches the theme, these are the questions the theme brings up:

(a) What am I not succeeding in, or where am I not doing well? What is something for which I could use some encouragement? Is it at work, in love, in family interactions, creative pursuits, or some group activity? What is it that I need to persist with?

Or, stated another way:

(b) What in myself, my attitudes, ideas, or thoughts do I feel really down about, or feel inferior about, that I may need a dose of encouragement for? How could I find this encouragement?

THEME-TO-LIFE MATCH

In this case, the dreamer was feeling very down about his career. He had succeeded in many ways, but overall he felt he had not really achieved what he wanted to in life and began to feel like a failure in some ways. This dream came at a time when he was giving his career and life direction a lot of thought, and wondering whether to just settle for what he had attained.

Knowing that his work and career goals seemed to fall short, he easily matched the theme to his career and his thoughts about career goals. Once this life area was placed, he could clearly see the dream's advice: Take heart, make a new plan, and try, try again. The dream accurately summarized the dreamer's secret feelings and fears about his future. It helped him turn his fears and discouragement into a new thrust, and as a result he is now on a new life and career track, finally actively pursuing the career he had always wanted.

* * *

To summarize the steps so far, first examine the emotions and emotional reactions of a dream. Then summarize the actions and plot as a theme or story line, and see what area of life or what attitude or action the theme reminds you of. If the theme is done right, the matching comes easily, and each time you get a match, it gets easier to do it the next time. You know you have a match because it "resonates," as an "ah-ha," as if a lightbulb goes on, which makes you feel good. Next take a good look at the symbols.

Step 4: The Symbols

After defining emotions and themes and determining the area of life that the theme matches, look at specific details and symbols in the dream. Start with the symbols and details that create the most reaction in you, or that strike you the most in some way. Keep in mind that symbols are unique to you and your own personal experience. For example, a red rose may remind one person of love because they received flowers from a loved one on Valentine's Day. It may remind someone else of sorrow and grief because roses were plentiful at the funeral of a loved one. Trust your own experience (rather than a dream book on symbols) to get meanings from your own symbols. Take a playful attitude toward symbols, as though you are playing a game of charades. In charades, the picture a person mimes to you is one that you translate into a new meaning or version. The same thing happens in dreams. You turn one picture or symbol into a new meaning that is a play on words or a play on images. There are two methods or approaches to use in dealing with symbols, as follows:

THE ASSOCIATION METHOD

The first way to approach symbols was brought into popularity by Sigmund Freud. It is the idea of "association," whereby you take a symbol and see what it reminds you of, then do it again—that is, go backward from the first association to another association. Keep doing so, and at each point ask yourself how each association from the past relates to the present dream's theme and overall thrust and symbol. Keep doing so until some meaning "clicks." For example, I once dreamed:

DREAM:

I am in a department store in the coat section. On one rack is a row of pink coats in different styles and shades, but I pass them by and go to a rack that has only gray coats. I pick out a light gray one. I am happy with this selection and yet at the same time I am disappointed.

In trying to figure out this dream, I picked the symbol "pink coat" in the dream and applied the association method. At first I could remember nothing in my past about pink coats. Then suddenly it occurred to me that a few months before I had been in a department store with my college roommate as she was shopping for a coat. That was the first memory. Then I took that memory of the shopping trip and asked myself how that related to my dream, and came up with a blank. Then I suddenly remembered that as we were shopping, I had actually seen a rack of pink coats, and had seen a coral one that I liked. That was memory number two, going backward in time. Still, it made no sense in terms of the meaning of this dream. So, going backward in time once more, I asked myself what I was thinking at the time as I was browsing in the department store, and bingo! It flashed through my mind that when I had seen that coral coat which would have looked lovely and feminine on me, I had said to myself, "Well, maybe . . . when I meet my true love and feel secure in a relationship, I will then consider buying such a coat."

As soon as this memory flashed before me, I knew what my dream meant. I realized it referred to a relationship question. In real life there was a new man I was beginning to like, and around the time of the dream I had asked myself if he could possibly be my "true love." Alas, in the dream I had picked out a gray coat, which gave me my answer very clearly. The dream was bringing to my attention the fact that this man was not the one for me. This proved correct, for he and I soon parted ways despite my wishful thinking. However, the dream helped me keep my feelings under control and provided a framework in which to question more broadly what I really wanted in a committed, long-term relationship. This is one example of how to use the association method to understand a major dream symbol: Keep working backward until some memory resonates in relation to the dream.

THE AMPLIFICATION METHOD

The second method of using symbols to derive meaning from your dreams was pointed out by psychologist Carl Jung, and is called amplification. In this method you take a symbol and instead of going backward in associations, you think of all the parallel meanings or associations it has for you in the present. For example, if you dream of a rose, instead of asking, "When was the last time a rose was important to me?" you list all the things a rose means to you. It might mean love, beauty, a wonderful smell, gentleness, softness, and so on. Or, if a rose reminds you of a relationship that was broken off or that ended sadly, it may remind you of feeling alone, feeling jilted, feeling sad and blue, and so on.

Then take all these meanings and see if they ring a bell in the context of the dream. Often you will discover that the meaning does resonate somehow with the dream theme or symbol. For example, in the above dream, if I took the meanings of coat and what they mean to me, I would say: warmth, security, and protection; and these are all qualities I would like to feel when I am in a committed relationship.

Both methods, those of association and amplification, are worth exploring and trying out often in order to understand at least the major symbols in your dream. As each symbol draws out new depth of meaning of the dream, you will gain more and more understanding of the dream's message.

SYMBOLS AS COLLAGES AND A CHARADE GAME

Symbols are often a play on words or a reminder of a common expression. Your psyche uses symbols to create a collage—that is, it creates a new picture from bits and pieces of other pictures. For example, someone saw a person with her head missing. Here the dream was using the expression "she lost her head" to make the point that someone was acting rashly. Someone else dreamed of a torso turned backward from the waist up so that both the head and the bum now faced forward. The dreamer was familiar with the expression "doing something ass backward," which meant that something was being done poorly. That dream image was asking the dreamer to examine what he was doing backward or poorly at the time.

YOUR GAME PLAN FOR SYMBOLS

Your psyche does not use symbols or expressions that are unfamiliar to you or deviate from the way you normally express yourself. Examine how you express yourself. If you are normally polite, symbols and stories in the dream will tend to be polite. If you are poetic and like to elaborate at length in your conversations, your symbols and scenarios may be elaborate and profuse. Or if you are a person who likes to express yourself in a direct way with as few words as possible, your dreams may try to pack much into little, like a summarized dream version, making your dreams relatively short. There was a writer in one of my dream groups. Her dreams usually came in three acts: the introduction, the major plot, and the resolution or conclusion. The hero and heroine were always easy to spot and the plots in her dreams were worthy of Metro-Goldwyn-Mayer. As a writer, her dreams were a clear example of her normal style of thinking and communication. In the same way, the format in your dreams reflect the way you normally think and express yourself.

Another way of thinking of the symbols in your dreams is as though you were playing a game of charades. At first it may seem like a strange thing to have to take an image or symbol and translate it into another image and another meaning. But even words that you take for granted, that make up how you communicate, are merely symbols. Consider the letters s/u/n/r/i/s/e; they have no logical link to the actual event of the sun rising above the horizon in the early hours of the morning. In fact, as you can see from this example, most "meanings" come to you in some symbolic, indirect way—that is, as a translation of something other than what you actually observe. Notice also the implication in the expression "A picture is worth a thousand words." It suggests that you are easily able to ascribe more meaning to an image than a mere set of words would give it. Thus, you can give yourself permission to feel at home with your dream symbols, just as you already do with other symbolic representations such as words. Translating symbols into meaning is as natural and as easy as getting the punch line of a joke. And always decide what a symbol or image means in relation to your own memories rather than the meaning others would give it; after all, it is your dream, and your own meaning.

SHARED SOCIAL MEANINGS OF SOME SYMBOLS

Though most symbols are unique to your own personal experience, we do share cultural and social meanings that give us shared meanings of certain symbols. Noting some of these shared symbols can supply a starting point to work with your own symbols. For example:

Animals
Our four-footed and feathered friends are convenient stereotypes for our own traits, both positive and negative. An animal you see in your dream almost always refers to a trait

in you, and generally it's a negative trait because it is easier to see a negative trait in an animal than to "own" it as part of yourself. This was the case with a woman who began to sleep in later and later, and had a harder and harder time getting out of bed in the morning. One morning she dreamed she was watching a huge, brown-eyed cow lazily chewing cud in her bed. She promptly awoke and jumped out of bed. It took her only an instant to realize that her psyche was calling her a lazy old cow; after that, she had no more trouble getting out of bed at her usual time.

Cars

Cars and vehicles in a dream often refer to your body (the vehicle with which you travel through life). Or they can reflect the direction you are choosing in life and how you are handling it. However, if you deal with cars as a hobby or for a living, they can take on more complex levels of meaning for you. They may, for example, have career or job-related meanings. Remember to always go back to your personal experience and associations with a symbol before deciding on its final meaning.

Children

Because a child is generally a symbol of something new and joyful, a child in a dream may refer to a new project, a new phase in your life, or a new activity. How the child fares in the dream is how the life counterpart is doing. A child can also refer to the open, innocent parts of yourself or the negative counterparts of immaturity and childishness, depending on the context in which it appears.

Clothes

Clothing is something you change to suit your moods, your needs, and the different roles you play in your life and career. Clothes are a good symbol for your attitudes and moods, which also fluctuate daily according to changing circumstances. And like clothes, attitudes and moods are the masks and roles you put on to cope with various situations. One woman dreamed she was going through her wardrobe and found that the styles of clothes in her closet no longer pleased her, and nothing seemed to fit anymore. The dream was telling her she had "outgrown" all her old attitudes and perspectives ("all" because the entire wardrobe was involved). The dream was therefore suggesting that she was going through a transformation, just like shedding a new skin. This meaning coincided well with major changes taking place in her life, beginning with changes in attitude and perspectives toward life.

Death
Almost all dreams about funerals, death, and dying refer to change, usually a major or a drastic change in either your life or your attitudes and inner self. Dreams about death can also be a symbolic confrontation with your own fears, whether of some change or an actual fear of death. For example, a young woman had been close to her father, when he died suddenly. Months later she began to dream regularly that her mother was about to die, even though her mother was in good health. She knew that she had no valid reason to think her mother was in danger of dying. Thus, the dream was more about her fear that since she had suddenly lost one person by death, maybe she could lose others. Because this underlying fear and anxiety was draining her emotions and limiting her actions in life at the time, the dream came to mirror this fear back to her as a way of telling her that she needed to come to terms with this fear of losing loved ones.

Twenty years ago, death was a subject you did not discuss because it has many frightening and threatening emotional links for most people. This is why it becomes a good symbol for what is threatening. And since death is "the ultimate change" you will encounter at the end of your life, it works as a symbol of major change.

Faces and Features
Parts of the body are often connected to their actual func-

tion and use. For example, teeth that look hideous can refer to speaking in a vicious or destructive way, because words are what come out of your mouth. Or a head that's too large for its body may refer to a "swelled head"—in other words, thinking too highly of oneself. Hair that is stiff can symbolize "rigid thinking." Hair and the scalp generally refer to what's on your mind because the head is where you do your thinking, so to speak, and hair is the visible result. Thus, by the same token, the state of your hair, head, and scalp is a good analogy for the state of your mind and your attitudes.

Houses, Buildings, and Rooms

These often point out the area of life that a dream is bringing to your attention. An office setting can literally refer to some situation at work, or, in a more general sense, it may refer to your career goals or skills or perhaps to attitudes you have toward work. A kitchen may refer to actual food habits or to the needs of the physical body. Or it can be an analogy for "what you're cooking up in life" in general, with details of how and what you are cooking showing a parallel to how you are handling some real-life counterpart.

Money and Jewels

Seeing money or jewels in a dream is often a way of asking you to think about what you value or to examine your attitudes toward material possessions. Someone who dreamed of stacking dollar bills high on a shelf yet felt the money was unsafe there recognized a parallel in a life situation where keeping values and standards high in order to stay secure within one's own integrity, made sense. By the same token, the common dream image of winning a lottery ticket usually refers to success in a goal or some area of life rather than to cash that will come to you for no reason.

People

The people you see in your dreams are another way your psyche mirrors aspects or traits of yourself back to you.

Generally, they are traits or attitudes that you either need to develop, or, if negative, ones you need to let go. When you dream of a person, ask the question: What are two traits I like about this person and two traits I dislike? Answer this spontaneously and quickly, and then take an honest look to see if you can recognize both the pluses and minuses you noted—in yourself!

For example, I dreamed of a friend who was preparing a banquet for a reception in a church hall. The tables were so beautiful, laden with wonderful delicacies that take hours to prepare, and spread out in a wonderfully attractive and appealing way. In addition, I was captivated by the delicate hand-made lace tablecloths in the dream. The qualities of this friend that I had always admired were her kind and caring ways with people, her diligence and her faithfulness to duty. I realized that at the time of this dream I was beginning to "goof off" regarding certain group responsibilities. The dream was hinting that if I would remain dutiful and caring in my responsibilities to others, the results would bring rewards and something as beautiful as the exquisite banquet tables. Thus, the dream was about me and what I needed to measure up to and stay faithful to, even though my friend was the main character in the dream. Other people in dreams tend to work that way—as representatives of parts of yourself—whether they are strangers, famous personalities, family members, or friends. Once you do find a wholeness and balance in yourself, however, some dreams may actually be about others. These may be warnings about the health or difficulties loved ones are experiencing, or about talents that you can help unfold in those around you, and so on.

Step 5: The Application

Once you decide on a theme, match the theme to a life area, and associate symbols to actual memories, one or more insights from the dream emerge. As a final step, you need to think about how to apply the insight. Does it invite a change in attitude, a change in heart toward someone, a clearer perspective on a decision you are trying to make, or an insight about a project or an activity? Rather than being simply amusing or entertaining, dreams are meant to be used in a practical way. Keep in mind that whatever you are applying is normally consistent with what is already in progress in your life. Thus, under most circumstances, applying the dream's insight produces a constructive and natural change for you, not a scary or unnatural one.

PARTING WORDS: EXPLORING THE LANDSCAPE

It is my belief that all dreams come with a "purpose." The purpose can be an insight to transmit, an attitude to change, an idea or activity or action to encourage, a talent to point out, or an emotion to adjust or to create. That is what Section II of this book is about. It lists 27 dream types and the purpose each type comes to carry out.

Most dreams are about you and refer to what is actually going on in your life, your personality, your relationships, or your actions. The question is not "What does this dream mean?" Rather, the question to ask is always "To what in my life, personality, or actions does this dream refer?" In other words, dreams mean something only in relation to you or to your life; they are not a separate story line appearing out of the blue.

In addition, keep in mind that dreams are a two-way street. The attitude with which you reach out toward your dreams and psyche is important. Dreams and your psyche reach out to you with a message, but your own attitude and willingness to receive the message facilitates the process, and allows all kinds of wonderful insights to come through easily. All dreams are friendly and come with a helpful purpose, even if they appear to be frightening. Thus you can approach your dreams as a positive adventure in getting to know yourself and in obtaining insights about anything and everything. In that sense, dreams are a way of mining for gold.

Know that you can proceed at your own pace. If you can't make sense of a dream, leave it for a while. Important themes are repeated and an undeciphered dream reappears in different forms with fresh perspectives as long as the topic remains an issue. Remember, too, that dream interpretation gets easier with practice. You "grow into" dream interpretation, like a muscle that slowly builds. Your psyche works with you by presenting new levels of dream gymnastics, if and when you are ready to absorb them. With these points in mind, you are well on your way to understanding your dreams, quickly and clearly. I hope your adventure in self-exploration is as exciting and glorious as mine has been, and continues to be.

SECTION II

◊

The 27 Dream Types

PART I

◊

Dreams Related to Basic Life Issues

CHAPTER 1

Body and Health Dreams

For of the soul the body form doth take;
For soul is form, and doth the body make.
—EDMUND SPENSER

WHAT THEY DO

Experience shows that your psyche, the part of yourself that is aware of everything about you, appears to monitor the exact condition of your body. This is like having your own built-in doctor who can tell you how you are at all times. Body and health dreams reflect this automatic monitoring system. They can tell you if a food disagrees with you, or how to raise your energy levels when they get low. Or, if you are hyper or nervous, they can suggest how to calm your body down.

At a more specific level, body and health dreams tell you if a health problem is building up in your system. In general, if there is a health condition building up, they warn you far enough in advance so that you can correct it, and they even include helpful hints as to how to rebalance the condition. However, if you are not in touch with your dreams along the way, and haven't received the help to avoid the problem, body and health dreams provide insights as to how to work with your body in order to regain perfect health.

How is such a feat possible, that the mind and psyche can diagnose its own body's condition? Psychologist Henry

Reed, a pioneer in the dream field, had a striking dream that explained this uncanny health-monitoring process of the psyche. It hinted that this ability is a gift that stems from the soul, and is a grace from God. In this dream he experienced a mystical mind-body connection:

> *My body is a million cells. Each one is me and each one has consciousness of the whole. It's a deeply moving vision of some transpersonal truth that I have been allowed to glimpse.*

Somehow, in some mysterious way, each of your cells contains a consciousness that communicates with the whole. Mystics claim that the reverse is also true, that your mind and spirit (which I call the psyche) communicates with each cell and each body part. As a result, the psyche, by scanning the body, can evaluate your health and submit a report that you experience as a body and health dream.

The fact that the body and mind can communicate with each other and communicate back to you via your dreams may sound fantastic. But as a parallel situation, consider a hologram you might have seen at a science exhibition. A hologram is a three-dimensional picture created by splitting light beams and reflecting them back in special ways. When the whole hologram is broken down into its halves, thirds, quarters, and so on, each segment, no matter how small, contains the complete, original picture. If it's possible for man to create or discover such visual mechanics, why wouldn't it be possible for the Almighty to create a mind-body communication link that can be viewed and reviewed in dreams?

It is what mystics of all cultures have always claimed— that your body contains the wisdom of the universe. One well-known adage states: "As above, so below," meaning everything on earth is a reflection of the universe and the Divine. By extension, it implies each atom is a mirror of the infinite, and, like a hologram, is capable in some mysterious way of containing the whole. Science acknowledges this mind/body link in its study and practice of biofeedback research and psychosomatic medicine, which are now commonly accepted features in the medical field.

Nevertheless, let's be sensible about this. I trust my psyche because I have worked with my own dreams for years. Therefore, thanks to experience, I can use body and health dreams with confidence. You, too, need to establish such a trust with your own dreams before setting out to use body and health dreams, so that you can do so wisely. But dreams are only one tool of many to maintain your best health. You can and should use your dreams as well as a physician to stay healthy. Thus, you need not announce to your physician that you'll no longer need his or her services, unless you want him to be concerned for more than your physical health. A doctor's skills and experience are a vital part of maintaining our best health.

EXAMPLES OF BODY AND HEALTH DREAMS

1: A Health Dream Attempts to Communicate a Health Condition That Is Building Up over the Years

Angela is an active, intelligent, middle-aged woman who took her good health for granted. For many years she demanded that her body see her through long hours of work, irregular sleep, and eating on the run. When she became exhausted she would rest, but aside from that didn't pay much attention to her body and how her stressful lifestyle was affecting it.

Over a period of five years she had recurring dreams about a house. At first it was a large old house in good shape and pleasant to live in. In a later dream the house needed cleaning. Still later, the house in the dream was accumulating more and more dust, until all the corners, nooks, and crannies were filled up. Then Angela saw that the plumbing needed attention, and the walls and ceilings showed cracks. These dreams intrigued her, but since she was not yet a student of dreams, she ignored what they were trying to tell her.

Over the period of five years this house in her dreams became more and more run-down. At first it was only mildly in need of care, but later its defects became more serious. The beams tilted under the weight of its heavy structure, and rust attacked the pipes. In the final stages of this dream series, the house was greatly damaged by severe storms. There was sand under its foundation and the final dreams warned that the house could slide down the hill on which it stood.

By the time the last few dreams occurred, Angela was in a dream group, telling the others about it because it intrigued her. The house was in such bad shape that its walls were sagging and a dream said the house could fall apart during the next storm. The very last dream showed a city inspector condemning the house and asking for enormous taxes. The landlady was with him, demanding that Angela make amends and fix the house.

When Angela began to study her dreams, it was suggested that this dream image of a house needing repair could relate to her health. Because Angela was feeling more tired than usual, she finally went for a thorough medical checkup. Doctors discovered a serious condition, and though she needed strong treatment, it was caught in time, so that her life was not in danger. This was a body and health dream in which the house was a symbol of her own body. It kept trying to bring the deteriorating condition of her body to her attention. If she had begun earlier by removing the dust that was accumulating and fixing rusted pipes—which might have referred to maintaining good eating habits and perhaps removing the body's toxins by doing regular exercise—she might have averted the illness altogether. Notice that when Angela finally acted on the message—went to a doctor—her house dreams ended.

2: A Health Dream Helps Someone Keep Her Energy Levels High During a Busy Period

You may already be in excellent health. In that case, body and health dreams can suggest how to keep you at your best. Emily was a perky young lady with a busy schedule. In fact, she had so many activities in her life that at one point she realized she was straining herself to fulfill some new and challenging ones, and wondered how she would have the strength to do it all. A body and health dream answered her question:

> *I'm lying on a sofa, listening to my favorite classical music. A melodious woman's voice in the background says to me, "Music reenergizes you."*

Thanks to this dream, Emily discovered that when she took regular "music breaks," by lying down at times for fifteen to thirty minutes and listening to her favorite records, they revived her. This technique helped her maintain vibrancy during an especially busy and challenging time of her career.

3: How to Beat a Persistent Flu—A Health Dream Helps Someone Find the Unique Medicine for Her Body

Roberta is a strikingly beautiful, tall woman with long black hair poised in a mass of curls. An accomplished career woman with intelligence and a lively sense of humor, her natural and direct personality make her popular with many. During her early thirties, which are normally years of peak health, she went through several winters of extreme fatigue. Her tiredness was so dramatic that not even a hectic schedule could account for it. Living in a cold, wintry climate, the doctor's diagnosis of a persistent flu virus did make sense, but she just couldn't shake it off.

Taking the doctor's sound advice of rest and vitamins,

Roberta's energy increased, but would flag again. These energy cycles of two steps forward and one back continued for months. Roberta became exasperated. As a student in a dream class, she discussed her frustration as a gossip item, until someone suggested she ask for a body and health dream. The dream group pointed out that body and health dreams often give clear and direct advice. She decided to try it and within a few days dreamed:

> It's lunchtime. I see a salad in front of me with beautiful leaves of lettuce placed invitingly in a glass bowl. It's so fresh, so green, and so appealing. I take a whole fresh lemon, squeeze it over the lettuce, and begin to eat. It's simply delicious. Words can't describe how good it tastes.

When she reported this dream to the dream group, everyone was delighted, as it was clearly a response to how to beat the flu. When someone asked how anyone could possibly eat a salad with only pure lemon juice squeezed over it, thinking it would be too sour to eat, Roberta explained that she loved salads that way, and furthermore confessed that she had been neglecting eating salads all season. Taking the advice of her dream, she began eating fresh salads with lemon juice and was amazed that her energy level did indeed return to normal within days. Now anytime her energy begins to flag or the flu threatens, Roberta has a salad with a whole fresh lemon squeezed over it.

4: A Series of Body and Health Dreams Helps a Man Recover from Cancer

Ivar was a quiet, good-natured carpenter with a large body frame, well over six feet tall, with blue eyes and a nature as gentle as a dove's. By any standard, Ivar was a "hunk": muscular, tanned, and handsome. In his early thirties he was recuperating from a bout with lymphatic cancer. Having taken dream seminars, he tried using body and health

dreams to enhance his recovery, reaching out for the full vitality and health that is his and everyone's right to claim.
So Ivar regularly asked himself for dreams to appraise his
body, and I agreed to work with him on them for a while.

His First Dream Brings Up an Issue of Cleansing:

*I'm in the corner of a large football field and see only
my back. I see a large yellow puddle forming, and know
my urine has been overflowing. I'm surprised at how big
the puddle is and think it shouldn't be there.*

This clear, direct image hinted that something involving
elimination and his kidneys was involved in his health
problem. It's always wise first to investigate the obvious, so
I asked Ivar what his drinking habits were, knowing kidneys use water to cleanse your system of toxins. This
turned out to be an important question, since his recent illness had been linked to the lymph glands, which are related
to the cleansing system in your body. It appeared that this
dream was hinting that Ivar's kidneys were not cleansing
efficiently. Was the image of the football field a metaphor
for his stomach, and the "leakage" of urine in a corner a
hint that toxins were accumulating in his body due to poor
or insufficient elimination?

To my surprise, Ivar admitted that he drank almost no
liquids on a regular basis except for a cup of coffee or two.
(The norm is to drink six to eight glasses of liquid a day.)
It appeared as if the dream had hit upon something. Ivar's
lack of liquid intake, particularly water, to help cleanse his
system may have contributed to his illness. Noting this, he
decided to see how he would feel if he drank water on a
regular basis. Because Ivar had a hunk-size body, he agreed
to try drinking ten to twelve glasses of water per day in an
attempt to cleanse his system thoroughly.

Ivar began religiously to drink water, more than he had
ever done in his life. He was determined to regain his full

health and vitality, and to keep it. Once the dream pointed out the need to do so, it made sense to him that his body needed liquids to do its cleansing and he felt good about this new habit. Within a few weeks he had a dream or two about a steamboat, and how enjoyable it was to feel the wheels rushing through the water, which was a health dream saying that drinking water was beneficial to his system. It was a pat-on-the-back image, confirming that his body felt good with fresh water rushing through his system.

However, within a few weeks, Ivar had a follow-up dream that left us roaring with laughter:

His Second Dream Shows a Sinking Ship:

I'm the captain of a steamboat, enjoying the journey down the river. However, as I walk on deck one day, I notice my feet are getting wet. I see the lower deck is flooding, and that the hold is full of water. I realize I have to reduce the water level so that the boat won't sink.

Ivar had no trouble associating this dream with his new habit of drinking water. This was because his new habit of drinking ten to twelve glasses of water per day had brought on a second new habit—frequent trips to the bathroom! This follow-up dream clearly gave him permission to "reduce the water level," that is, to drink fewer glasses of water per day. When he went down to six to eight glasses per day, he achieved a sense of balance he could live with. As in Ivar's experience, dreams match your exact physical needs as accurately as your unique fingerprints.

As part of the continuing saga of wishing to regain his health and a normal life, Ivar continued to monitor his dreams for health dreams. After a period of recuperation from his lymphatic cancer, Ivar began to contemplate returning to work. He wanted to be active again and do what

he loved to do, which was to work as a carpenter. In regard
to the question of returning to work, he dreamed:

His Third Dream Indicates That Rest Is Still Needed:

*I'm a member of a building crew, and we're building
something. There are four circular wooden frames within
which concrete has been poured to make pillars. The
concrete isn't dry yet, but the workmen, in a hurry to
proceed, are taking off the pillars' wooden supports. I'm
watching them uneasily, knowing the structure isn't
strong enough yet to support itself. I turn to the manager
standing next to me and comment that I don't feel safe.
I wake up feeling uneasy.*

These were dream images that a carpenter could easily understand. If he were putting up a building, Ivar would never
dream of removing its supports before the concrete had set,
lest the whole building fall apart. In the same way, his body
and health dream was telling him that his body still needed
the support of rest. The image of concrete needing time to
set was just the right analogy to show that his body needed
to "set into strength." Ivar recognized this as a vivid hint to
curb his impatience, lest he damage his now-healing body
by straining it with work before it was ready. Being a wise
fellow, he followed his doctors' orders, which corresponded
to his health dream's advice, and stayed home to rest
awhile longer.

Later, an even more serious question came up for Ivar.
Although he had recovered from his bout with cancer, during a regular checkup his doctor suggested further radiation
treatments, just in case. This puzzled Ivar. If he had a clean
bill of health, why have further radiation treatments? He
was feeling strong and healthy again, and wanted to maintain that surge of energy returning to his body. Wondering
whether such treatments were really necessary, Ivar asked

his psyche for another health assessment. It was a matter of great urgency to him, and he received a body and health dream that same night:

His Fourth Dream Shows a Perfect House:

I'm in the hospital with the doctor and some of his associates. They're all excited, running up and down the hallways, talking and arguing. They can't seem to reach an agreement and act very agitated.

The scene changes. I see a dollhouse I've just built. It's beautiful and intricate, reminding me of fine lace because of the beautiful carvings all through the wood. Going over the house, I know it's perfect. It's just right the way it is and needs no more work done on it. I'm so pleased and feel at peace.

In the first scene the dream shows the doctor's concern as one of agitation and distress, and shows that there is not much agreement as to a decision regarding treatment. This may be a metaphor for Ivar's distress, with him as the doctor needing to make a decision. Or it may have reflected the real doctors' actual uncertainty regarding the best course of action for Ivar.

The meaning in scene two of the dream is obvious. During recuperation Ivar had treated his body with due concern and respect, as though it were a delicate creation, just like a dollhouse. The intricate carvings, as a parallel to the nooks and crannies of a body, are perfect images for a carpenter. Surveying his body, the psyche replies, "All is perfect and beautiful, just as it is." Ivar took this as a suggestion that no further radiation treatments were necessary. The decision proved correct for him, as he continues to live in perfect health many years later.

Note that Ivar's dreams were clear to begin with, and that where critical decisions were required, he had a dream expert's help in deciphering his health dreams. Notice, too, that the decisions Ivar made were generally in harmony with the doctor's advice. Even though he refused further radiation treatments, the doctor had himself admitted this might by unnecessary and that he recommended them only as a precaution. You can and should work with all known medical facts rather than against them. Thanks to both his doctors and his dreams, Ivar regained his health and his sense of inner peace. Note that when a dream touches a part of you that feels true, it creates a sense of peace in you, as it did for Ivar.

5: Body Dreams Inspire Someone to Improve Her Eating Habits

Every person has his or her own set of standards regarding health: how much you eat or don't eat, eating meat or not eating meat, how much fat to take each day, how much you can weigh, and so on. Since weight is often an issue, especially for women, if your own standard is to achieve and maintain a certain body size, your dreams will work with you, as body dreams worked with Nancy.

Nancy is your average office worker: hardworking, efficient, and with an occasional streak of the devil in her when, to the delight of her coworkers, she imitates her boss's foibles. After successfully quitting smoking, Nancy gained about twenty-five pounds. Since she had been slender to begin with, the extra pounds didn't look all that terrible, so for a couple of years she accepted the new, larger edition of herself. She felt it was wise to let her body stabilize after quitting smoking before tackling the extra pounds.

But the time came when Nancy got tired of her extra weight and wanted to deal with it. As a member of a dream group, she already worked with her dreams regularly and knew they would help her. So before starting to diet, she asked for body and health dreams to motivate her and give her the strength she would need. As anyone who has tried to lose weight knows, it ain't easy, so she tried to muster all the help she could get via her dreams.

Body and health dreams on the topic of her weight did begin to appear for Nancy. In one dream she was at a high school reunion with friends. They had all managed to stay slender, except her, which annoyed her no end and awakened her competitive streak. In another dream she was in a pastry shop ordering a delicious, gooey French pastry. But it fell onto the floor before she could take it and became an awful mess of raw eggs and flour and dough, an image that repulsed her. Afterward, every time she headed for the bakery, this dream image would come back to her, and she would lose her appetite for pastry.

Such dreams helped her to begin to cut down on portions and helped her to improve her eating habits. However, the following dream brought out every ounce of fury and vengeance in her and provided the final motivational boost that got her into serious dieting. Nancy dreamed:

> *I'm at a sidewalk curb with a pretty young girl who looks like a younger, slimmer, and prettier version of me. Even though I envy her looks, I decide to let my good nature rise above my feelings and be nice to her. We have both just received parking tickets, and three handsome officers approach to take the money we owe. I give them the full amount of what I owe and they take it routinely, hardly noticing me. The young girl approaches them and gives them her money. They check her amount and find she has paid only half her ticket, but to my chagrin, they don't care. They smile at her kindly, mesmerized by her beauty, gladly overlooking what she owes. I realize they were made happy by the gift of her beauty.*

Nancy awoke from this dream thoroughly annoyed. Why should good looks excuse the pretty woman from paying half her parking ticket while she had to pay the whole amount? It was only a dream, but Nancy fumed all day at the thought of a woman gaining advantages based only on her looks. When Nancy finally calmed down, she examined what was really bothering her and admitted that the dream's implication was a truth every woman knows. When a woman is pretty, people are more responsive and cooperative to her because we all admire beauty. What really bothered her, she admitted to herself, was that she wanted those kind of advantages and would have to lose weight to earn them again.

The dream reminded Nancy that looking good allows a woman to feel more powerful and effective, which brings more opportunity her way. The dream pointedly reminded her that it was time to get back on track with her appearance and weight. The dream had created an emotional reaction, first of resentment, then of inspiration and facing the truth about her priorities. Those feelings then translated into the motivation to get back her youthful, slender looks. Shortly afterward, Nancy went on a serious diet and lost her extra pounds.

IDENTIFYING FEATURES OF BODY AND HEALTH DREAMS

1. Medical Imagery

Sometimes body and health dreams are symbolic, so that a car or a house stands for your body. But often they contain direct medical images such as doctors, operations, X rays, pills, hospitals, or discussions about health, and so on. These can be clues that you've had a body and health dream. Typically, there may be an opening scene with a medical image to tell you it's a body and health dream, and then the scene changes into a metaphoric one that explains what is going on. It may well end with a hint regarding what to do.

2. Metaphors for the Body

Watch for images that can be metaphors for the body. As noted above, common ones are houses and cars. Less common, but often seen, are images of pipes, bathroom cabinets or drawers, and dishes and pots and pans (especially if they are dirty or rusted). These can be stand-ins for the body or parts of the body. The state of the symbol tells you something about the body part. For example, a rusted pipe can suggest that eliminations are poor or that eating habits leave unhealthy residues in the stomach. Or a leaking pipe can suggest a perforation in the stomach, implying an ulcer, or may hint that a woman's menses are abnormal, with a flow that does not stop. Look at metaphors as playing a game of charades, and figure out what the image or the action stands for.

3. Foods and Eating

Body and health dreams often have images of actual foods and eating. Sometimes these are symbolic references to another issue, but often they are directly related to your health. For example, seeing yourself eat a certain food with gusto can be a suggestion that you require more of that food or food group for your optimum health. Or seeing a food you normally love, such as cake, become ugly and unsavory, may hint that it's not good for your system at this time. It's a hint that if you continue to eat it, you do so to the detriment of your body.

4. Direct and Literal Quality

Many dream types are completely symbolic in nature, but body and health dreams can have a very literal, direct quality to them. References to specific foods and eating patterns are often literal scenarios of your body's unique needs. References to medical images or discussions about your body in a dream are also often very literal. Body and health dreams may have some element of a metaphor in them, but in general they tend to be more direct and literal than other dream types.

CHAPTER 2

Relationship Dreams

Do not walk ahead to guide my way,
Do not walk behind to shield me from harm's way,
Walk beside me, and be my friend.
                                        —JOEY CRINITA

WHAT THEY DO

Relationship dreams give advice as to how to interact with people. Often, deciding whether to react in anger or with patience at something that annoys you is a difficult choice. It's easy to be unsure as to how to react to someone, or how to approach someone in a particular situation. A relationship dream comes with the specific purpose of showing the way in such questionable circumstances.

It can give guidance about how to handle a friend's crisis, or how to encourage your child's musical talent. Or you may wonder how to react to a supervisor at work. Or you may want to know how higher-ups perceive your career potential. If so, ask your psyche to provide a relationship dream. It will give accurate information about people and interactions with them, whether they were relationships in your past, in the present, or are possible future relationships. Many types of dreams include insights about other people, but the relationship dream deals specifically and fully with your ability to interact appropriately with others.

Montague Ullman, a psychiatrist and major pioneer in

the dream field, believes dreams link us to our own psyche, but even more important, that dreams link us to each other. In his view, ". . . dreams serve the purpose of maintaining and repairing our connections with others". To Ullman, the very purpose of dreams is to break down our illusion of separateness. In a dramatic statement he says:

> *Dreams monitor the struggle to be truly human, to be truly committed to other people. The main focus for us while we're awake is separateness and individuality. While we sleep, there's a shift of focus to the more basic state of our relatedness to others.*

Getting along with others is important for happiness as well as for success in life. Since dealing with people is a two-way street, relationship dreams answer two questions: How do I affect the other person? and How do they affect me? As feedback on how we treat each other, dreams sometimes throw us a bouquet, and sometimes swing a brickbat at us, but either way, a relationship dream gives you accurate reflections of where you are in relationships. Their ability to give accurate insights about how you relate to others is quite amazing, as you can see in the following examples.

EXAMPLES OF RELATIONSHIP DREAMS

1: A Relationship Dream Puts Someone at Ease Regarding an Upcoming Party

Patrick was asked to take part in a skit at an upcoming company party. Normally, he's shy, but when he does get onstage, he comes alive. Yet the upcoming acting part made him anxious, and he worried whether acting the fool at a party would put a dent in his professional image. The possibility haunted him for a few days, but then he dreamed:

*My boss is having a party with important guests. I'm
there too, watching them make popcorn. A large bowl
fills up as the popcorn begins to pop. At first everyone
looks formal, but as the popcorn pops and all generously
help themselves, people are put at ease and everyone
laughs. The scene turns into a relaxed, loving, and joyful
setting. I wake up filled with mirth and good cheer.*

People usually munch on popcorn when they are relaxing at
a movie or are at home with family and friends, so it's a
good symbol for cozy, happy feelings. The dream hinted
that just like eating popcorn, the skit would help people
open up, be happy, and relax. This relationship dream encouraged Patrick to go ahead and do his skit onstage. In the
end he was glad that he did, because it was the hit of the
party. Rather than harm his reputation, people admired his
versatile talents and his ability to play the clown. In this
way, the relationship dream helped Patrick get closer to others and be happier with himself.

2: A Relationship Dream Encourages Someone to Be There for a Friend, No Matter How Busy She Is

Brigitte was well-liked and enjoyed being with people, but
an active life sometimes made her spend less time with her
friends than she would have liked. Yet if someone needed
her, she was there for them. One day she learned that a
friend was in trouble and even though she was swamped
with deadlines, Brigitte took time to help her. Her soul
commented with this dream bouquet:

*I'm running around looking after a million things. I
see a friend walking nearby, carrying heavy packages,
her arms too full. I offer to help, but she says no, feeling
she'd be imposing on me. I insist, so she puts a package
down and I take it. She's relieved at the help, and I feel
good about it.*

This dream told Brigitte: "No matter how busy you are, your priority of making time to help the people you care about is super. Keep up the good work." This pat on the back made her feel terrific, and gave her a confirmation from the deepest part of her soul that her life and priorities were on track.

3: A Relationship Dream Shows Someone How Poorly He Is Relating in a Situation

Ed was making a lot of headway in his career and could finally see himself reaching his goals as a successful engineer. However, at one point, when he was pushing very hard to get a promotion for a senior position that had just opened up, Ed dreamed:

> *I'm on-site in a mountainous, hillbilly area where a black man has arrived to take a literacy test. He wants something but isn't getting it. So he says aggressively, "Yes, you will teach me!" It sounds militant and overpowering, but I know he won't get what he wants despite the adamant way in which he's asking.*

Ed wondered who the black man was. If you're not sure what to make of a person in a dream, whether a stranger or a familiar face, try the following trick. Off the top of your head, name two positive traits and two negative traits you associate with that person. Thinking about the black man, Ed associated positive traits of survival and courage with him, and negative traits of overassertiveness and a need for more education.

Then see if you recognize these traits in someone you've been dealing with, or in yourself. When Ed did this, he recognized himself as the black man, realizing he had been more aggressive than usual with his boss, trying to push himself into a promotion. In fact, he had almost demanded it, just as the dream implied. The dream correctly pointed out that Ed needed more experience before he would deserve that promotion. By helping him put his own behavior into perspective, Ed eased up and became more patient with his own agenda for progress. Ed's dream helped him realize that advancement alienated him from those around him, and it wasn't worth the price.

4: A Relationship Dream Helps a Timid Lady to Assert Herself

Molly was a sensitive young woman, and so cooperative and eager to please that people found her an easy mark and often took advantage of her good nature. She was trying to become more self-assertive and was using her dreams to understand herself better. A fast-talking salesman who had noticed her willing nature tried to sell her an expensive set of fine china, which she didn't need and couldn't afford. Molly was not yet assertive, but she had at least learned that not making snap decisions was a step in the right direction. But not yet able to say no in a firm way, Molly agreed to let him call on her again. A few days later he spoke to her a second time, and did so several times more, wearing Molly down. She began to seriously consider buying the set of dishes, especially since she could pay it off in three installments. Nonetheless, it would put a strain on her finances. But the following relationship dream gave Molly feedback about the questionable dynamics going on:

A smooth-talking radio disc jockey organizing a beauty contest is on the phone asking me to participate. He explains there will be three rounds, and says he already knows the score in each round, saying that I'll be a winner for sure by the last round. He's a smooth talker and very charming and I want to please him, so I'm tempted to participate in the contest even though it doesn't appeal to me and deep down I know I shouldn't. I know there's no way I could actually win a beauty contest.

Two features of this relationship dream gave Molly the perspective she needed in order to deal with the salesman properly. In real life, she knew she was nice-looking but wouldn't make the cover of *Glamour*. Secondly, it was clear in the dream that something was being pushed on her, that it was something illogical and something she didn't want. Analyzing her dream, the image of the beauty contest intrigued her. As Molly pondered sexy women vying for attention in a beauty contest, it occurred to her that she looked forward to hearing the salesman's voice even though she didn't want his product. As a shy and lonely young woman, his charm had stirred her feelings, which was why she had trouble saying no to him.

Buying a product to gain a salesman's attention with romantic illusions is illogical because his attention is not a valid part of the deal. Because of her dream, Molly saw how foolish her behavior was. The next time the salesman knocked at her door, he received the reply he should have gotten in the first place—a firm no and a clear message not to call again. For Molly, this dream insight was a major step in understanding her need to assert herself more.

IDENTIFYING FEATURES OF
RELATIONSHIP DREAMS

1. People You Know

Relationship dreams accurately portray other people and how you relate to them, even though they may use symbols, metaphors, and story lines to do so. If you dream of someone you know, she may be a symbol for some of your own traits or characteristics, or, you may be having a relationship dream about that person. Take the time to check out the alternatives.

2. What People Represent

Other people, whether strangers or those we know, sometimes appear in a dream in order to mirror our own traits back to us. This is because we are more willing to see certain traits, especially negative ones, in others than in ourselves. In psychology this phenomenon is called projection. The people in our dreams, both acquaintances and strangers, are often projections of our own traits.

If you are puzzled by what a person in your dream means, try the following trick. Whether it's someone you know, a stranger, or a well-known celebrity, name two traits you like about that person, and two that you don't. Do this quickly, taking the first things that pop into your mind. Once you've written down the two positive and two negative traits or actions, ask yourself two questions. First, do these traits remind you of anyone you know? Second, do they remind you of yourself even if they reflect a temporary state of mind or attitude? If so, then the person in the dream portraying those traits is you, or is someone else close to you, in order to elucidate how those traits are affecting your relationships.

3. Current Relationship Dynamics

The first thing to do to understand any dream is to find its theme (see the Five-Step Method of Dream Analysis, page 20). The theme is a one-liner that bests describes the dream's action and overall sense but leaves out the details. If the theme of the dream distinctly reminds you of how a current or past relationship is going or how it is affecting you, it is likely a relationship dream. Remember that the purpose of a relationship dream is to give you insight regarding interactions with others in general. Sometimes it uses dynamics from past relationships to shed light on present ones.

4. Literal Information

A relationship dream often contains literal as well as symbolic information about actual people you know. The information is provided in order to help you interact with them with more understanding. So look for literal information as well as symbolic information about your relationships.

5. Feedback About Your Own Behavior

Most relationship dreams give you information about you and how you are handling your relationships. Because we tend to be better observers of other people's behavior than our own, relationship dreams are a way of balancing this out by giving feedback about your own behavior. Once you decide on a theme of a new dream, ask yourself if the dynamic or trait portrayed between people could possibly apply to you. Naturally, you prefer not to see yourself as short-tempered, a mite lazy, dishonest, or dodging the truth, but 'fess up. In all fairness, relationship dreams are a test of your ability to grow up and to own up to your less-shining side. As such, if you dare to face the truth about yourself— both the greatness in you and the not-so-great—you can become the best you can be. Be assured that relationship dreams are really there in order to bring you to your full strength and ability; thus in the end, any pointing out of your negative side is merely a housecleaning, not a rap on the knuckles.

6. Exaggeration

Relationship dreams give insight according to society's normal rules of behavior, but they especially take your own personal standards into consideration. But remember that because dreams often exaggerate an attitude, an action, or a personality trait in order to get a point across, so people are often portrayed as caricatures, even you. Go ahead and get the point of the dream, but be kind to yourself and others

as you interpret it. Therefore, the in-law you are feuding
with is not, in reality, a devil, even if you saw him in a
dream with two horns, nor is your mate an angel, even if
she glows in a dream. By the same token, if a relationship
dream shows you punching someone out while others cheer
you on, it is not likely urging you to hit someone. Instead,
it may be suggesting that you need to assert yourself more
with a person or a situation, but for heaven's sake, do it
sensibly and kindly. Dreams do tell us the truth, but it is
our responsibility to measure those dream truths in proper
perspective.

CHAPTER 3

Decision-making Dreams

Once to every man and nation
comes the moment to decide.
—JAMES RUSSELL LOWELL

WHAT THEY DO

Your psyche has the unique feature of helping you make decisions and solve problems. Like a computer, it has the capacity to review all the present facts in light of your goals and your past experiences, and then predict what the outcome will be, based on those facts. This guessing game is often done with computers and is known as modeling. Thus decision-making dreams are an important time-saving tool, allowing you to hold an option in your mind as you go to sleep, and request a dream about the potential outcome of that option.

I believe the psyche also has a hotline to the soul so that if you want to be in touch with the Divine Will, advice is available to you from your soul. Such soul guidance helps you to achieve maximum wholeness and satisfaction for this eternal spiritual journey.

But there is a logical as well as an intuitive portion of the decision-making process that is acknowledged by the psyche and honored in your dreams. For example, a critical preliminary step in making a decision requires that you first review your options. If you haven't examined your options well, the decision-making dream will point out that you need to go back to square one and reappraise the possibilities. Thus, dreams and your psyche won't do your conscious, waking-life work for you, but they will give you feedback as to whether or not you are on track and provide hints when you are stuck.

When you make a decision, you are comparing your options to what you really want—your ideals and standards in the situation. Checking with your ideals and standards is an optimum way of making a decision that allows you to live in full integrity. Alice demonstrated this need to figure out what she really wanted and why when she met the White Rabbit in Lewis Carroll's famous tale. Running breathlessly, Alice came to a fork in the road and wondered which way to go. Along came the White Rabbit, so she asked him which road she should take. In response, the rabbit politely inquired, "And where do you want to go?" "I don't know," answered Alice, to which the rabbit replied, "Then it doesn't matter which road you take." This illustrates a most important part of decision-making—that you must have an ideal or a goal first, against which to measure a decision. If you don't know where you want to go, how can you make a decision?

A decision-making dream first requires that you have fully defined the problem for yourself while awake. Once you have done that and begin to think of options you can take regarding a decision, your dreams will work with you to help you make the choice that is best for you from every perspective. The dream psyche goes through the same steps in assisting you with a decision as you do in your waking life: It compares your decision to your overall goals and standards; it scans your options; and it tries to guess the effect the decision will have on you and on your life. Often, decision-making dreams send you back to redo one of these steps, because that is where the problem lies. The psyche may suggest you redefine your goals more clearly, or it may direct you to consider a wider range of alternatives, or it may show you a potential outcome should you take a certain option.

EXAMPLES OF DECISION-MAKING DREAMS

1: A Decision-making Dream Hints at a Need to Reexamine Goals and Standards

Julie was a born romantic, so finding a husband and partner was a major preoccupation. As a pretty brunette with a saucy smile, she had no trouble attracting men. As an artist who enjoyed poetry and images, she liked working with dreams. When she met Bill, she fell head over heels and thought she'd like to marry him. However, he remained completely elusive about a commitment. In the throes of confusion, Julie dreamed:

> *I'm with my sister who is throwing out boxes of old jewelry and makeup. I go through them with her, and put aside a few things she intended to throw out, thinking they could still be useful. I see two rings and am surprised at the one she is throwing out because it looks like a real diamond. I ask whether it's the one she intended to throw out. Did she get the real diamond mixed up with the fake one? She thanks me for pointing that out and tries to decide which is the real diamond and which is the fake one. She waves her finger through the air while fishing for an answer and begins to say, "Oh, the real one is . . ." but she can't really decide.*

In terms of goals, Julie knew she wanted to settle down and have a traditional marriage. The image of sorting out old boxes hinted that she should evaluate her old ideas and premises regarding a relationship. The jewelry was a good metaphor for what one values, so what Julie needed to reappraise were her values, to reassess what she really wanted in a relationship. A diamond ring is easily a symbol of commitment, so Julie's psyche hinted that she should examine what was going on in terms of a commitment between herself and Bill.

As she thought about it, Julie realized that Bill genuinely

liked her, yet was totally noncommittal. Like her sister in
the dream, Julie had been overlooking a key item of
information—letting herself remain blind to the fact that
Bill was not interested in settling down. Both jewelry and
makeup are adornments, since they make us more attractive
but aren't essential things to wear, so she wondered whether
the dream also hinted that Bill's values were too superficial
for her needs. It seemed possible. In reviewing the pros and
cons stimulated by this dream, Julie began to suspect that
Bill was not her Romeo!

However, because the course of love does not always run
smooth, the saga of Julie and Bill continued. Although she
began to see that Bill was not marriage material, she still
had strong feelings for him. The next time they spoke, her
resolve to let him go crumbled, so she continued to secretly
desire more from Bill than he was willing to give. Julie was
sincere in her attempts to sort things out, but her mind and
feelings were at odds, keeping her in constant turmoil.

Even though you may initially ignore or reject the advice
of a decision-making dream, your psyche will keep working
with you. In Julie's case, it sent more dreams to try to help
her resolve her obsessive yet unsatisfying relationship with
Bill. Another fake-versus-real decision-making dream
pointed her back to examine what her real values were:

*Two golden-haired dogs belong to the same couple.
The dogs look alike yet are quite different. One of the
couple asks me, "Are the dogs alike?" I reply, "Oh, no,
one is a pedigree Pekingese, the other is an ordinary dog
of mixed breed."*

Julie and Bill are both blond, so Julie reckoned the dream
was about their relationship, hinting at two "unmatched
dogs." In checking dream images against real-life reactions,
Julie realized she didn't want a Pekingese dog because the
breed was too finicky and high-strung. It was more of a
show dog than one that could be a true friend and companion. It then occurred to Julie that Bill was a bit of a dandy,

finicky in dress and manner and reminding her of the Pekingese. Because he was charming, good-looking, and popular, she enjoyed being with him and liked to show off
what a dashing boyfriend she had. But as a friend he wasn't
much of a pal, often preferring to do things on his own.
Julie was open, friendly, and practical, whereas Bill was exciting and intriguing, but high-strung and reserved. From
this perspective, the dream posed the question: "Is your
down-to-earth nature a good match for his critical, more reserved style?"

Many months and dreams later, Julie realized that she
was behaving in an obsessive-compulsive way toward Bill
that was not healthy for either of them, and let him go. She
used her dreams to ask questions and finally discovered for
herself, as the dreams had hinted all along, that they were
really not a good match. Notice that dreams don't make decisions for you. As in Julie's case, the psyche presents relevant questions and provides hints toward a particular
direction. But it was Julie's conscious, waking mind that
evaluated the information, made a decision, and carried it
out when she was ready, and only when she was ready.

2: A Decision-making Dream Shows a Need to Rethink Options

Decision-making dreams sometimes display similar objects
from which you must select one. These reflect the fact that
you need to make a choice, but may first need to reexamine
the options. Christine was a pretty, intelligent, and sensitive
sixteen-year-old participating in a dream therapy session for
young drug offenders. She volunteered this dream:

> It's nighttime. My friends and I are going out. We go
> to a building on the outskirts of town, which is a meat-
> packing plant. We enter one of its cold-storage rooms
> and I have to choose one of the sides of raw beef hang-
> ing there in long rows. I find this repulsive but feel I

*must do it so as to keep their friendship. I feel cold. I
wake up feeling turned off and unhappy.*

Discussing the dream informally, Christine checked her
own experience to get a sense of what meat, as a symbol,
meant to her. She rarely ate meat and in general didn't like
it, so it was a symbol of something foreign and unappeal-
ing. And the theme was saying: "I'm feeling forced to
choose something I really don't want." In addition, if you
look at the cold-storage room as a symbol, we often equate
"cold" with lack of love, so that the cold-storage room was
an image for feeling unloved. These were the pieces of the
puzzle Christine had to put together.

This dream took place around the time Christine was getting involved with peers who were drug users and it gave
her glimpses of where she really stood in her own motives.
The dream begged the question: "Where in your life do you
feel pressured to choose something you don't want or like,
because you feel unloved?" Christine was pensive as it
dawned on her that the dream accurately described her situation. She let herself be influenced by the others just to
keep their love and friendship. In effect, she didn't really
want to take drugs; what she really wanted was to feel
loved. This dream had a positive effect on Christine.
Whereas young ones may reject an adult's direction, they
are surprisingly open to their own psyche's dialogue in the
form of a dream. Dreams hold direction and healing for us
all.

3: A Decision-making Dream Projects How a De-
cision Will Turn Out

Ellen was clever, active, and a superb organizer. While actively engaged in several projects already, she was invited
many times to take up a position in an international group
involving volunteer work. She thought highly of their activities, but the invitation came when she already had too
many irons in the fire. However, the position appealed to

her, so Ellen wondered if she could take it on as an extra project. Ellen works with her dreams regularly, so her psyche picked up on this flirtatious thought regarding more work and presented the following modeling dream in response, as if to say, "If you take up this responsibility, this is what it will feel like":

> *I'm looking after a group of children. A bus is coming and I flag it down to take us somewhere. Everyone else has climbed aboard and the bus is waiting for me to get on board, so I'm delaying its departure. I'm carrying baggage as well as peaches and other fruit in my hands and literally begin to juggle them, but there are too many things in my hands, so I fumble and drop everything. What's worse, I'm about to miss the bus. I stand there, keenly distressed and feeling foolish. I wake up wanting to free my hands.*

The theme here is obvious, that "someone is trying to juggle too much," or "someone has their hands too full!" Ellen realized the dream confirmed her own misgivings. If she took on one more activity, it would be one too many and she could end up doing everything poorly, and being totally ineffective. Feeling at peace with her decision, she declined the position that would have been prestigious but overburdening.

4: A Decision-making Dream Projects What Someone's Decision Will Lead To

Sabrina was ambitious, worked hard, and wanted to get ahead in life. People admired her good judgment and charm and respected her dedication to her career. At one point Sabrina unwittingly entered a job which she intensely disliked. Her coworkers were bad-tempered and unpleasant, there was little cooperation between them, and even less communication. Yet as a junior still building her career credentials, she could not risk leaving a job too abruptly or on unfriendly terms.

Sabrina began to have dreams about wanting to travel somewhere. She would see herself waiting at a bus stop, trying to get to a new destination. However, even if the bus came and she boarded it, the trip would be a mess and the bus never took her where she wanted to go. Sometimes the bus was too full and she couldn't board. Or she would miss the bus, or wouldn't have the right fare. Whenever she did get on a bus, she knew she wanted to go somewhere, but had no idea where.

These dreams paralleled Sabrina's uncertainties about making a job change. She knew she had to make a change but wasn't sure which direction to take. At the same time, the job market was depressed and the competition was heavy, so switching jobs was difficult. Her getting-nowhere dreams continued for two years, paralleling several unsuccessful attempts to find a new job. Because the job scene was bleak, it showed up in her dreams as empty highways and large uninhabited stretches of land. Finally, after two years, Sabrina's goals became clear to her and the job market picked up, at least for her. Sabrina then dreamed:

> I had entered a lottery, and am now being informed by telephone that I have won first prize—a red sports car. I am very excited by this. It feels absolutely wonderful. I wake up feeling terrific.

This dream was a projection, that is, a modeling, that she was about to get the job she had been trying so long to find. Sabrina was finally going on a career trip that she had always wanted to take. Just like being in the driver's seat of a brand-new red sports car, Sabrina did indeed find a job and lifestyle she felt in control of, found exciting, and could have fun with.

Such dreams of taking a trip are a common version of the projection decision-making dream, reflecting attempts to estimate the outcome of a potential decision. A trip is a parable that says: "When you go in this direction, it's going to turn out like this, and the outcome can be like that." You may travel by plane, bus, or train, or just be somewhere in transit in your dream. Whether or not you arrive at your destination and what happens during the trip are models (projections) for what you will encounter along the way if you make that decision. Finally, the end of a trip shows how a decision is likely to turn out overall, given the present facts and circumstances. So be forewarned—if you never arrive at your destination, you are likely barking up the wrong tree of options.

IDENTIFYING FEATURES OF DECISION-MAKING DREAMS

1. Real Versus Fake

When a dream shows an item that makes you question whether it is real or fake, this is a clue that it is a decision-making dream. Examining whether something is real or fake is a way of asking you to examine what is true or false for you. Or, put another way, it invites you to check your standards, ideals, and goals regarding your question or situation. Once you know where you stand on an issue overall, you can make a specific decision about it.

2. Picking One from an Array of Many

Watch for decision-making dreams that show you trying to pick out one item from among many of the same kind. It may be picking a piece of clothing from a rack, or a dish from a buffet table, or whatever. Such pick-one-from-many scenes are telling you to look at more options, or examine your options in more depth before making a choice. Notice whether or not the dream ends in your making a choice. If it doesn't, then you have more options to examine than you've looked at. If a choice is made at the end of the dream, the dream includes a hint regarding an option that you do have, and the mood of the ending predicts how the choice will turn out.

3. Trips and Travel

Seeing yourself take a train, a bus, a plane, or any other mode of transportation is also a metaphor for an attempt to make a choice or a decision. It is a way of saying: "If you go in this direction, the journey will be like . . ." If you end up at a destination, see if you like it in the dream, because it is a projection of what that choice would actually lead to. If you are unable to catch the bus or plane but keep wanting to, either you are not ready to make that decision or you are unwilling to pay the price to get to where you want to go, and therefore you are not ready. Thus, trips and journeys are often metaphors for choices and decisions. What happens during the trip depicts how you are dealing with available options, while the end of the journey hints at the decision's overall outcome.

4. Modeling or Projection

The dream psyche is capable of predicting, in a fashion, what an outcome will be if you make a certain choice. You can test this by saying to yourself before your fall asleep, "If I do such and such, what will the result be like?" and then watch what the dream you get is like. If it is dreary and difficult, then the decision is not advisable. But if all is sunny and the dream leaves you feeling happy, it would be a good choice. You can even color-code your projections. For example, you can say: "If such and such a path is the better one, show red in the dream." Or if there are three options, color-code each one in writing for yourself, then ask for a dream that will contain the color of the best option for you. It works.

5. Notice Reactions in Yourself

Sometimes, when there is an invitation from a deeper soul level toward a decision, deep feelings are stirred. These can be positive feelings, or feelings of thoughtfulness, regret, longing, or depression. Such intense feelings upon awakening, which you can't shake off during the day, can be a clue that a dream had an invitation for you toward a certain choice or direction in your life, so examine the dreams of that night carefully. If you can't remember a dream but wake up with deep feelings, ask for a clear dream the following night to explain your feelings. Remember, your conscious mind may be the captain of the ship you are steering consciously through life, but the soul is the ship's owner and has a vested interest in how things work out in the long run. So even if you consciously think a certain path is the correct one, occasionally the soul steps in and stirs things up in order to steer you in a different direction. If followed, soul invitations ultimately bring you the most happiness.

6. Look for Dreams as Three Parts, or as a Series of Three

In order to help you make the best decision possible, decision-making dreams frequently give an overview of the whole picture. Such an overview often appears when the situation is very complex, or if you have had a great deal of trouble making a certain decision. The overview comes in the guise of a series of three dreams in a row the same night, or as a dream that has three parts. Part one deals with the past and the present, how things actually stand. Part two examines what has been done or acted on to date, and why that hasn't worked. And part three suggests a constructive option that would help bring a resolution so that you can make the decision properly. In general, look at the end of a decision-making dream for a hint regarding what action or attitude to take. It often contains just that, like a pot of gold at the end of a rainbow.

CHAPTER 4

◊

Male-Female
Rebalancing Dreams

Male and female created He them . . . .
—*Genesis*

WHAT THEY DO

This is one of the more difficult dream types to notice and understand. Renowned psychologist Carl Jung was the first to discuss how each male or female contains traits of the opposite sex, which need to be integrated into the overall of who we are. Thus when appropriate, a man needs to be able to express his feminine qualities such as gentleness, sensitivity, and nurturing. If he cannot, he becomes overbearing, tyrannical, and antisocial. A woman needs to be able to use masculine qualities of initiative and self-assertion. If she cannot, she becomes overly dependent, lacks confidence, and is anxious about life. Those who can call upon any trait feel happier, have better relationships, and tend to cope better in life.

The purpose of male-female rebalancing dreams is to help you achieve your balance of male-female traits. You recognize a male-female rebalancing dream by the appearance of an opposite-sex figure as a main character in the dream, which we can call the "animus" and the "anima." The animus is the essence of the male in a woman's dream, while the anima is the female essence in a man's dream. Because you are always growing and changing, such opposite-sex traits need to be rebalanced once in a while. Assertiveness is a positive trait in a woman, but if she becomes too aggressive, it defeats her own purposes by alienating others. Tenderness in a man is highly desirable, but if he becomes so sentimental that his emotions get in the way of what he is trying to accomplish, he has taken on too much of a good thing. Balance and perspective is always the key.

The man's anima is recognizable in a dream, for he will dream of a woman he admires: an actress, a spouse, a parent, or a relative. A woman's animus can show up in a dream in the disguise of a male friend, her husband, or her father. For either sex, the opposite-sex figure can also be a stranger such as a movie star or a politician, or it can be an archetypal figure such as a priestess or a wise old man, but it's always someone we greatly respect and admire.

EXAMPLES OF MALE-FEMALE REBALANCING DREAMS

1: A Positive Animus or Anima Figure Appears in a Dream

Despite a financially underprivileged background, Marnie decided to go to college. It was tough going all the way, having to do it alone and by her own steam, but she had learned to look to her dreams for guidance and inspiration. One night she dreamed:

> I'm climbing a very high, steep mountain. I'm tired, but I am determined to reach the top, where there's a marvelous school I can attend. I see my father, who has died, nearby, and I am so glad to have him near me. He's applauding my efforts, which makes me very happy.

Marnie's father, as the opposite-sex figure whom she greatly admires, is her animus in this dream. As an image, he plays the part of the male qualities that are available in Marnie. Marnie is exhibiting initiative and strength, which are stereotypes of male qualities, and traits her father had. By applauding, he's giving Marnie feedback, telling her how well she's using these strengths which she needs to complete her education. This dream says to Marnie: "Well done!" and at a deeper level it says: "You are using initiative and strength to achieve your goals. Keep it up." The dream reflects her successful integration of masculine qualities.

2: A Negative Animus or Anima Figure

Alan is the kind of husband many women would love to have. He's easygoing, always a gentleman, always cooperative, and always in a good mood. His wife Mattie genuinely appreciates him; and in her own down-to-earth nature and easy humor takes her good fortune in stride. Alan was a successful manager in a large firm. Because of his good nature, he was well-liked by both colleagues and subordinates. Yet one day he dreamed:

> I'm in my office at work. A blond woman, an employee in my division, comes in. I begin to shout and scream at her with enormous anger, waving my arms wildly and becoming a madman. I'm totally out of control, carried away by my anger.
>
> My mother-in-law is standing nearby. I'm astonished because not only is she calmly watching my behavior, but she actually nods in approval. This horrifies me, since I am very upset at my behavior. I wake up greatly disturbed.

It was unusual for Alan to remember his dreams, and he was particularly upset by this one, so Mattie called me to discuss it. I had met Alan, but didn't know him well, so I asked Mattie to verify a few details. Checking how literal the dream was, I asked if he was ever prone to temper tantrums. Or could he become overly aggressive at times? Mattie replied that he was just the opposite, consistently unflappable and enormously good-natured. She said he was born under the astrological sign of Taurus, and true to his sign, he was as solid and as placid as a rock. Furthermore, he was always nice to people, especially to women. Mattie confirmed he would never act like that toward anyone, or even show any anger, especially toward a woman.

Checking further differences between the dream and real life, I asked about Alan's mother-in-law, because she's a central figure in his dream. Did he have the stereotypically difficult in-law relationship with her? Mattie again replied that the opposite was true. In fact, Alan and her mother were the best of friends and they spent many happy hours together. In fact, Mattie went on to say, "Alan greatly admires my mother." Then it occurred to me, since she was an opposite-sex figure whom Alan admired, that she was an anima figure in his dream. But what did the dream mean?

Because the dream showed Alan at work, I asked how his career was going. Mattie indicated that Alan enjoyed his work, was a successful manager, and was well-liked. But then Mattie remembered a recent problem Alan had described in very emotional terms to her, about a new employee, a blond woman who behaved very rudely to him without any provocation. She would deliberately ignore his requests or challenge them, which made him furious. This information was very helpful in terms of understanding the dream because it paralleled how he felt toward the blond woman in the dream. Then I got it; the meaning of the dream became clear to me. In real life Alan was trying to deal with this new, difficult employee as he did with all employees, with discussion and kindness. But she had been unresponsive to this approach, which secretly made Alan frustrated and angry—a natural response. The result was that he could not handle her.

This was the last piece in the puzzle necessary for the dream to click. Here was a man who was successful, happily married, held a good job, and enjoyed his work. Aggression, even verbally, was a no-no to Alan, especially toward a woman. Along comes a woman at work who behaves terribly and challenges his authority. He feels anger toward her but can't express it because he's a real gentleman. Then a dream appears with an anima, his mother-in-law, who approves of behavior that he would normally not exhibit, losing his temper and showing real anger.

This was a male-female rebalancing dream. It came to tell him that while his sensitivity to others and gentlemanly ways were positive traits, they were perhaps a mite too well-developed. He had become so sensitive and good-natured that these traits interfered with his ability to become angry when needed, and prevented him from dealing with a difficult person.

The main clue of the dream's meaning comes from the image of his mother-in-law's approval at his angry outburst. Despite his shock at her approval, his psyche was telling him that it is all right to get angry at this difficult employee. As an emissary from his feminine side, his mother-in-law was saying that being tender and caring need not stifle anger when appropriate. Note, however, that the dream was not suggesting that he go into an uncontrollable rage. Instead, the rage scene was simply an exaggeration in order to put him in touch with his genuine anger, and help him break his inhibitions at getting angry. Like a caricature, the dream exaggerated the trait in order to get a point across, as dreams often do.

Alan and Mattie agreed this interpretation felt right. Last I heard, Alan is still one of the most good-natured and well-liked people around. However, he is now willing to put an employee in her place with a smattering of anger, if needed. And the day after we discussed this dream, guess who got her due?

3: Several Animus or Anima Figures Appear in a Single Dream

Having been abused as a child, Sarah received little in her childhood to give her a feeling of emotional support. She was a beauty to look at, slender, with high cheekbones and a glint of defiance tempered by unabashed friendliness. When Sarah enters a room, people notice. Yet few knew that scarred by her childhood, all Sarah wanted to do by the time she was in her late twenties was to die. She carried out her work well and went through the motions socially, but underneath it all constantly felt miserable.

Fortunately, Sarah was bright enough and brave enough to choose to enter extensive therapy. Her therapist was versed in dreams, and Sarah took to dreams easily, often having clear and vivid ones. Determined to find healing and happiness, Sarah applied herself with a vengeance to the therapeutic process.

At first her therapy rambled on, just investigating loose ends. Then she began to see insights as to what triggered her depressions and feelings of being overwhelmed. In time she found ways of snapping out of periods when negative emotions took over. Later Sarah discovered that enormous rage lay behind the depressions, a rage born in childhood at all the misery she had suffered, a rage she was afraid of. But she was learning that within anger and rage there also lies strength, a strength she started to draw on.

Soon Sarah began to convert some of the old anger into self-assertion, and her bouts of helplessness, which were brought on by past memories and patterns, became fewer and fewer. Somewhere along the line Sarah even found it was possible to forgive the adults in her past who had caused her such pain, and began to let the past go. Doing so, she found the happiness that had eluded her thus far, not the jumping-for-joy variety of happiness, but the serene peacefulness and optimism of knowing she, not a goblin from the past, was now in charge.

Sarah's dreams are a fabulous account of how to find

yourself with the help of dreams. As a reflection of finally coming into her own, one dream in particular is very revealing. Toward the end of her therapy, Sarah was savoring her new feelings of strength and happiness, knowing that she could now have such feelings and keep them going. Well, almost. Although she knew these effects were permanent, a streak of uncertainty remained. Sarah still needed a final, full assurance that her newfound courage, assertion, and ability to define her life, all of which tend to be masculine traits, were permanently hers. A male-female rebalancing dream with a number of opposite-sex (animus) figures, showed she was ready to graduate into maintaining these traits permanently:

> I'm with a television hero, a handsome black man who always triumphs over evil and wins the day. He's muscular, strong, and appealing. Others are afraid of him; I'm not as afraid, but treat him with caution. He embraces me and we kiss. It feels powerful, sweet, and soft. I then take the initiative and cautiously kiss his neck. From my feelings and his reaction, I know I don't have to be afraid of him, and that he'll protect me and care for me.
>
> In the next scene, the black man, a white man, and I are walking through a school. There's a criminal nearby, a white man, and the task of the three of us is to find him and permanently stop him by killing him. We find him. He's flimsy and weak, an insipid creature reminding me of a mere outer shell of a human being. His body hangs limply as I take him by the lapel, hold him at arm's length, and bring him outside.
>
> I position the culprit in the middle of a road, still holding him at arm's length. The two men get in a car and whiz by to run him over and kill him as is our mandate. At first they miss, but finally they successfully run over the weak man, driving back and forth over him several times, and he dies. The three of us walk back through the school. I see the dead man's desk. Seeing his empty seat, I know he is now gone forever.

This dream has two themes. The theme in part one—Sarah's encounter with the black man—is that someone loses their fear of something very powerful and possibly dangerous. This was meaningful to Sarah as an image of both her initial anger and the strengths hidden within anger, because when she first had discovered her rage, she was afraid of what it could do, unleashed. Some of that fear had lingered right to the time of this dream. So the powerful black man was a symbol of all her repressed anger, as well as of her strength. In her dream Sarah is respectful of the man's great strength, yet initially cautious, aware that he may be dangerous. By kissing the black man's neck, Sarah finally overcomes her fear and shows her willingness to explore the last portions of the deep, dark, and powerful parts of her animus. As she proceeds, she discovers that rather than being dangerous, this black hero who fights for justice makes her feel loved and secure. In this moment of time, Sarah integrated a strength in herself that had formerly been blocked by fear. Such integrations, or insights, that bring wholeness to you can take place while you are awake or, as in this case, while you are asleep, due to a dream mechanism. This is one reason dreams are very helpful in the therapeutic process—they, too, can act as mini-therapists when the person is ready.

In part two, the theme describes the execution of a weakling. There's a white man, weak and guilty, who has to be permanently done away with. Sarah and her two male friends skillfully collaborate to accomplish his demise. By driving over him several times, the psyche might be having fun via a pun, suggesting the death needs to occur as an "overdrive"—that is, a pun on the fact that Sarah really needs to overdo the image in order to finally "get it." This would be a way of saying to Sarah: "You want reassurance that the weak, passive part of you, your old negative animus that used to leave you feeling helpless, is dead, so let's drive over him not once, but several times, just so you'll be sure he's dead." The final scene, walking through the school and seeing the empty desk, is one more final confirmation.

All three men in the dream represent different aspects of Sarah's animus. The executed man was the victim part of Sarah, the memories of her past that would sometimes take her over and immobilize her strengths, thus allowing depression and passivity to surface. This shell of a man, someone weak (her negative animus, that is, a strength turned into a weakness), had emerged during her childhood as a coping mechanism during abuse. When it was in charge, even as an adult Sarah acted passive, frozen, and miserable, caught by the fears and distortions of her childhood. Thus, his symbolic death in the dream was a victory, a way of completing and finalizing her triumph over her past.

The white man who helps out shows the part of Sarah that got her through a difficult childhood, through college, and through therapy. This white man could cope, and thus he was the portion (but not the whole) of her animus that she could draw upon. But the white man could not do things on his own yet, and needed the black man's help. The black man was the remainder of unclaimed strength hidden in her old rage, which she finally recognizes as constructive and reassuring. Thus the black man and the white man, combined, represent Sarah's full strength of masculine traits, her full animus. The black man, the white man, and Sarah finally become good buddies, and get rid of the weak one who kept sabotaging her.

Sarah's past is finally behind her, for the most part. She may experience ups and downs, but no longer withdraws into a lifeless shell. These days people see only Sarah's vibrant, assertive, happy personality that always longed to come out and play. Her dreams, such as this male-female rebalancing dream, played a part.

IDENTIFYING FEATURES OF MALE-FEMALE REBALANCING DREAMS

1. A Positive, Central Opposite-Sex Figure

If there is a major opposite-sex figure in a dream, it may be a male-female rebalancing dream. When the figures are positive, they evoke admiration and respect from you. Sometimes they take somewhat of a background role, observing what is going on but giving feedback via words or a marked reaction. At other times they participate in the main action of the dream. The feedback, support, or reaction of this central figure represents the main message of the dream.

2. A Negative, Central Opposite-Sex Figure

The major opposite-sex figure can also be a negative figure, someone the dreamer fears because it is threatening in some way, or because it is trying to get you to do something that makes you uncomfortable. The negative opposite-sex figure is also bringing a message. Generally, this message relates to an opposite-sex trait that is either undeveloped in you or, less commonly, is overly developed. Look at the ending of the dream containing this negative, opposite-sex central figure. If you triumphed and overcame whatever needed to be overcome, usually as an attitude change in the dream, there will be a happy ending. If the trait still needs to be rebalanced and worked with, the ending will leave you anxious or unsettled.

3. Feedback Cues from the Opposite-Sex Figure

Look for feedback cues and clues from the opposite-sex figure. The feedback can come as words, as actions or reactions, as a facial expression, or as implied actions or reactions that you could make. This feedback portion is the

most important part of the dream, telling you what the
problem is and what the solution can be.

4. Multiple Opposite-Sex Figures

A male-female rebalancing dream can contain more than
one main opposite-sex figure. This can come as a dream in
several parts, with a different central figure in each one, or
a single dream can contain several figures, with each playing out a trait, or each reflecting a different intensity of the
same trait you are working to rebalance.

5. A Process of Elimination

Aside from noting a major opposite-sex figure, deciding
that a dream is a male-female rebalancing one is frequently
a process of elimination. Often, the theme of a dream you
have just had does not seem to fit any obvious situation or
issue in your life. So as a step along the way to finding out
what it means, ask yourself if it might contain a metaphor
for rebalancing an opposite-sex trait. I guarantee that once
you discover your first male-female rebalancing dream, noticing others becomes easier.

CHAPTER 5

Strength Dreams

My strength is as the strength of ten,
Because my heart is pure.
            —*TENNYSON'S* "Sir Galahad"

WHAT THEY DO

Strength dreams act like meters that register how strong or how vulnerable you feel, and mirrors it back to you as a dream. We don't always feel strong and we don't always feel vulnerable; instead, those feelings go up and down, depending on situations and our own attitudes at the time. Strength dreams let you know where you are on the range between feeling very powerful and feeling very vulnerable. It is important to stay in touch with how strong or how vulnerable you feel, because it helps you to maintain your best confidence level, thus enabling you to accomplish what you need to in life. It's easy to lose touch with your actual feelings and hide behind a comfortable mask, but pretending to be what you are not holds you back. Getting out of touch with inner feelings is generally more true for men than for women, because men are often taught to project a macho, always-strong mask, while women are allowed to be sensitive and thus have more permission to show their vulnerability.

When changes come into your life, especially unexpectedly, the best thing you can wish for is to have inner strength. This is because changes, even positive ones, tend to shatter safe and familiar patterns. Whether due to happy or challenging events, you feel vulnerable in new situations. Mystics say we have to learn to accept change as an inevitable part of growth, learning to go with life's flow. Nevertheless, changes shake you up, often leaving you feeling as though you are walking an emotional high-wire. As a built-in meter that registers your degree of feeling strong or vulnerable, strength dreams help you maintain this strength/vulnerability balance. Such dreams also come to prepare you for a difficult change before it enters your life, so that, as Scouts know, by being prepared, you can react with strength.

EXAMPLES OF STRENGTH DREAMS

1: Being Chased Shows That a Young Woman Feels Vulnerable with Men

As a senior in high school, Brenda became involved in a relationship a little too soon for her sensitive nature, and when it ended, it left her confused and traumatized about love and sex. Her grades plummeted, leaving her even more demoralized and confused. After taking two years off to re-orient herself, Brenda returned to school to pick up where she had left off, resolving to finish her education. But she had dreams that left her feeling tortured:

I'm in the city in the middle of the night. The streets are gloomy and empty. Suddenly I see a dark, sinister figure approaching and know he wants to catch me. He has knives and throws them at me intently, but misses. I run for my life and manage to escape. I wake up feeling very frightened.

Dreams of being chased are common. I've been chased down city streets, through subways, along highways and underground passages, and through halls of large, old buildings.

I see only shadowy, indistinct figures, but know my assailants are sinister and dangerous. In Brenda's case, sometimes there was one man, sometimes many, and she, too, was chased in subways, along streets, or in old buildings.

Having just returned to school, Brenda had two reasons for feeling vulnerable. Because of low grades before quitting, she had fears regarding her intellectual capacities. And though she had put the traumatic relationship behind her, her dream images of knives (stereotypes of masculine energies) were clues that she still had leftover fears about men. These dreams helped Brenda take the first step toward healing by making her realize these fears. Brenda slowly began to regain her strength and went on to achieve fine grades and gradually establish new relationships. As she did so, her chase dreams disappeared, reflecting her newfound feelings of confidence which replaced the old vulnerability.

The chase dream is a classic image of vulnerability, but there are others. Who hasn't dreamed of being in the middle of a crowd scantily dressed, feeling embarrassed? A lack of clothes or being dressed in inappropriate clothing is another way of registering vulnerability in dreams. These images tell us: "This situation is making me feel somewhat helpless or out of place." If you have such a dream scene, examine what in your life is making you feel vulnerable, and take steps to regain your footing of strength.

2: Falling in a Dream Indicates the Loss of Something Precious, Which Parallels Feeling Quite Vulnerable

Dreams of falling or losing something precious are another common form in which strength dreams register your feelings of powerlessness. Keep in mind that like a caricature, dreams exaggerate in order to get a point across, as happened in Jeremy's dream:

> I'm standing on the balcony of a high-rise apartment. My young son is with me, whom I love more dearly than

*my own life. Suddenly I see him leaning on the rail,
which is wobbling. I shout at him to get away from it and
rush toward him, but before I can get hold of him, the
rail gives way and he falls over. I feel complete agony
and helplessness watching him falling through the air,
knowing he's about to crash and die. I wake up with a
scream, in utter terror.*

Fearing that his young son might actually be in danger, this
dream shook Jeremy up so much that he came to me seeking an explanation. Direct warnings of actual danger do appear in dreams, but they tend to be rare. So we first tried
to understand his dream as a metaphor related to something
else. In Jeremy's dream, the action plot, or theme, shows:
"Someone loses something young and precious and is in
agony about it." A child often portrays something new that
we've started, so I asked Jeremy whether he had started
anything new in the last year or so. Following the dream's
imagery, it would have to be something new and very
meaningful to him.

Looking at it in these terms, Jeremy realized that what
was new and constantly on his mind was a part-time business he had begun eight months before. Even though it was
not his main source of income, he really hoped to see it get
off the ground and was giving it a lot of time, emotion, and
energy. After I asked how things were going with that business, Jeremy admitted that a lot of red tape related to li-
censing of imports was preventing him from making
headway. This was causing him a lot of pressure and frustration. In other words, as I pointed out, the situation was
"wobbly," just as was the railing in his dream. I then suggested to him that according to this dream, those issues of
red tape that were causing the wobbling in his business
could well lead him to lose the part-time business venture.

Jeremy was relieved to see that the dream images fit what
was going on with his new business rather than expressing
an actual danger for his son. As something precious and
young, his son had become a symbol for his new business

venture, and the dream was warning Jeremy that he "would not be able to get a grip on it," and would lose it. Making matters worse, a number of friends were involved as business partners, so his biggest loss would be prestige and credibility in his community. Such a public loss of face in a small town where success is applauded and tongues wag at failure would be hard to take, and would indeed cause even a strong man like Jeremy to feel quite vulnerable.

Sure enough, it was not long before licenses were refused, squelching Jeremy's budding business venture before it had a chance to begin. He had to admit to himself that he had gone into it without first researching it thoroughly. It was a mean blow to his ego, corresponding to the shock and terror with which he had awakened from his dream. This strength dream appeared beforehand to try to prepare Jeremy for the shock that was about to befall him, that he was completely powerless to prevent, just as in the dream. It was traumatic and did make him feel vulnerable, but the dream had helped him prepare for it and also to accept responsibility for how things had turned out.

3: A Strength Dream Shows Scenes of War and Combat to Register Extreme Levels of Vulnerability

War and combat dreams, assuming they're dreams of civilians who have not been in the armed forces*, are a more severe, escalated version of a strength dream, showing high levels of vulnerability, almost to the edge of being overwhelming. In the lower-level chase-dream version, the psyche registers your vulnerability to a new or difficult situation. It's a signal that you need to take a look at circumstances and attitudes and develop more strength. As

*If you are a veteran and have traumatic recurring dreams related to war and combat, you may have degrees of post-traumatic stress disorder (PTSD). It requires treatment from those trained in recent years to deal specifically with PTSD. Nightmares of actual veterans are unique, and in this book most are related to recurring nightmares. See Chapter 16, Frightening Dreams.

you do so, the chase dreams end. However, if you don't adjust to the new challenges, confidence may erode even further and bring even more vulnerability into play than before. At high levels of vulnerability, war and combat dreams, or any scenes with a huge amount of destruction in them, can appear.

War and combat dreams often take place in foreign countries with whom your culture has a history of war. Sounds of exploding shells and battle scenes are common, as are guns and tanks. Typical scenarios include dead or dying bodies. Sometimes the dreamer, feeling in great danger, tries to hide, as in the following example.

In his fifties, Ernie was a reliable office worker, but he admittedly was not ambitious. He preferred putting his time and energy into family and friends and could always be counted on by Cub Scout Troops, Boy Scouts, and Little League baseball teams. Yet despite the fact that he was easygoing, good-natured, and optimistic, he began to have combat dreams regularly. They escalated in intensity until the final one appeared as:

> I'm in a hut in a foreign country like Thailand or Vietnam and our village is about to be invaded. Many leave, but those of us who stay lock ourselves up in our homes, but the locks are crude, simple hooks and can be easily broken. Although it's futile, I take great care to lock up, but know it's useless even as I'm doing it.
>
> The enemy arrives without bloodshed or violence. It's a peaceful takeover but I'm a prisoner and will have to work out a two-year sentence before I'll be freed. Yet the captors are kind and will let me work out this sentence at my regular job, so I decide to carry it out in a good-natured and sincere manner. Despite the two-year sentence, I wake up feeling very peaceful, knowing that in two years I'll be free.

At the time of this dream, the small company that Ernie worked in had been bought out by a huge international corporation. Under new management, many workers left, and many, like Ernie, stayed on. Ernie's division got a new supervisor, who changed the office dynamics for the worse. In the face of the new supervisor, continued cutbacks, and unpleasant office politics, his work environment had become hard to face.

Some employees made a fuss and tried to fight the situation. Ernie was also upset at what seemed a priority of dollars over people, but knew that outbursts from a fifty-eight-year-old employee like himself would be dangerous. Knowing his job was already precarious, he kept his opinions to himself. Outwardly, Ernie rolled with the punches; inwardly, he was a bundle of nerves. As pressure built up, those combat dreams began to appear regularly. Just at the point when Ernie was thoroughly worn down by his own anxiety and the negative environment, that dream had appeared.

Ernie shared this dream with his dream group. The dream pointed out that his work environment felt so overpowering that Ernie felt like a stranger in a strange land. The crude locks in the dream hinted that resistance to the new administration was futile; there were no defense measures to take against a large corporation without putting his job in jeopardy. Yet the takeover had been smooth. Like the takeover by the enemy in the dream, the new owners had left most things intact. Ernie knew he was stuck, a prisoner of the situation just as the dream described. Yet the dream hinted that though it was unpleasant, all he had to do was accept the status quo, concentrate on getting the job done, and not make waves. By doing so, he would feel peaceful again, just as he felt at the end of the dream.

He decided to take the dream's advice and take on a good-natured and sincere attitude instead of sulking as he had been doing, and he immediately felt better. Just by his own change of attitude toward the job, a huge weight lifted off his shoulders and his old energy and enthusiasm returned. As Ernie discovered, attitude can make all the difference between feeling miserable and feeling happy.

But there was one further point of interest. Ernie was fifty-eight years old at the time of the dream and did not expect to retire until age sixty-five. Why did the dream specify a sentence of two years, after which the enemy would free Ernie? Someone in his dream group suggested that this could be a hint of ESP, a hint that the situation would change for the better in two years. And it did! Two years later the company opened up an option of early retirement for which Ernie was eligible. Having worked for that company for thirty years, Ernie happily retired and now devotes his life to the people he loves.

4: A Strength Dream Shows a Hero or Heroine to Indicate Development of Strength

In a hero or heroine dream, there's always a difficult or dangerous situation that calls for the dreamer to step in to save the day. Such scenarios indicate the dreamer is learning or has learned to handle difficult situations or emotions in a constructive way. On the meter showing powerfulness versus vulnerability, such dreams show a turning point toward gaining strength. Or they are like receiving a gold star from your psyche to let you know you've just achieved great strength! Note this dynamic in Eileen's strength dream.

Eileen was an adventurous young nurse. In her early twenties, she liked socializing and having a good time more than changing bedpans. She fantasized about quitting her hospital job to travel around the world. Such fantasies made her so restless that she even began to condemn her work as dull, drab, and insignificant.

She swung from one exaggerated fantasy version of her life to the other, never seeing that both versions, that of playing the bedside attendant and that of the world traveler, were exaggerations. Despite these episodes of restlessness and indecisiveness, a dutiful streak somehow kept her going as a nurse. Yet Eileen began to despise herself for not having the guts to quit, thinking that if she were braver, she would do so and begin traveling. Feeling depressed, she had the following dream:

> I'm on the bank of a river, wearing my nurse's uniform. People are swimming in the water. As I move closer, I notice one of the bathers is holding up a beautiful baby and that a former teacher, who was one of my favorites, is close by. The parents who are holding the child become distracted. I see a large wave coming and know the baby is in danger of drowning, which the parents can't see. My teacher sees it, too, and swims toward the baby to rescue it. Suddenly I know my teacher could rescue the baby, but because she's now elderly, she'd lose her life in the process. I am the only one who can save the day. I dive into the water and save both the child and the teacher. Noticing what had been happening, everyone is relieved.

As an image of new life, the child represents Eileen's fresh new career as a nurse. Water is often a metaphor for emotions, and in this case the child bathing in water is a reflection of Eileen's recent, highly emotional state. At first the baby is safely held up by its parents, an image suggesting that Eileen's basic values, like the dutiful streak by which her parents raised her, were standing her in good stead and "holding her up."

Her teacher's presence is significant. People in our dreams, whether friends or strangers, often act as stand-ins for traits we associate with them. To Eileen, her former teacher symbolized self-sacrifice and devotion to others, values she wished to emulate. She realized she could best develop these qualities by staying in nursing, a conclusion supported by the dream's image of her standing by the water in a nurse's uniform. Her psyche was suggesting that by staying on the job, she was gaining the inner power that would unfold a life as admirable as her former teacher's.

Yet the large wave comes along, threatening destruction. Turbulent water is an excellent image for a menacing emotional state that could sweep away Eileen's new life as a nurse. It refers to the negative attitude she had acquired toward her work, and to her fantasy of quitting. Her psyche is communicating that unless she draws on her strength and continues to build on it, Eileen will destroy something very precious—the child, which represents her career, and she will also destroy the teacher, a metaphor for the traits she really admires and wants to live by.

This dream helped Eileen accept that what she really valued could be found in a nursing career. It reminded her why she had gone into nursing in the first place, as suggested by the teacher whom she most admired. Eileen discovered that humble service was the real adventure she was striving for, that it would give her the strength and feeling of inner power she sought. Realizing this, Eileen rose to the occasion. Just as she had saved the child in the dream, the corresponding heroic act in her real life was her realization that she could be a nurse who used her vacations to travel. And while still young and single she could even take long-term assignments in foreign countries. In effect, she could have her cake and eat it too, or, rather, she could be a nurse and travel as well.

As in Eileen's case, a dream often presents a choice you can either accept or reject, right then and there, even as you are sleeping. At some soul level, whether awake or asleep, you are making choices to grow or to stay as you are. By accepting the call to be a heroine in her dream, Eileen turned a serious corner in her life. As a hidden but powerful energy that shapes our lives, the unconscious and its decisions are the seed from which the flower blooms. Eileen's turning point came when, remembering her old teacher, she changed her perspective on what she was doing. This was the same challenge that two ditchdiggers faced. Asked what they were doing, one replied sourly that he was digging a hole. The other calmly answered that he was building a cathedral. Eileen decided it was more fun to build a cathedral after all.

IDENTIFYING FEATURES
OF STRENGTH DREAMS

1. It Acts Like a Meter

A strength dream acts like a meter, showing what level of empowerment or vulnerability you are feeling at any given point. A strength dream tends to appear only if you begin to show levels of vulnerability that need some rebalancing. It is important to be aware that you are feeling vulnerable, because by being aware of your vulnerability, you can turn it around. But if you repress such feelings, they get worse and lead to erratic behavior or to levels of unexplained anxiety. At the other end of the meter's scale, a strength dream will also appear to show that you have made progress in becoming strong. So it can also be a pat on the back to make you feel very good about yourself. If you allow strength dreams to put you in touch with your best levels of strength, you can be empowered to accomplish much.

2. Low to Medium Levels of Vulnerability

Low levels of vulnerability are seen in a variety of ways. You may see a scene of wearing few or no clothes. Or you can be chased down dark streets with varying degrees of terror. Dreams of falling also register that you feel powerless and out of control, mirroring back a higher level of vulnerability. By the same token, the loss of something very precious to you, whether a material item such as a purse or jewelry, or someone you love, also indicates a higher degree of vulnerability. All such strength dreams have an important quality in common: They put you in touch with how vulnerable you really feel. Feeling powerless and out of control in a dream is a clue to how you really feel in waking life. Yet, even though strength dreams put you in touch with your weak spots, they are dreams of strength rather than weakness, because they enable you to see where the pain and the problem lie. Then you can begin to heal.

3. Extreme Levels of Vulnerability

Strength dreams put you in touch with high levels of vulnerability or helplessness by using images of war, combat, or a great amount of destruction. This can include images of violence done toward you such as rape, or of your surroundings becoming very vulnerable, such as dreaming there is a bomb in your home. When such dreams begin to come, especially if they appear regularly, it is a warning that you need to change your attitude or change the situation that is making you feel vulnerable. If you cannot do so on your own, seeking a counselor's or therapist's help is a good idea. Keep in mind that such dreams tend to appear while there is still time for healing to take place. Such strength dreams showing extreme vulnerability are an important warning signal, but one which can be dealt with.

4. Heroic or Unusual Feats

At the other end of the meter, strength dreams can show that you have attained fine levels of inner strength when you see scenes of a heroic act such as saving lives. Or they can be scenes of unusual feats such as flying or of lifting objects that are unusually heavy. Or a positive strength dream may show something transforming from the ordinary into something beautiful and extraordinary. Such dreams are definitely an A-plus rating of strength that you can be proud of. They come to let you know you are strong now and ready to achieve all that you want to in life in full confidence, and without any fears to hinder you.

5. Taking the Initiative or Remaining Passive

By now you can see that feeling powerful is a two-sided coin. On the constructive side, strength implies that there is no fear, that you can take the initiative to accomplish what you need to and want to, and that you feel an optimistic sense of empowerment. Thus, dreams showing you or someone else taking the initiative are, like hero and heroine dreams, also strength dreams, putting you in touch with what you can do.

On the negative side, feelings of vulnerability can make you feel powerless and can produce depression and passive behavior. Therefore, scenes showing passiveness, sadness, or depression are another way of registering vulnerability. If and when you do get glimpses of yourself as either vulnerable or passive, don't be too alarmed. Everyone fluctuates regularly in how strong or how vulnerable he or she feels, and such dreams generally show temporary patterns, unless they persist for very long periods of time. Remember that these are helpful dreams, merely pointing something out to you so that you can set the meter straight. Strength dreams should make you feel relieved rather than alarmed.

6. Aggression Versus Assertiveness

Remember, too, that aggression can be strength run amok. Sometimes dreams showing very aggressive scenes can hint that there is great strength to draw upon, but that it is being used unwisely. If the aggression is being done to you, then it is merely an indication that you are feeling vulnerable. However, if you are carrying out the aggression, take stock of whether or not you are turning into a tyrant, a bully, or a self-centered so-and-so who always wants your own way. In the final analysis, strength is an inner quality, so the true warrior is not one who battles the world, but one who is able to overcome obstacles in order to achieve constructive goals. If you are truly empowered and in touch with your own strength, there is no need for aggression.

CHAPTER 6

Sex Dreams

Love is only for the young, the middle-aged, and the old.
—ANONYMOUS

WHAT THEY DO

Technically speaking, sex dreams don't "do" anything; they simply reflect the topic of sex. However, not all sex dreams are about sex, so it's worthwhile to observe the range of what sex as a symbol can mean.

In the early 1900s, Sigmund Freud believed that sexual drives influenced most dreams, but psychologists now agree that this is an exaggeration. With no tangible starting point of how to map out the human mind, my guess is that Freud picked a perspective that was of great interest to him— sexuality and how dreams deal with the subject. After all, he lived in the Victorian Age, and though it was not acceptable to talk about it, sex was still very much alive. Freud's emphasis on man's sexuality freed us from the Victorian Age, but his view that sexual drives inspire almost all dreams is no longer accepted.

What we now know is that dreams that deal with sexuality occur for a variety of reasons. A sex dream can occur in order to awaken the sexual urges of someone who is inhibited. Or its purpose may be to calm someone down who may be too driven by sex. Along other lines, sexual imagery can be a metaphor for getting close to another person, because that is about as close as we get to another hu-

99

man being. What about sex dreams as simply wishful thinking? There are times that sex dreams are a substitute for actual urges, but in my experience that tends to be rare. So if you have a dream containing sexual imagery, don't jump to conclusions. Sexuality is very much a part of our body's rhythms during sleep, and very much on our minds sometimes, but in dreams, sexual imagery has a wide range of purposes which vary as much as people do.

EXAMPLES OF SEX DREAMS

1: Sexual Images Heal a Past Sexual Trauma

Some sex dreams are about sexual issues, but not necessarily about sex. The first time Donna fell in love she was in her late teens. Thinking she was in love, she became sexually involved before she was emotionally ready. When her relationship ended, her illusions of romantic love crashed, and so did Donna. Deeply traumatized, she avoided dating and was mildly depressed for three or four years. A recurring theme began to appear in her dreams, so Donna's mother brought her to a counselor versed in dream analysis. By that time Donna was in college and often dreamed:

> *I see my male professor or some other man at school whom I really admire. We talk. Later they give me a hug or a kiss. It makes me feel good, but worries me.*

As a young girl, Donna had a lot of feelings to unscramble, but it was easy to spot what her dreams were trying to do. Despite her worries, her dream embraces were mild and gentle sexual encounters that made Donna feel special. Using images of men she liked, she was practicing what it would feel like to get close to a kind and respectable man again. Along with counseling, such dreams helped Donna lose her fear and anxiety about men. Her dreams were telling her: "Some men are nice and it can feel good to interact with them." In that sense, her dreams were a practice session for seeing men in a more positive light again rather than through the eyes of her past trauma and fear. In time those scars healed, and Donna dated again.

2: Overcoming Sexual Inhibitions

Some sexual issues relate to attitudes that need healing. Tracy and Winston made a cute couple. She was tiny and slender, with a sweet personality and a calm, vulnerable disposition. Winston had a Mr. Universe physique and manner, yet a gentle, winsome smile that had won Tracy over. After their first few dates and a few hugs and kisses, Winston confided that he felt inadequate in the love department because his confidence had been ruined by unsuccessful lovemaking with his former girlfriend. Tracy tried to reassure him, suggesting that maybe the chemistry between them had been wrong and the experience did not reflect something permanent. They just kept talking and getting to know each other, and she suggested that they not make it an issue. But what Winston did not know was that Tracy was also dealing with an issue, one of sexual shyness. And the fact that he talked about his own fears encouraged her and made her more confident about reaching out to him. The night after their long talk, she dreamed:

> I'm in a supermarket on a Sunday evening. It's deserted except for a few boys emptying boxes at the back. I walk toward the back to get something, and meet one of the clerks. He's about seventeen, much younger than me, and I sense he wants sexual favors. Because I'm older, he thinks I have a lot of sexual experience, and wants to discuss a book with me that he has about how to excite himself. He's very aggressive and I'm afraid of him, but can't let him know it.
>
> I realize that in order to befriend him, I have to put him in his place and this will make him respect me. Then I'll have to seduce him aggressively and prove my sexual

*superiority. Wasting no time, as we walk down the aisle
to get his book I put my hand into his pants and take
hold of his penis, squeezing and stretching it till it becomes three feet long. This proves to him that I know all
about how arousal is really done!*

*I'm sure I'm hurting him, but he's not complaining, so
we keep walking to get his book. The outer skin I'm
holding is so stretched and loose that I wink and tell him
I'll tie a knot, just to keep it tidy. I don't really intend to
do this, but it impresses him. Finally, I loosen my caress.
His penis is soft and lost in folds of skin. I shake it up
a bit like fluffing up a pillow and return it to its natural
shape. All his aggressiveness is gone. I've proved my
prowess, and have made him an ally who respects me. I
wake up feeling really terrific, as though I've achieved
something very important.*

Just as Winston needed to prove his manhood, Tracy
needed to prove she could get past her inhibitions. In this
sex dream, Tracy was practicing letting go of her sexual
shyness. A short while later she and Winston spent the
night together. Now that she understood his concerns, and
had her nocturnal practice session, she had no qualms about
taking the initiative in the encounter. Concentrating on releasing him from his fears, they spent a delightful and satisfying night. It was an especially unusual night of ecstasy
for Winston. One might say that to Winston's delight, she
stretched his capacities to their limit. Winston regained his
confidence, and Tracy developed a new level of uninhibited
sexuality.

3: A Sex Dream Helps a Young Girl Make a De-
cision Related to Sex

Kit was part of a group of late teens who gloried in dreams
of success and what life's unlimited horizons had to offer.
Sharing their daydreams over pizza, they took good times
and the exploration of their sexuality for granted. All except

Kit. Kit liked to date, but didn't feel ready to spend the night with any boyfriend. Her friends sometimes teased her about this, but Kit knew what she wanted. Having already tried it both ways, she knew sex wasn't meaningful to her unless she cared in a deeper way for someone, and that hadn't happened yet. In her eyes, love meant more than sharing a night of pizza and rock and roll. At one point, when the teasing had escalated, Kit had second thoughts. She searched for answers that were right for her, and had this dream:

> A group of us are at an outdoor café. A girlfriend whose attitude toward sex is easy sits down with me at a table for two, and we enjoy some girl talk. We laugh and have fun, and she describes her escapades with boys. It's right for her and I'm happy for her. A street vendor comes by selling Popsicles and ice cream. My friend says, "Help yourself." She waves a few brightly colored Popsicles, takes a couple herself, and enjoys them. I like Popsicles but decide to save my appetite for some ice cream, later. I wake up feeling good.

Kit's mother was into dreams and was glad to discuss this one with her. Overall, it described someone choosing what kind of treats she wanted, and when she'd have them. Kit's friend symbolized the issue of casual sex. The ice cream vendor represented the wide range of choices a young person has these days. An open-minded and realistic woman, Kit's mother assured her it was okay to make whatever decision felt right for her. Her mother felt it wasn't a question of whether she had sex before marriage or not, but whether it was right for Kit at this point in her life.

Letting her mind wander to the Popsicles and ice cream, Kit pondered what these meant. Both were tasty. But as a diet-conscious young woman, it occurred to her that Popsicles had only a few calories, so one could eat them freely, while eating ice cream came with the responsibility of burning off quite a few extra calories. So a person could have Popsicles thoughtlessly, but she had to plan ice cream treats as part of her day's overall calories.

This sex dream was a playful analogy that compared free love to a long-term relationship. Like Popsicles, free love comes easily and has few consequences, but leaves you emotionally hungry. Eating ice cream demands more thought and responsibility regarding caloric intake. Likewise, it takes commitment and forethought to establish a deeper, long-term relationship, but such a relationship is also more satisfying. By choosing to have ice cream in her dream, Kit was telling herself from a place deep within her own soul that she'd rather wait for a long-term relationship. As colorful phallic symbols, no doubt even Freud would have enjoyed the multicolored Popsicles!

4: A Sex Dream Breaks Down Negative, Nonsexual Psychological Walls

Regina was proud and stubborn, traits that ran in her family. So when she and her brother had a terrible row, she swore she'd never speak to him again. He felt the same way. Weeks went by, and though she felt a little guilty about it, Regina's heart had hardened to the point of no return. Still seething with anger every time she thought about their raging quarrel, she resolved to cut her brother out of her life forever. But a few weeks later Regina dreamed:

I wake up in the middle of the night and notice a handsome man in bed with me, but because it's dark, I can't see who it is. We make love with wild abandon and it feels good. As morning dawns, I notice it's my brother, and I am horrified. I wake up deeply troubled.

As Regina awoke, she wondered whether the dream meant she had a secret attraction toward her brother. Yet she had no reason to think so, because her brother felt exactly like a kid brother, and only a kid brother. Consulting a friend who was familiar with dream analysis, Regina discovered that dreams deal with what's actually happening in our lives. This dream's theme, her friend pointed out, said: "I'm surprised at who I love." So the question the dream was putting to Regina was: "Who in your life do you love that would surprise you?" Or stated another way, it was asking, "Whose love is hidden and yet is forbidden?"

Regina began to see this dream did relate to her brother. Despite their fight, it put her in touch with the fact that deep within herself she still loved him, but her recent adamant rejection of him now made him a "forbidden" love. The dream was a reminder of deeper feelings for her brother that she was trying to hide from herself, feelings of sisterly love. Though it used sexual imagery, the dream stirred her loving thoughts and feelings about her brother and succeeded in helping Regina let go of her anger toward him. As in this case, sexual symbols can be a metaphor for deeper, nonsexual feelings. And who can be angry at someone with whom you've just had terrific sex?

5: A Sex Dream Renews a Woman's Dormant Sexuality

This is an example of a sex dream that is truly about sexuality and describes an amazing sexual healing. Jeanne had been happily married for six years when, to her dismay, she discovered she had breast cancer, which led to the removal of her right breast. The emotional and physical shock of losing a breast devastated Jeanne. Though her husband was greatly supportive of her feelings through her long illness, it was a major disruption for him, too, and he was confused and distressed at the break in what had been, up until then, a joyful and healthy sex life. For more than a year after the surgery, Jeanne would not let herself get close to him. Neither knew what lay ahead, taking the year of sexual abstinence in silence.

By spring, Jeanne's body had healed, but her emotional state had not. Despite her husband's assurances that he still loved her, Jeanne felt unattractive and depressed and refused to even consider having sex. Yet she longed to feel feminine and satisfied again. One night, Jeanne dreamed:

> *I see myself as the essence of womanhood. I am a wood nymph, scantily dressed in a brown, soft suede outfit, walking happily through an enchanting forest. Suddenly I come to a clearing and find a man waiting for me who is known for his sexual prowess. He seduces me on a bed of moss, and we enter a period of total, complete, and utter lovemaking of an intensity I've never experienced. After many encounters, we finish, and I feel totally and completely refreshed and renewed.*
>
> *My lover leaves, but another man, one of the most handsome men I've ever seen, appears. We make love, and his sexual powers are equal to those of the first man. Much time passes, and after I am totally satisfied, he leaves. As I rest, a third man appears, whose gentle, laughing eyes entrance me and lead me into another encounter of complete and ecstatic lovemaking.*
>
> *After I have had encounters with six different men, each with different yet amazing qualities, I am finally alone again. It's dark now. I see brilliant colored sparks of light beginning to appear in front of me. Like fireworks, the sparks of light take the shape of a graceful and exquisitely beautiful bird that flies away. Like the fireworks, only a memory remains.*
>
> *I feel like mother earth, with a sense of wholeness and abundance sufficient to embrace and comfort the whole world, and I feel strong and whole. I wake up feeling sexy, incredibly energized, and at peace.*

Jeanne woke up totally changed in attitude. Rather than feeling depressed and unattractive, she once again felt whole and happy in her womanhood, with a restored sense of sexual prowess. Following this dream, Jeanne and her husband resumed their sex life, entering a new era that brought more excitement and fulfillment than ever before.

Her experience shows that we have much to learn about the power of dreams to heal and to balance sexuality.

IDENTIFYING FEATURES OF SEX DREAMS

1. Healing Sexual Attitudes

Some, but not all, sex dreams are about sex. The most common purpose for sex dreams to appear is to heal some attitude or past trauma related to your sexuality. Sex dreams are easy to identify because they contain sexual and intimate imagery. The theme of a sex dream will be the major clue as to whether it is actually about sexuality or whether it is a metaphor for some other issue.

2. Insight and Healing for Psychological Problems

Many sex dreams come for the purpose of healing nonsexual problems. In this case, a sex dream uses sexual imagery as a metaphor related to a psychological problem, attitude, or nonsexual emotion. Since sex is an image of "getting close," it easily stands up as a metaphor for getting closer, or for situations where things have become too close for comfort. It is always the theme that will help you differentiate whether the dream is actually about sex, or about some other issue.

3. Breaking Down Barriers or Putting Up Needed Barriers

Some sex dreams come to evoke feelings that break down unhealthy barriers. This is often the case when you dream of having sex with someone you can't stand. By having enjoyable sex with that person in a dream, you can't help but look at them with new, more positive feelings thereafter. By the same token, sometimes sex dreams come to warn you to stay away from certain relationships that are not good for you. For example, if you dream you are having sex with someone and feel disgusted by it, it is a clue that the relationship is not a good one for you.

4. Individual Standards

Keep in mind that dreams are not judgmental. When sex dreams make evaluations related to issues in your life, they are based on your own standards of sexuality. So whether you have more relaxed standards or more stringent ones, your dreams reflect your personal beliefs and needs, and no one else's.

PART II

◊

Dreams That Help You to Remove Life's Roadblocks

CHAPTER 7

◇

Rebalancing Dreams: Dreams That Rebalance Your Emotional States

Speak what we feel; not what we ought to say.
—SHAKESPEARE'S *KING LEAR*

WHAT THEY DO

Rebalancing dreams do just that—they rebalance your emotions. Sometimes emotions or attitudes go overboard. Your anger gets out of control, or you become oversensitive, too fearful, or even too optimistic. Part of the psyche's normal housekeeping duties are to spot emotional imbalances at an early stage and work with you to nip them in the bud. The rebalancing dream is the medicine sent by the psyche to accomplish this.

The psyche acts as an automatic meter in many ways. As far as emotions are concerned, it keeps track of your normal range of emotions and reactions, and then notes when they are a little off track or going way overboard. There are two types of medicines rebalancing dreams send. The first is a dream that acts as a mirror. The mirror-version of the rebalancing dream simply shows you that you are off track, just to bring the situation to your attention. Because it's likely a small imbalance, just bringing it to your attention helps you get back on track.

The second type packs more of a punch, because it relates to a stronger imbalance. It's a rebalancing dream that acts as a catalyst and works by actually initiating a reaction and change in the dreamer. Such a catalyst version of the rebalancing dream takes specific aim at the imbalance and provokes a strong emotion in the dreamer that acts as an antidote for the imbalance. Such a catalyst effect can feel like a nurturing hug or a kick in the seat, depending on what you need to get you out of a temporary emotional imbalance or dysfunction.

EXAMPLES OF REBALANCING DREAMS

1: A Mirroring-Back Version Rebalances Scattered Feelings

Amanda's work required frequent travel, often on short notice. Between trips she was a homebody but stayed active in the community, happily involved in her children's school and the church choir. One night Amanda dreamed:

> I'm at home, walking downstairs to the den in the basement. I notice the door leading to the garage is open, and when I go to close it, I glance inside. I'm horrified to see someone has left the garage door wide open and that wild neighborhood kittens have entered and are having a grand old time running over everything. The garage is still okay, but the kittens are chaotic and out of control and could do some damage. I close the door leading into the house just in time and am relieved the kittens didn't get into the house. But I don't relish the thought of clearing them out of the garage.

Kittens are a good symbol for rushing around but accomplishing little. So the dream describes scattered energies that through carelessness have invaded a normally orderly space. Amanda was normally highly organized and carried on her life in an efficient manner. Looking further at the dream's images, a garage is where we keep a car, the vehicle that takes us places, and it can be a metaphor for our direction in life. The dream thus hints in several ways that someone is scattered and needs to readjust her sense of direction.

Due to this dream, Amanda took a quick inventory of her life. She began to realize that she had in fact been feeling scattered lately, like the kittens in the garage, and tried to figure out why. She began to see that people were draining her, and that she was giving too much of her time away to those who could actually help themselves. This tendency to let herself be taken advantage of was paralleled in the dream by the metaphor of leaving the garage door open, which lets the stray cats enter. Amanda did reorganize her priorities, and feeling more at peace, felt her calm energies and feelings return.

2: A Mirroring-Back Version of a Rebalancing Dream Helps Unplug Feelings Stuck in the Past

A rebalancing dream can also mirror back too much of a good thing, as it did for Kelly. Smart and sassy, Kelly had been totally engrossed for a year as chairman of a national conference. There were endless details to look after, and since it was her first time organizing a conference of that scope, there were also endless anxieties. However, Kelly succeeded with flying colors, and the conference accomplished its goals and provided memorable social events. Kelly rightfully accepted bouquets and accolades for this achievement. A month afterward, she was still floating on air from her success. While vacationing by the seashore for a few days, she dreamed:

> I'm walking back and forth in the hospital corridors where I work. There are long tables laden with banquet leftovers like smoked salmon and salted herring, my favorite dishes. I just gaze and feel the wonder of it all and am pleased at how beautiful the table is, with its matching linens and flower arrangements. I'm walking along,

*floating on air, just overjoyed. As I walk, I invite others
to help themselves, though there's not much left. Yet
there's a feeling of sumptuous plenty and of something
important going on.*

The dream portrayed someone savoring the joys of a meal
that has virtually already been eaten, as per the image of a
banquet where the guests have already come and gone. This
was an image that spoke volumes to Kelly, for a banquet
had been one of the highlights of the conference. In the
dream she's still soaking it all up and still inviting guests to
partake of the leftovers.

Now on vacation, Kelly had a right to feel good about
her success and to savor it. As her favorite dishes, the
smoked salmon and herring in the dream portrayed how
personally satisfying the experience had been for her. And
as a review, the dream helped Kelly feel a sense of accomplishment and completion about the event, nurturing her
feelings of self-confidence and self-worth.

However, her psyche was reminding her with this
rebalancing dream: "Yes, it was wonderful, but you've been
floating on air long enough. Relive it one last time, and
then move along." The leftovers are the clue to this advice
because it doesn't take long for leftovers to go stale, as
would happen to Kelly's energies if she kept thinking
about the past. As an avid follower of her dreams, this one
made the difference between enjoying her laurels and resting on them. Rebalanced, she looked once more to the future to decide on further uses of her talents.

3: A Catalyst Version of a Rebalancing Dream Reverses Mild Depression

Heather was feeling blue for a few weeks. Nothing was
wrong, family and friends were well, and she knew she was
loved. She didn't know why her sadness continued, but it
did, settling in like a fog that wouldn't budge. Her psyche

took the initiative to remove it, by providing the following rebalancing dream as a catalyst:

I'm on a bus. There's a group at the front laughing and having a good time. I'm sitting at the back, feeling lonely and distant. I'm sure the gang up front is nice, but they're just not my type. Then I see my beautiful young niece coming toward me. She gives me a huge hug and asks for her black doggie, a stuffed animal. Her love flows through me, and makes me feel so good.

When Heather awoke she was happy again, feeling nurtured and comforted. The blues had disappeared and didn't return. She didn't know why they had come or gone, but it didn't matter. She could have explored the symbols in the dream to find out what they meant, but she didn't need to because the dream had already accomplished the task of dissolving her blues. This is a characteristic catalyst version of a rebalancing dream, where some emotional reaction it creates provides the cure for what ails you.

4: A Catalyst Version of a Rebalancing Dream Reverses Someone's Dark Mood

The winter caught up with Carrie. Normally she took good care of her appearance and paid attention to whatever she did. But now she had a bad cold, was feeling miserable, and wanted to shut out the whole world. Yet because she was responsible for deadlines and work no one else could take care of, she went in to work even though she felt miserable. Each day Carrie felt more and more grim. Sensing her mood, colleagues were smart enough to leave her alone, but her psyche would not leave her alone, and she dreamed:

I've just gotten out of bed, washed my face, and am putting on my makeup. I've been groggy, but suddenly I notice my eyebrows are black and thick. I shudder at how overgrown they are, dark and half an inch wide.

They look like the eyebrows of a villain in an old movie, and obviously need immediate attention. I smooth oil over them and see what needs to be plucked.

Carrie woke up feeling some drastic improvement was necessary. This dream shocked her into waking up and evaluating her appearance, and it was so real that the first thing she did was walk to the bathroom mirror to check her eyebrows! To her relief, they were still light brown and shapely. But then she noticed the expression on her face, a scowl, and began to understand the dream.

It took her only a second to realize that it was her black mood, not her eyebrows, that needed improvement. This catalyst dream shook her up enough to notice that she had allowed pessimistic and cynical feelings to rule her, causing her to become antisocial. Carrie quickly turned her inner feelings around, making herself and her colleagues happier with a more pleasant attitude and a more optimistic mood, which was her normal, true self. Soon both the cold and the bad mood had lifted.

You've now seen two kinds of rebalancing dreams. One mirrors back what you're feeling that is out of balance, and the insight alone helps you regain your footing. The second kind acts as an instant catalyst, dissolving imbalances that have left you emotionally stuck. Both types of rebalancing dreams are common in our dream landscape, and I cherish this automatic role of rebalancing of my psyche. Keep in mind that the psyche is like a dear friend; it won't trespass beyond the limits with which you feel comfortable. This also means that the transformations available in rebalancing dreams come only after we consciously acknowledge an openness to constructive growth and change.

IDENTIFYING FEATURES
OF REBALANCING DREAMS

1. Strong Emotional Issues or Personality Traits

A rebalancing dream deals with a strong emotion you've been feeling at the time of a dream, or a personality trait that may have gotten out of balance. These can be negative or positive traits or emotions that have gotten out of balance. Try to note whether the dream is dealing with a strong emotion in you that is unbalanced, or whether it evokes a strong feeling in you. Either situation indicates that it is a rebalancing dream.

2. It Acts as a Mirror

One form of rebalancing dream acts to simply mirror back your feelings to you. So if a dream has a strong emotional content or theme, ask yourself whether it reflects how you are actually feeling. If it does, check whether the dream is hinting that these feelings are either overdone or off track.

3. It Acts as a Catalyst to Initiate an Emotional Reaction

Another form of rebalancing dream is one that actually creates an emotion in you. The purpose is to produce a reaction to a feeling or attitude that is out of balance, so that the reaction it creates becomes the antidote.

CHAPTER 8

◊

Review Dreams: Dreams That Review Past Events or States of Mind

Wherever the wind takes me I travel as a visitor.
——HORACE

WHAT THEY DO

Review dreams literally go over a past event in order to extract information that you missed and is important for you to have. Imagine you had lunch yesterday with an old friend you hadn't seen for a while. You part ways but are left thinking that your friend seemed strained. Remembering an ambiguous part of the conversation or some emotional reaction, you wonder if he was hiding something or had something to tell you but just couldn't get it out. However, it's a busy day, so you don't have time to dwell on it any further.

That night your psyche goes over the incident as part of its automatic daily review and clear-up duties. It evaluates your unresolved emotions and questions about what was really going on between you and your friend. Your psyche has access to wider, subliminal cues such as telepathy, to which you don't have conscious access. The psyche's post-review evaluation comes back to you in the form of a review dream and puts the incident into perspective. But the review dream does more than just scan the event; it also

118

adds some new insight, such as what you should do next, if anything.

Review dreams cover a range of situations. They can review an incident that occurred yesterday, but they can also review a situation you have been dealing with for months, or even years. For example, you may have been working on a business deal for three, six, or eight months and it has finally come to its conclusion. Having been intensely involved with it for a while, you need to relax and clear your brain before taking on something new. This is like resting after eating; the stomach needs time to digest what it's just eaten as part of its natural rhythm. In the same spirit, a review dream can recap the highs and lows of what happened with the project over the last few months. There are lessons to be assimilated and successful moments to be savored and put into perspective before you can put those months behind you. This is the purpose and function of the review dream. It's a way of digesting an event or a cycle in your life so that you learn the most from it and then can let it go and go on.

A review dream can also review past attitudes, accomplishments, or incidents in your life. For example. if you ask the question: "Have I been a good father to my children?" or "Have I learned to take charge of my life rather than be a victim of circumstances?" a review dream can give you a reply. Dreams can review a marriage of fifteen years that has just ended, childhood episodes that still affect you, or habits that are hanging on and need updating.

There is yet another kind of review dream, one that comes in cycles. The cyclical kind appears when you are letting go of one phase of your life and are about to begin a new one. At such transition times, review dreams often appear as a way of preparing you at a deeper level for the change from the old to the new. It's like taking inventory of the past in order to see what's still useful for the future and what isn't, or like going through the cupboards to get rid of the clutter and make way for new things you'd like. Review dreams help you take a fresh look at attitudes, lessons, and inner progress that you've made in the last round, kind of like going through your soul clutter. Once done, it leaves you so prepared for the new phase of your life that you positively sparkle.

EXAMPLES OF REVIEW DREAMS

1: A Positive Review of a Recent Attitude

A review dream can give positive feedback. Georgia is a gorgeous redhead. True to her colors, she can be quick to anger and quick to subside, but most of the time a sunny spirit permeates her energetic personality. One day Georgia was planning to meet her sister for a day of shopping. Her sister was notoriously late. That day Georgia remembered how her past fits of temper at her sister's lateness had put a damper on their pleasant excursions, so she decided she would not lose her temper, and, despite the fact that her sister was a little late, she kept her peace. That night she dreamed:

> I'm walking down the street wearing a pretty light-blue dress. A car passes abruptly, driving through a mud puddle at high speed and spraying mud all over my dress. I'm furious, but there's nothing I can do. To get to where I'm going, I jump into a narrow river and swim across. The water has a strong undercurrent and looks dangerous, but I make it across. When I get to the shore, someone says, "It's a good thing you didn't get caught up in the strong current." I feel calm and pleased to hear this. For some reason, it's high praise.

A veteran with dreams, Georgia laughed as she woke up, knowing instantly what it was about. She knew the question to ask herself was "What current did I not get caught up in yesterday?" She remembered that, as expected, her sister had been late, an act of inconsideration symbolized by the spray of mud on the dress in the dream. Though this normally left Georgia sizzling and in bad temper, she settled for a wry comment to her sister, and then let the incident go.

Since water is often a symbol for emotions, the current Georgia escaped was obviously her own temper. Georgia had dealt with her anger and went on to enjoy a day with her sister, a wonderful day of shopping and catching up on gossip, a day that she would not want to trade. Her psyche reviewed this success and, by giving positive feedback via a review dream, applauded it.

2: A Review of a Recent Decision

Joan is an associate in the dream field. We were scheduled to give a talk at a major convention, and met to work out the material and the presentation. After a brainstorming session, we agreed to get together once more for a final practice of the presentation. Before our final meeting, I had this review dream which discussed our brainstorming session and our attempt to put together an interesting talk:

> I see my sister leaving for a conference. At first she's wearing a brown business suit. Then she changes her mind and decides to wear something brighter, a dress with green and red coloring. People are cheering us on, and we're cheering each other on, which seems to be important.

When we met the following day, Joan and I talked about our dreams, knowing they might provide a commentary on our efforts to make an excellent presentation. Joan immediately recognized the thrust of my dream. Clothes are a good symbol for the impression you want to make. Thus, the initial drab business suit in the dream suggested that our material was too dull and businesslike.

Checking this out, we realized that we indeed had too much theory and too few real-life examples, and it's the ex-

amples that make the understanding of dreams come alive.
The review dream had accurately pointed out that we had
overlooked the most interesting part of the presentation—
the stories. Taking the dream's advice, we added lots of
amazing stories which made our presentation interesting
and vibrant. Our success was reflected in the fact that we
spoke to a standing-room-only crowd who couldn't get
enough of what we had to offer regarding the rewards of
using your dreams.

3: A Review of Long-Standing Habits and Attitudes

Reviewing what has failed and what has succeeded in the
past can provide important clues for present decisions.
James knew this, and as an aspiring advertising executive,
he kept an open mind toward all tools that can help solve
complex problems. When he began to compete for a major
promotion, he looked to his dreams, as well as to other
sources, to guide him through this highly charged period.

When the opening came up for a vice presidency in his
company, there was no shortage of qualified candidates, but
he, too, wanted to take his best shot. Trying to impress his
superiors by drawing in new clients, James became more
aggressive, setting up lunches and meetings and writing
outlines of possible campaigns.

But as the months passed, he had not managed to get
many more clients or the promotion. James reacted by trying even harder and getting even more aggressive, thinking
that the company wanted a real go-getter. Instead, all he
achieved was getting frustrated and clashing with one or
two other associates, who felt their territory was being in-
fringed upon. In the midst of this confusion, Jim dreamed:

> *I have a small child in my arms. He's normally quiet
> and easygoing, but sometimes gets upset and aggressive.
> We're on an excursion far from home in a room with
> white walls and long hallways. The child badly needs to*

*go to the bathroom, so I search for one. We glimpse the
sidewalk of a mall through the window and a friend suggests we'll find a bathroom in the mall. But it turns out
that the mall's bathroom is not next door, as we hoped,
but seven buildings farther down. It's late and we're too
tired to walk that far.*

*So I try something else because I don't want the child
to suffer. I go into a restaurant nearby and explain the
child's dilemma to the manager. As I talk, I hug the child
with great affection and feel very protective. The child is
suffering, but despite his great discomfort and turmoil, he
remains loving and patient. I expect the manager to let
us use his executive toilet, but instead, he puts some
medicine on his finger and puts it on the child's tongue
to dull the pain. I protest that this is no solution, but the
boy licks the medicine. I'm dismayed that the manager
doesn't seem to care and doesn't help.*

The child was an apt symbol for something new Jim was
attempting, trying to get the promotion by proving how
much of a go-getter he was. Like Jim, the child is normally
tranquil and loving, but can get cross and aggressive. Jim's
executive offices are in a building with white halls and long
hallways, which tipped him off to the fact that this dream
related to work. And if the dream had a title, it would be
called: Seeking Relief but Not Finding It.

Just like the child, James's attitude toward work was initially laid back and cooperative. He became aggressive because he thought it was a quality that would win him the
coveted promotion. But when it didn't work, James needed
relief from his frustration. The dream hints that he'll just
have to bear the pain, for instead of getting a key to the executive washroom—which would be like getting the
promotion—James's child receives only balm. So the dream
was predicting that he was not likely to get the position he
coveted whether he used aggressive tactics or not, which
turned out to be correct.

What, then, was the dream suggesting would be the right

attitude for Jim to take? Licking the medicine despite protests is one clue, suggesting that he bear his disappointment
and accept circumstances as they are. Since the bathroom in
the dream was far away, it suggests he still had a long way
to go before he could find relief, that is, before he would
get such a coveted promotion. The fact that the usable bathroom was seven blocks away could have been a hint that it
would take seven years for him to earn such a position.

But there's another interpretation that's even more likely.
In numerology, the number seven has mystical and spiritual
implications of which our unconscious is intuitively aware.
Since symbols are picked very carefully by the psyche, the
dream may have been implying that Jim's path of progress,
at least for the present, lay in the path of spiritual and inner
growth, which is what the number seven represents. This
rang a bell for James. He realized he liked working hard for
the company, but felt most at peace when there was enough
time to go hiking, visit museums with his wife, go to
church picnics, and build a tree house with his young sons.

The dream's symbols came back to him full circle and
suddenly it all fell into place for Jim. Feeling a burden lift
from his shoulders, Jim went on his way, finally feeling at
peace, and realizing that the time with his loved ones and
in spiritual growth was more important to him than a promotion that would demand extra work.

4: A Review Dream Examines How an Incident Affected Someone

Grace was visiting an out-of-town friend. After dinner they
sat in the living room talking, enjoying each other's company. The conversation turned to the importance of looks,
and the hostess, Lorna, an attractive but average middle-
aged woman, confided that she had little confidence in her
appearance.

Trying to say something reassuring, Grace pointed out
that many women have low self-esteem regarding their
bodies, even when they look good. She went on to say that

everyone instantly recognized her hostess's intelligence and warmth, intending to convey that beauty should be of secondary importance to personality. But it was a sensitive issue for her hostess, who chimed back in mock anguish, "Well, thanks a lot!" She sounded as though she had barely won third prize in a beauty contest with only three contestants. Grace realized that without intending to, she had hurt Lorna's feelings, but didn't take it too seriously since Lorna had quickly changed the subject. That night she dreamed:

> *I'm receiving a book as a prize and the award is announced as "... to someone who is less than desirable physically, but who has a beautiful mind." This is a backhanded compliment. I'm hurt and annoyed and want to throw an egg at the master of ceremonies. I half-heartedly throw a ball of scrunched-up paper at him, which lightly hits his shoulder. Then I feel foolish for showing my resentment.*

As all avid dreamers do, Grace analyzed her dream as soon as she woke up and knew it had reviewed that incident. She realized her psyche was pointing out that Lorna was more hurt by the remark than she had shown. By experiencing how the contestant in the dream felt, the dream put Grace in touch with Lorna's true feelings. Vanity may make us all a bit unrealistic, but we all need to feel like Cleopatra to some Antony in order to feel confident. Grace had accidentally taken that harmless illusion away from Lorna for a brief moment.

Grace was happy to dream this while still visiting Lorna, and the incident was fresh enough to fix. Over breakfast she managed to discuss Lorna's basic attractiveness, especially her flair with clothes. Her hostess looked reassured as she glowed under the genuine compliments.

IDENTIFYING FEATURES
OF REVIEW DREAMS

1. Theme Can Be Related to Something Recent

Always begin by finding the theme of a dream (the action stated in one sentence). If the theme fits something that happened recently—an event or an attitude or a feeling—it can be a review dream.

2. Images from Your Past

A review dream may contain images from your past, especially if it is reviewing a longer period. You may see scenes of a childhood home or school, old friends, or articles you once had. Such images from your past may be hints that it is a review dream.

3. Processing Leftovers

If something from your past is bothering you, look for a review dream on the matter. This may be something from either the recent past or the more distant past, or even from your childhood. Review dreams process all leftover thoughts, feelings, and situations that leave a hangover effect on you, but you won't notice them unless you are looking for them. Because dreams in general deal with what is already on your mind, if something from the past is bothering you, look for a review dream. In fact, instead of waiting for one to appear, you can ask your psyche to provide one.

CHAPTER 9

Nonsense Dreams

Through sense and nonsense, never out nor in;
Free from all meaning, whether good or bad.
                              —JOHN DRYDEN

WHAT THEY DO

Dreams sometimes contain features that appear absurd, but
when they are looked at as a pun or a play on words in the
context of the entire dream, they make sense. For example,
watching a clock run down the hallway is absurd, but the
pun it creates, that time is "running out," makes perfect
sense for some situations. Or a person's head may be
grossly enlarged; though it looks ridiculous, as a visual cha-
rade game it speaks of "a swelled head," which is a pun for
someone who thinks too highly of himself.

Such pinches of absurdity in dreams are like a hint of
spice that adds tang to a dish, but the spices blend harmo-
niously, just as some unusual dream images add up to a
meaning. Such visual puns are not what nonsense dreams
are about. Instead, nonsense dreams are entire dreams that
are so far beyond making any sense that the absurdities,
distortions, and contradictions they contain make no sense
at all. In effect, nonsense dreams leave you baffled because
there really is no sense to them. However, true nonsense
dreams are rare, so just because you can't extract the meaning in a dream does not make it a nonsense dream.

Yet paradoxically, by being in fact entirely nonsensical

and baffling, they contain a message after all. Nonsense dreams are actually warnings about contradictions and distortions in yourself, which, if noticed and caught in time, can save you from messy consequences. So even though genuine nonsense dreams are rare, they are worth checking out.

You may dream of yourself eating a tennis shoe, and shudder. The actions are illogical, but because you notice how absurd it is, you are saved by the awareness of your own absurdity. Such a nonsense dream may be trying to warn you about something unreasonable going on around you. Perhaps your husband is planning something ridiculous like selling his business and moving to a farm, and your dream is suggesting that his plan is as indigestible as eating a tennis shoe. Or maybe your extroverted daughter is planning to major in library science, a program suited to introverts but not to your outgoing daughter, so the dream suggests it will agree with her about as much as eating a tennis shoe. It's a warning that she needs more guidance from someone with whom she can sort things out. Thus, nonsense dreams alert us to confused, distorted, or contradictory behavior in you or in others that needs attention. If the confusion and distortion is caught in time, it can help prevent the messy consequences that would otherwise follow.

A final note. The dreams you have during a fever or other illness do not count as nonsense dreams. At such times, you may typically experience weird imagery that makes no sense. These random images are not messages; they are merely peripheral images experienced as the body attempts to heal itself. Such random, meaningless imagery may also occur just as you are falling asleep, which is called the hypnogogic state.

EXAMPLES OF NONSENSE DREAMS

1: A Nonsense Dream Shows Someone Doing Something Totally Absurd

Bernie was a successful businessman. He was proud of the fact that he had become president of his company by the time he was forty, but paid for his success with a broken marriage along the way. Handsome and debonair, he rightly thought of himself as attractive to women but was puzzled and taken aback when a young, woman in her early twenties rejected his advances. It made no sense to him that she could prefer her young, but inexperienced, boyfriend to him, someone twice her age, so he persisted in trying to win her over. One night Bernie dreamed:

> *I'm sitting at the keyboard of the teletype machine in our communications room. The machine is broken but I keep pounding away at the keys. I'm determined and desperate to make it work.*

Bernie shared this dream with his therapist, who pointed out his illogical behavior in the dream—trying to force something to work that couldn't possibly work. This matched Bernie's continued efforts to sway the young girl despite her consistent and firm rejection. The dream was pointing out that by refusing to take no for an answer, Bernie was behaving in an illogical, distorted manner. It was Bernie's attitude that was broken, not the teletype machine, because his attitude was no longer logical. Normally Bernie was practical and down-to-earth; after this dream he duly noted his illogical behavior, brought on by his infatuation with a pretty young thing.

2: A Nonsense Dream Warns of Another's Upcoming Absurdity

Glenda worked as an administrative assistant in a university. Involved in a student-placement service, she enjoyed being in touch with students and employers and generally fit in well with the relaxed and charming atmosphere of the campus. On occasion, the department head to whom she reported would need to preen his feathers and strut about to show his importance, often demanding attention just for its own sake. At those times, his judgment seemed out of whack, although he was generally good at what he did. At first these inconsistencies annoyed Glenda, but basically he was good-hearted, so she learned to let occasional foolishness pass. One day Glenda dreamed:

> *I'm sitting at my desk, absorbed and enjoying what I'm doing. An acquaintance who can be foolish and irritating comes in. He's my boss. He struts by very importantly to the thermostat on the wall at my right and turns the temperature up to 140. I see it's an absolutely crazy thing to do, but I know it's pointless to confront him about it when he's in that frame of mind, or, for that matter, at any time.*

It didn't take Glenda long to put two and two together. Sure enough, the day after her dream, her boss went through an exotic song and dance routine, carrying on about an issue in a way that made no sense. Thus, Glenda's nonsense dream also had an element of ESP, as it noted a future event. Forewarned and remembering the dream as her boss began to rant and rave over something ridiculous, Glenda listened patiently. Thanks to the nonsense dream's insight, she simply humored him, knowing that this, too, would pass. A nonsense dream can, with the help of a bit of ESP, warn us of another's upcoming, convoluted, crazy behavior.

3: A Nonsense Dream Explains a Person's Absurd Behavior

Isabel was a caring person, and when her mother became ill, she naturally went to stay with her. Her mother had always swung from behaving in a good-natured and easygoing way to getting crotchety and difficult, so Isabel was prepared to be patient. Yet dealing with absurd conversations in which her mother regularly and irrationally contradicted everything was frustrating enough to drive even a saint to distraction. As a dream user, Isabel looked for dreams to put things into perspective, and dreamed:

> I see Mum has just started a hairdressing and shampoo business and I'm delighted she's showing initiative and doing something constructive. The phone rings, indicating someone wants to make an appointment. But I notice there's no way to receive the call, because, for some reason, mother has taken the phone off the hook. I find it strange that she's in a business that depends on calls but that she isn't taking any calls.

This dream shows someone behaving in an illogical way, and Isabel easily saw the parallel to her mother's behavior. As a theme, the scene of having her own business but not taking calls was saying: "I want to be independent and I don't want to be bothered by others." The dream pointed out that behind her mother's ornery behavior was a terrific desire for independence, and yet, since she was sick, her mother had to accept Isabel's care. And because her mother did feel contradictory, she behaved in a contradictory manner, so even her illogical behavior was in some sense logical. This insight helped Isabel remain patient during a month of caring for her mother.

IDENTIFYING FEATURES
OF NONSENSE DREAMS

1. Part Versus Whole

The first thing to note is whether an absurdity is a part of a dream and makes sense as a pun, or whether the entire dream is simply absurd. If it is the entire dream, it is likely a nonsense dream.

2. Everything Is Illogical

When everything is illogical and nonsensical in a dream and there are no visual puns or plays on words involved, you have a nonsense dream. These dreams are warnings of distortions, confusions, and absurdities in people or situations around you, or in your own thinking, feeling, or actions. But keep in mind that dream warnings generally come to you in time to avert a negative consequence if the warning is heeded.

3. Did You Notice Absurdities While Dreaming, or Upon Awakening?

Ask yourself when you noticed that you were having or had a nonsense dream. Were you aware of the high level of nonsense while actually dreaming, or only after waking up? If you noticed it while dreaming, there's a good chance the dream refers to absurdities around you, such as in other people or in unavoidable situations. If you noticed it was a nonsense dream only when you woke up, it may reflect contradictions in you, since we tend to tune out our own absurdities. In case you do have a nonsense dream at some time that is about you, rest assured that everyone has moments of nuttiness, especially when highly emotional issues are involved.

CHAPTER 10

Recurring Dreams

Our echoes roll from soul to soul,
And grow forever and forever.
— TENNYSON

WHAT THEY DO

Recurring dreams are often precipitated by a major life change or a significant challenge or event in your life. Something related to that event leaves an impact, which acts either as a block, a catalyst, or a reminder of something that you need to know. Generally, its message is very important, and therefore is repeated over and over again through recurring dreams. The dream's message may be related to something in your personality that you need to develop. Or it may reflect a past trauma or current problem or area of life that's blocking you.

Once you are aware of the message behind the recurring dream and begin to deal with the issue, it stops. This is one way of knowing that you've found the correct meaning. Recurring dreams deal with needed changes that, if carried out, would make a crucial difference in your life. Recurring dreams tend to deal with difficult themes, often putting you in touch with traumas or trouble spots you would rather avoid. Thus, like touching a wound, they often leave you feeling frightened and distressed. Nevertheless, recurring dreams contain potential breakthroughs that bring you greater adjustment and happiness. They are not about pain, they are about good news.

Just as there are recurring dreams, there are also recurring nightmares. A nightmare is related to some trauma, fear, distress, or anxiety. Yet our psyche rarely throws frightening images at us just to frighten us. What is really going on is that your own fear and distress mask potentially positive and helpful images, making them look like frightening ones. It is as though you are wearing glasses that have accumulated dust that make what you see look grim, although it actually isn't.

In other words, there are no frightening dreams, only frightened dreamers. Recurring dreams are common, but the recurring nightmare is rare. If a recurring nightmare persists, it's an indication that the dreamer needs to work with a qualified therapist, preferably one versed in the use of dreams. But the recurring nightmare does illustrate the fascinating though painful twists and turns our minds can take in attempting to recover from trauma, which is why this example is included.

EXAMPLES OF RECURRING DREAMS

1: A Recurring Dream Speaks of an Emotional Blockage That Needs to Be Removed

A retired senior citizen, Mary, was in good health and had led a full life raising a family and working. When she and her husband retired, they had enjoyed a quiet life of gardening and visiting with family and friends. Her husband was her closest friend and companion, so when he died, Mary was devastated. Within a year of his death, she began having this troubling recurring dream:

> *I'm at my husband's funeral. I see his funeral take place in exact detail, just as it actually happened. I go up to the coffin to say good-bye to him before it is closed.*

I'm shocked to see that instead of my husband lying there, it is me lying there. I wake up terrified and in tears.

The main image of this dream is death—her husband's and her own. Mary asked if it was a forecast of her own death, which is a common assumption. I assured Mary that nine times out of ten, death is a symbol for change, because it is the ultimate change we encounter. However, Mary sounded so miserable that I wondered whether dying appealed to her. Was Mary's dream a death wish? This was possible, but my work with dreams led me to believe that such wish-fulfillment themes are rare.

I gently asked about her life since her husband's death. Weeping, Mary lamented the joy they once had. Her whole life had revolved around him, and now that he was gone, she felt she had nothing to live for. She never went out, had no hobbies, and rarely saw friends. She spent her time watching television, which was her only respite from days filled with lonely, aching memories. It was obvious that since her husband's death, Mary had spent her time brooding and had not progressed beyond that.

The dream was saying: "When I see someone else's death, I see my own," or, one could say, "He's dead and so am I." And indeed, though Mary was alive, by staying so completely engulfed in her grief, she was, in a very real sense, dead too. The image of her own funeral was a message pointing this out to her, and though it frightened her, this dream was trying to provoke Mary to see her unresolved grief, and deal with it. By facing her sorrow, she might be able to grieve fully and then go on with her life.

The purposefulness of a dream never ceases to amaze me, as if it comes with a game plan. Mary's dream first brings her back to her original trauma—her husband's actual funeral—as if it is saying: "This is where your blockage began." In step two, packing an emotional punch, the dream shocks her with the image of seeing herself in her own coffin. This was a dramatic way of asking: "You're acting as if you're already dead! Is that what you really want?" With this jolt, her own psyche, attempting to heal her, hoped that Mary would see her deteriorated state and do something about it. In a kindly way, I suggested to Mary that she seek professional help to deal with her grief, which was obviously crippling her ability to live.

2: A Recurring Dream Acts as a Cue to Remind Someone to Draw On Her Strength

Olga was in her fifties. Like many immigrants, she had come to America by boat at a young age. The trip to America represented not only a new life in a new country, but it was also the start of her life as a young bride. She and her husband were glad to be in America, and in their first years worked very hard. By persevering, they established a modest yet comfortable life for themselves and their family. Yet for thirty years Olga had this recurring dream:

> I'm on a ship in the middle of the ocean. I feel stranded, and don't know which way to go. I look out over the ocean; sometimes the water is choppy or stormy, sometimes it's calm. But it's always deep and fearsome. Yet in the end I always find myself on the shore, relieved to be on land again. I look out onto the ocean and feel happy to have arrived at my destination.

If you've ever spent a pleasant vacation by the seaside, the ocean will be an image for you of rest, peace, and renewal. But for Olga, the ocean was a symbol of the hardships of her voyage to a new country and of her new life there as a young bride. The trip had been difficult, with cramped quarters and the tension of uncertainty as to what to expect. Thus to Olga, an ocean voyage became a symbol of great adjustment and change, which she successfully dealt with. So the dream's theme was saying: "Faced with new circumstances, you cope well."

Each time Olga had her dream, she was replaying her

voyage to America. I asked what went on in her life, more or less, when this dream appeared. Did it come during a happy time, during crises or difficulties, or when she felt anxious or challenged? Olga decided that her recurring dream appeared at difficult times. Her journey to America had become a cue for periods of challenge in Olga's life. The dream always had a happy ending, that of a happy landing, so that it was an encouraging dream reminder for her that when faced with difficulties, she always made it. It's purpose, then, was to remind Olga of her own strength and courage, qualities she could draw upon whenever the voyage of life got rough.

In this case the recurring dream had become a cue. If the dream acts as a cue, its message is still important, but not as urgent as when it speaks of a blockage or a challenge that needs to be overcome. In this case, it is simply a reminder of something you need. As cues, recurring dreams remind you of associations and emotions you can draw upon, such as courage or confidence, and so on. Entire dreams that recur can act as cues of qualities we need to draw upon, and sometimes symbols alone recur and also act as cues. When a symbol takes on a recurring quality, it goes through minor changes paralleling dynamic changes going on in your life and acting as feedback for something important.

3: A Recurring Dream Reflects a Woman's Marital Difficulties

Norma was married to a domineering, demanding man for five years. Alcohol was involved, and physical abuse was often a threat and a reality. She regularly dreamed:

I'm standing on the edge of a busy highway and I have a heavy load on my back. I'm trying to get across, but cars whiz by too fast and I feel I won't make it.

Unable to convince her husband to get help, Norma wanted to leave him but felt too overwhelmed to try. Finally, after many years of continuously trembling in her own home, she found the courage to leave him. Just before she left her husband, Norma dreamed the final version of her recurring dream:

> *I'm on the edge of a busy highway. I leave my parcels by the roadside and run across, afraid but determined. I reach the other side safely and feel a sense of relief.*

Commenting on her intention to leave, the last in this series of recurring dreams encouraged her to do so by saying: "By letting go of what you are holding on to, you will make it across, and you will feel relieved."

4: A Recurring Nightmare

In general, a recurring nightmare would indicate a serious emotional issue or a trauma that might often, though not always, require the help of a therapist to sort out. Recurring nightmares are very common after a trauma. This example is included not as a model for treating them, but merely as a way to understand what can happen to people, and how sleep disturbances are related to actual life conditions. If you know someone who has recurring nightmares, don't try to interpret the nightmares; be understanding and support him in seeking counseling. Here is an example of how the source of a traumatic nightmare was unraveled.

Steven was a nineteen-year-old college sophomore who was having the same recurring nightmare three to five times per week. It had begun at about age nine, and created such intense fear that he would wake up with bloodcurdling screams, often waking his parents and four older brothers. He would jump out of bed, run from his bed violently, and crash into a wall with such strength that bloody wounds on his head were common.

When I met him, I was charmed by his well-built good looks, chestnut-brown hair, intelligent and sensitive face, and obvious calm and confidence. Any family would have been proud to have him as a member. No stranger would guess that this handsome young man was suffering from intense, regular nightmares that were tearing him and his family apart with worry. Consulting a family doctor had failed to help, so his mother asked me to speak to him and try to decipher the cause of Steven's distress. According to her, there seemed to be no reason for any great anxiety in his life. She insisted her son was a good student, happy, and well-adjusted, and part of a loving, upper-middle-class family. This hardly sounded like a circumstance that would cause severe nightmares.

Meeting Steven, I found his personality easygoing and polite. He was eager to cooperate and to find a cure for his distress. Over lunch he described his life. He shared that he was attending college and was an A student taking a fine arts program with a view to finding work in a museum, perhaps eventually as a curator. I guessed from his sensitive and gentle manner that his chosen career would suit him well. Despite the litany of normal conditions, he exuded an uneasiness, but I couldn't pinpoint why. Steven's recurring nightmare took this form with predictable consistency:

> A small animal sneaks into my bedroom. Often it's a dog, but sometimes it's a mouse or some other creature. At first it appears as a small shadow in the corner of my bedroom. Then it becomes larger and larger, till it fills the whole room. It begins to approach as if it will attack me. I become terror-stricken and flee with all my might.

This was a dream describing someone who first sees something small and innocuous, but which quickly escalates into something very threatening, filling him with terror. Knowing the dream began around age nine, and that a recurring dream is often linked to some change or challenge that occurs, I asked whether he remembered anything happening or changing at that time. Had his family moved to a new neighborhood, had he changed schools, or lost a school friend? He thought carefully, but none of these situations applied. Nor could he remember any anxiety in his home life at that time. Yet I knew that a specific item was often linked to the beginning of a recurring dream. I also knew that memories, especially painful ones, can often be buried very deep as a protective shield.

As we continued to talk about his home life, his feelings, and his family, interesting points began to surface that contrasted with the original rosy picture. Steven admitted he was so distressed about his nightmares that he had begun to fantasize about committing suicide. He also explained how difficult it was being the youngest and most sensitive. His four older brothers were macho types who constantly teased him about his artistic inclinations, and about the fact that he liked to cook and help his mother with home decor.

In fact, one of their family stories was that after having four sons, his mother was sure that her last child was going to be a girl. She had already picked out a girl's name, but to everyone's surprise, she had another son. She never let the family forget this, and the family never let Steven forget that he was supposed to have been a girl. An unspoken and degrading implication went along with this family myth: ". . . and that's why you act so girlish."

I remarked to Steven that this family joke might be very threatening to one's self-image, especially in establishing one's masculine identity. This seemed to be the right moment to ask him whether his identity as a male was or ever had been a problem for him. He became uncomfortable but replied openly. He felt it had been a problem in his early teens, but now that he was older, he felt fine. Going into more detail, Steven admitted that the merciless teasing of his brothers and remarks made by classmates about his artistic interests, as veiled insinuations that he was effeminate, were hard to take, especially when he had been around the age of fourteen. By now, though, he felt that he had come to terms with it, so that it was no longer an issue.

I pressed this issue, asking whether at some unconscious level feelings of anger or fear related to these put-downs of his masculinity might still be disturbing him. Perhaps there were none, I explained, yet it might be worth examining, just in case. Without resistance to this train of thought, he genuinely pondered it. Then it occurred to Steven that one way his brothers heckled him, which bothered him a lot, involved the family dog. Steven didn't like their dog very much, so his brothers would entice it to growl at him, then would laugh, implying that even the dog thought he was a sissy! Come to think of it, Steven noticed, a dog was most often the creature in his nightmares that would grow in size, become an indistinguishable monster, and chase him. Remembering this fascinated him, and deep feelings began to stir as I saw his thoughts lingering on this insight.

My mind shifted back to his life at age nine. Why had the dream begun at age nine and persisted in exact detail for over ten years? All my experience suggested that such things were not a coincidence, and that some event or troublesome change should coincide with the dream's onset. Casually, as he was lost in thought, I brought up the question once more of what might have transpired at age nine. Again Steven tried to recall his ninth year, with no results. In a low-keyed voice I kept talking, expressing my surprise that nothing difficult had happened at that time.

Suddenly Steven's mouth fell open. The intent expression on his face hinted that something had finally jogged his memory. "Yes," he replied feverishly. "Now that you mention it, something did happen. How could I have forgotten?" he asked himself out loud. In a dazed fashion he described an event that had occurred while walking home from school after a music lesson when he was nine. A strange man in an alley had stopped him, taking him by the arm and leading him into the darkness. The man tried to entice him to stay awhile, fondling him in forbidden places as he spoke. Remembering the horror of this experience for the first time in ten years, with a taut facial expression and a strained voice Steven continued. Terrified, he had stood frozen. Then, feeling utter terror, he had managed to break loose and had run all the way home, which was a long way. He remembered the pain in his lungs as he ran and continued running even when it felt as if he could no longer breathe. He remembered going right to his room and sobbing, trembling all night and for days afterward. He slept fitfully for some nights after that.

He never told anyone about this incident. He was afraid to tell, because by coincidence, that day he had naughtily used his bus fare for ice cream, which is why he had to run all the way home and had been late. This early traumatic encounter, together with the family's teasing about his artistic and gentle nature, likely combined to produce and maintain Steven's recurring nightmare. He was relieved to remember it and resolved to begin to work with a therapist to undo his distress.

IDENTIFYING FEATURES
OF RECURRING DREAMS

1. They Recur

Dreams that keep coming back are recurring dreams. The point of the constant replay is that there is a message behind it, one that is so important in some way that the psyche keeps bringing it to your attention, hoping some semblance of meaning will come through. It's an invitation, so to speak, to explore some blockage, challenge, or direction of growth in yourself. If you discover its message, it will release or heal something in you. Therefore, a recurring dream is a very beneficial mechanism, even though it appears to be mysterious or vexing.

2. An Entire Dream Can Recur

Entire dreams that recur are most often messages of blockages. Sometimes the dream stays exactly the same each time. Sometimes it is the same story line, but details change in the replay, though it is still recognizable as the same dream. The block may be due to some early pain or painful event, some talent that needs to be developed that you are ignoring, or some change that needs to be made in your life or lifestyle that would benefit you. By not making that change, not developing that talent, or not healing a past pain, one is not whole. The point of a recurring dream is to help make you whole again.

3. Its Beginning Relates to Some Life Event or Change

An important step in understanding a recurring dream is to establish exactly or approximately when it began. Once that time frame is established, try to see what changed, or what happened to you around that time. Sometimes, if the dream began a long time ago, you won't immediately remember what might have triggered it, but if you think about it now and then, more and more memories of that time period will arise. Generally, there is either a striking change or an event at the time of the recurring dream's origin that is related to its meaning. Keep in mind that this change or event can be an actual event, or it can be some emotional, inner event that impacted on you very privately.

4. It Packs an Emotional Punch

A recurring dream often creates a strong emotional reaction in you. This is because the psyche is trying to get your attention regarding some hidden issue or agenda that you need to deal with. Stirring strong emotions is a tool it uses to get your attention. And there is some unconscious reason you are resisting it, either because you don't want to touch an old pain, or because you are not inclined to exert yourself toward growing. But these are important dreams, so it is worth your while to work with them. If you uncover its meaning, the dream gives you a gift, some change or healing in you or your life that will lead to more happiness. And that's worth a bit of struggle.

5. It Stops When You Get the Message

If you get the message of the recurring dream and act on its insight, the dream stops appearing. It has done its work and no longer needs to get your attention. So, unless it is a cue dream (see below) which occurs for another reason, one way of knowing you have healed or changed in the right direction is that the recurring dream stops appearing.

6. A Recurring Dream as a Cue

Some recurring dreams come as a cue of something you want to remember. Suppose that at a particular time in your life you had to muster great calmness in order to deal with a situation—say, a funeral. Then, later, every time you need to bring forth calmness in yourself, you might dream of some symbol related to that event, such as a certain type of flower that was present at the funeral. It's there only to say: At that time you drew on your great reserve of calmness; do the same now, and it will help you in the same way.

7. A Recurring Symbol

A symbol can also recur regularly. It is generally a metaphor for something either in you, such as an attitude or emotion, or something with which you are dealing in your life, such as a relationship, a career, or your spiritual development. The symbol can be a flower, a car, a house, or whatever. I have a recurring symbol of a black cat which is a metaphor for my unconscious and deeper, inner self getting in touch with me. What happens to the car, flower, or house metaphorically parallels what is going on in you. In effect, a recurring symbol can be a mirror or a report card regarding the progress of a particular item in you or your life. As such, it is a very handy tool, though one that is often overlooked.

PART III

◊

Dreams That Help You Realize Your Potential

CHAPTER 11

Signal Dreams: Dreams That Signal Something New

Only a signal shown and a distant voice in the darkness . . .
—LONGFELLOW

WHAT THEY DO

Signal dreams get your attention about something new that is about to come your way. This can be a new talent, a new event, a new job, or even a move to a new city or a new home. Signal dreams come to tell you what changes and new potentials are about to be at your disposal. A signal dream wants to get your attention about the new happening because, the more aware of it you are, the better you will be at taking advantage of it when it crosses your path.

A signal dream is like opportunity knocking. When you open the door, a stranger tells you good news and you're surprised by your good fortune. Dreams of winning a lottery are often signal dreams of some unexpected opportunity, but it's rarely about actually winning a lottery. Like the cliff-hanger telling you what the next episode of tomorrow's soap opera will contain, the signal dream discloses what new talents, changes, and potentials will be at your disposal in the next episode of your life.

The signal dream has a second amazing ability. It can signal the timing for events, changes, and states of mind, telling you when they will occur, or when the timing is right. Many people are able to wake up at a specific time without an alarm clock just by telling themselves before going to bed what time they'd like to arise. I find this practice convenient when I'm traveling. I suspect the timing-cue category of signal dreams is related to this amazing ability of the mind to accurately stay in touch with time. Because timing cues signal changes related to timing, I include them as a subtype of signal dream, though eventually we may see these as a unique kind of dream in itself. Timing dreams tell us when something will take place, or when it's appropriate to begin or end something. They can be seen as entire dreams or as fragments within a larger dream. As you will see in the following examples, such timing cues prove accurate and most interesting.

EXAMPLES OF SIGNAL DREAMS

1: A Signal Dream Shows New Opportunities on the Horizon

Anne was in a period of transition. She loved being active and had many accomplishments to her credit. But for the first time in a dozen years, Anne had more time than she knew what to do with, and was not happy about it. She began to fear that the best part of her life was over, and that only the humdrum awaited her. Feeling shaky about her future, she had this signal dream:

I'm outside and have to get something in the house. My young niece, whom I adore, is standing just inside the doorway. She tells me she can't stay, but says there are empty rooms inside I should look at. I'm surprised to hear this, as I thought I was familiar with every inch of the house. I walk over to where she's pointing and open a door. I am astonished to see a new wing of the house containing several large, empty, beautiful sunny rooms which can be used at a later time. I have to leave now because of a pressing engagement, but am glad to have discovered this wonderful new space available to me. I know it'll take a lot of time to decorate and fill it. I wake up joyful and enthusiastic about what I can do with it.

This signal dream replied to Anne's unspoken fears that her future might be empty. It was a signal that she still had much to do that would excite her, and was saying: "There's lots of room for you yet." The dream also gave her hints about a time frame for the new, since in the dream she had errands to do first, suggesting: "The time is not yet right." This proved to be true. Within a couple of years, however, Anne had shifted gears into a new life filled with enough interests to keep her active and happy for at least twenty more years.

2: A Signal Dream Reveals What Career Direction Will Be Next to Open Up

I spent years analyzing my own dreams and participating in dream groups. But initially, working with dreams was a hobby rather than a main preoccupation. I spent my days like everyone else, working at a nine-to-five job, seeing family and friends, and relaxing. My spare time was spent in volunteer work, but it was not related to dreams. But there came a time when my life was rapidly changing and I wondered where I should head next. I received guidance from this signal dream:

A serious request has come to analyze three dreams for someone. It was an honor to be asked to do so, and I feel elated about it. I begin to concentrate on working with dreams.

From the start, dream work was what most interested me in life. But because our society does not see it as a profession in itself by which you can make a living, it stayed just a satisfying hobby, or avocation, for many years. But it was and still remains where my heart really lies, so when I had this dream, I was delighted to discover I could actually turn it into a career. I left myself open to the possibility, and over the years it has come about. And just as the dream predicted, requests to use dreams in counseling began to appear more and more frequently. Later, invitations to present seminars on dreams skyrocketed, and I began to do media work on the topic. This signal dream gave me the impetus to pick up the ball and run with dream work as a profession in a way I never would have thought possible.

3: A Signal Dream Points Out That Someone Has Undergone a Significant Change of Attitude

Linda worked in an accounting office with a dozen or so employees; their office manager, Mr. Graydon, was a tyrant. Needless to say, he was not the most popular person around and associates gave up trying to coax him into being more tactful and less overbearing. One day Linda dreamed:

> *I see Mr. Graydon with a dark black beard. He walks out of the room, then comes right back in. I'm surprised to see he's cut off his beard and tell him he no longer looks like a tyrant.*

Because she works with her dreams, Linda recognized this as a signal dream predicting that her manager's attitude toward employees was about to improve. About this time, Mr. Graydon was publicly honored in the community for volunteer work he had done. After receiving the award, his manner softened, and though still reserved, his way with people visibly improved, confirming the signal dream.

Of course, Mr. Graydon doesn't have a beard in real life, nor would Linda have ever spoken to him in such a personal way as she did in her dream. But by using this set of double images—the shaved beard and her statement—her psyche was making sure she got the message that her boss was becoming more gentle in manner. Such multiple references to the same message show how hard our dreams work to get a message across. The old-fashioned view was that dreams try to hide messages. But in the modern view, as in this example, we see that many clues and symbols reinforce the same message. So, rather than trying to hide anything, the dream tries to do the opposite—bring it all to light.

4: As a Timing-Cue Subcategory, a Signal Dream Points Out That It Is Time to Take a Vacation, and a Second One Points Out That It Is Time to Get Back to Work

One summer, under the strain of an erratic and busy schedule, I couldn't decide whether to take a vacation, and if so, when. This was not a trivial question because, living in a cold climate at the time, it was important to take advantage of the sun's warm summer rays. Here it was, mid-June, and I still couldn't decide. Then I dreamed:

> I'm outdoors, in a country setting. I see my lovely niece Andrea nearby with some friends. She points to me playfully and says to her friends. "There's my auntie on vacation." I wake up in the same playful, happy, and relaxed mood.

As I woke up, I recognized that this was a timing signal dream suggesting I could begin to ease off from work and take a vacation. As circumstances turned out, it soon became easy to do so and a vacation naturally fell into place. I was impressed that my psyche picked up on this change in responsibilities before I did. I then playfully challenged my psyche, if it was so smart, to let me know when the end of my playtime came. I forgot about the challenge and continued to enjoy the slower-paced, pleasant summer days. Until . . . In mid-August, almost two months to the day later, this second timing signal dream emerged:

> I'm at a country retreat, feeling relaxed and mellow. I glance at the ceiling and see small cracks. Then I see

cobwebs and dust hanging here and there. It looks musty and in need of a good cleaning. I feel I want to roll up my sleeves and start to work to fix it all up.

I awoke, realizing this dream was suggesting it was time to get back to work again. Examining how I felt, I knew it was correct. I had indeed let a major portion of my work gather dust during the summer—with no regrets. But I had been getting restless, and now, having had a refreshing holiday, I was ready to dive into a sea of work again. Then it dawned on me that with this signal dream my psyche had answered my friendly challenge. I was very impressed that like a computer program, it was able to hold on to my instructions until it was time to carry them out.

IDENTIFYING FEATURES OF SIGNAL DREAMS

1. Something Unexpected

Signal dreams bring something new to your attention, something that you're not expecting. So when you have one, you experience a sense of surprise.

2. A Reaction of Disbelief or Amazement

Within the signal dream itself you often express some reaction, surprise, or disbelief. This can carry over as a sense of wonderment or amazement upon awakening. Just as news of something new and unexpected would shake you up when you're awake, in the same way something unexpected stirs your sense of "that's surprising" in a signal dream. This reaction by a main character in a dream (even if it's not you) is a clue that it's a signal dream

3. Encouragement of a New Potential

A signal dream often points out a new potential. It may be something you are already aware of but haven't used, or it can be a talent you don't even know you have yet. In the dream you may protest the new activity, but you are given lots of support and encouragement to continue. This is typical of a signal dream.

4. You Have to Enact the Potential to Make It Real

The signal dream alerts you to something new on your horizon so that you can better take advantage of it when it surfaces. But once you know about the new horizon, it's up to you to make use of the opportunity by applying yourself and living up to the implied potential.

5. It Signals Something That Will Unfold Soon

A signal dream alerts you to the fact that something new is on the horizon, and will appear soon. You can discover it in a few days or in a few months, or even up to a year or so. It's like a flower that's on the verge of blossoming, so if you get a signal dream, keep an eye out for changes around you, and how they may unexpectedly affect your life. "Soon" is the key.

6. It Signals Something Good

A signal dream is talking about something that you may have always wanted, or would like, but you weren't expecting to happen at all, or at least not yet. It is about something pleasant, some goal you have wanted, or a talent that was in you that is about to spring forth and become useful. A signal dream is about something that will bring you happiness and good fortune if you follow up on it.

7. Accurate Timing Cues

There is a subtype of signal dream that gives timing cues. This can be a reference to a season, a month, an exact date, or someone's anniversary. It is a timing cue that makes sense to you in some way, and is meaningful to you. If a signal dream contains a timing cue, it is an accurate one. It can refer to a time to begin or end something, or lets you know when a new opportunity will arrive. Look forward to that date, and note how something unfolds that is related to the signal dream.

CHAPTER 12

Promise Dreams: Dreams That Promise a Favorable Outcome

If only I could be set aglow.
—EMERSON

WHAT THEY DO

Promise dreams show the potential fruits of your labor. A promise dream resembles the signal dream covered in the last chapter in that both point to potentials in the dreamer's future, but they're different in the following ways. A signal dream announces something entirely new, whereas a promise dream shows something familiar and already in progress. The signal dream deals with something just around the corner, while the promise dream hints at something which is still far away. If you compare the signal dream and the promise dream to a flower, the signal dream shows the first bud whereas the promise dream shows what the potential will look like in full bloom. Both tend to come at critical turning points in your life in order to provide a needed impetus, the signal dream to start you upon a new direction, and the promise dream to keep you going toward a direction you are questioning.

The purpose of a promise dream is to provide encouragement by hinting at the longterm result. You might think of a promise dream as a morale booster which, if it works, helps you manifest a worthwhile result.

EXAMPLES OF PROMISE DREAMS

1: The Promise of a Career Path Opening Up

Hilary was a community organizer who entered media work accidentally. As the head of a group that often held seminars, she brought guest speakers to local radio and television stations to be interviewed. Producers met her regularly and discovered that she was an expert in areas of interest to the public, and so they began to interview her, as well, from time to time.

At first she accepted shyly, but in time Hilary became bolder and began to enjoy the media limelight in the large city where she lived. Within a year she had become a regular fixture on local talk shows and of feature stories. Enjoying the thrill of reaching millions of people, Hilary went along for the ride, charging nothing for the time and effort she put in. But because this was an extra activity, the wear and tear of these responsibilities caught up to her, and she wondered whether it was worth continuing. On the verge of giving it up, Hilary dreamed:

> *I'm in a newspaper office. The editor is interviewing people for a job and I am a candidate. His assistant, a woman, gives me the news that he decided against me because of lack of experience. I'm disappointed, but I know it's the truth. But the scene shifts to a later point in time. A blond woman telephones me to tell me that I have the job after all. I'm thrilled! A while ago I was sure such work was out of my reach, but here I am now, starting out as a journalist. I wake up feeling joy, enthusiasm, and energy, as though I finally have the career I've always wanted.*

This promise dream hinted that despite a lack of experience and apparent setbacks in media work, Hilary would get a break and find just the job she wanted. At the time of this dream, Hilary was associated with a major network. The management hinted at the possibility of regular work for her, but it fell through. Hilary was disappointed, but she remembered her dream, and therefore continued to accept unpaid guest appearances.

A year later, a competing station with an even wider audience unexpectedly invited her to do a regular series for a prime-time program. Delighted, Hilary met with her prospective producer, who had telephoned with the good news. The producer turned out to be a vivacious blond woman just like the one in her dream. They went on to create interesting features for many years and reached a wide audience. Hilary was grateful for the promise dream that inspired her to persevere.

2: Promise of Self-Transformation and Achievement

Laura was a college sophomore who came from a poor economic background. Finding herself among peers who had advantages such as accelerated educational programs and travel around the world, she felt awkward. Not surprisingly, her self-esteem was low, and although she entered college with fine grades, she always believed others were smarter than she was, and that she could never catch up. Nevertheless, Laura decided to make the best of it, and following up an interest in psychology, began to study her dreams. Soon after, she had a promise dream that changed her life:

> *I'm in a fine arts class, where a demonstration slide is being projected onto a screen. The slide is a picture of my art homework which the professor is about to evaluate in front of the class. I feel so ashamed, knowing that my work is so inferior. Sure enough, my canvas is a mass of ugly squiggles, like pieces of string thrown together. The professor's piercing eyes evaluate it, and as he examines it, the squiggles begin to move gracefully, like*

*fluid beams of light, and begin to take on a different
shape and form.*

*In a flash the loose ends turn into a breathtakingly
beautiful flower—a violet orchid so rich in color and yet
so delicate that anyone can recognize it as a master-
piece. I marvel at this transformation of my artwork. The
professor smiles at me approvingly, and I feel honored
and wonderful. I wake up knowing that the slide represents the "before" and "after" versions of me—what I
will become as I keep learning and growing.*

Even though Laura was new to dreams, her promise dream
produced a sense of hopefulness in her. It was as though
in the guise of an orchid, she saw something deep within
herself that made her feel special and put her in touch with
her own abilities. Afterward, whenever she began to get
discouraged, she recalled this dream and felt uplifted by its
promise. In time Laura stopped comparing herself to others and simply concentrated on her studies, and eventually
realized she had as much ability and potential as anyone
else. After completing college, she went on to live a full
life as a leader in her community. As it did for Laura, a
promise dream often helps provide the change of heart
necessary to turn many of us ugly ducklings into magnif-
icent swans.

3: A Promise of Advancement in Career

As a junior social worker looking for work in a depressed
job market, Jan was glad to find a part-time position. Her
sincere, sympathetic manner spiced with strength and wit
made her a natural for social work. She enjoyed her colleagues as well as her job of looking after the needs of the
disabled and wished she would be hired on a full-time and
permanent basis. But thanks to government cutbacks, no
openings were on the horizon.

Six months later, however, a veteran of the department
went on a one-year leave of absence, so Jan was hired as

a temporary junior replacement. She thought this was great, but it would take a year before anyone would know whether he would return and thus, whether the job would become available as a permanent position. And even if the position did open up, there was no guarantee that Jan would get it. Feeling insecure, she was torn between waiting for a job that might not materialize versus looking for work elsewhere. In the throes of this uncertainty, she dreamed:

I'm sitting at a table with place settings carefully arranged to match the pecking order of jobs at work. I'm describing my work to a blind person sitting beside me, telling him how I look after the emergency needs of the mentally and physically handicapped. Then the host gives me a choice. I can take a seat at the head of the table, where the setting is very fancy, or I can take a seat at the left, which is more humble but is appropriate to my experience. The seat I take is the permanent place setting for the person who carries out my work, a more modest seat, and I continue to talk about my work with enthusiasm.

The place settings are a metaphor for finding one's place at work, whereas talking to a blind person is a metaphor for helping someone to see. As both listener and narrator, Jan was explaining to herself in the dream how her job prospects were likely to turn out, suggesting to herself that she would be offered her present job on a permanent basis. Because it also uplifted her and gave her a sense of having a future, it was a promise dream. Thanks to her dream, Jan decided to be patient and remain where she was.

The image of a seat at the head of the table is interesting too. Those who know Jan recognize many leadership qualities in her. In its all-comprehensive and knowing way, her psyche was saying: "You know the more humble position suits you best at the moment, but someday you'll be offered a position as the head." A year and three months later, just as her dream predicted, Jan succeeded over other candidates in securing the position she was filling in a temporary capacity. I've no doubt that, as suggested in her dream, Jan's sense of confidence and dedication will one day lead to a job as department head.

IDENTIFYING FEATURES OF PROMISE DREAMS

1. Something Already in Progress

A promise dream speaks of something already in progress in your life. Its purpose is to encourage you to continue with it, because if you do, the outcome will be wonderful in time.

2. They Appear at a Critical Turning Point

A promise dream comes at a time when you need it. You have been working on or toward something, and may begin to wonder whether it is worthwhile. Or others may speak in discouraging terms about your goal, and their talk begins to influence you, so that you wonder whether to discontinue. A promise dream appears as an attempt to keep you on track with a prospect, because no matter how you feel, or what others of short vision might say, the initial impetus that got you started with it was correct. Trust yourself, and continue. The promise dream guarantees results if you persevere.

3. They Come as an Encouragement

As already stated in different terms, the main purpose of a promise dream is to encourage you to continue with something that is somewhat in doubt within you. Its encouragement creates a positive shift in your attitude, motivation, and purpose. In fact, you recognize a promise dream by the enormous sense of upliftment, peace, and enthusiasm it stimulates from a deep, inner part of you. Once you feel that sense of upliftment and peace, nothing can derail you from continuing.

CHAPTER 13

◇

Energizing Dreams: Dreams That Energize You

Are you in earnest? Seize this very minute:
What you can do, or dream you can, begin it;
Boldness has genius, power and magic in it.
Only engage and then the mind grows heated;
Begin and then the work will be completed.
—GOETHE

WHAT THEY DO

Did you ever wake up from a dream feeling an energy and inspiration rushing through you, an energy that carries you on its wings for hours or even days? If so, you had an energizing dream, which, just by having it, revived and renewed you. It can stir up a new and deeper spiritual level, a joy of life, a new self-confidence or a new interest in life, people, and activities—all at once.

Energizing dreams often appear at a time of great stress or pain. Unless you've had one, it's hard to convey how transforming energizing dreams are. But once you have one, you remember it fondly for life. Besides releasing a tangible energy, it provides feelings of upliftment and inspiration, and it can change your perspective into a fresh understanding of an area of your life that needs it. In a small but important way, an energizing dream permanently changes you. No one else but you may know about this change, but henceforth, a new you begins to emerge.

EXAMPLES OF ENERGIZING DREAMS

1: An Energizing Dream Helps a Man Find the Energy to Forge a New Life

Arun was an engineer who brought his wife and family from New Delhi, India, to New York to start a new life. He came to America with the unbounded enthusiasm of a young man in his early twenties and with all of life and its dreams ahead of him. He missed his ancient and venerable culture, but he and his young family were thrilled with their new home. Arun did his best to adjust to the radical differences of New York culture, language, and careers. But because starting over in a new land is never easy, the adjustment was long and difficult. So after the first few years when the struggle of adjustment was at its height, Arun wondered whether he had made the right move. Despite his efforts, people were slow to accept him and he often felt alienated. He worked twice as hard to prove his worth, but sometimes the going was just too rough, and Arun sadly began to contemplate returning to India with his family. At the point when he was most discouraged, he dreamed:

> *I see myself dressed as a North American Indian on the shores of the ocean. It's sunset and I'm riding bareback on a magnificent white horse with a long white streaming mane. The wind caresses my face and I feel incredibly refreshed as the ocean spray cools my face. I see myself with shoulder-length black hair, just like a North American Indian. There's an incredible sense of joy and freedom. I feel wonderful, relaxed, and very strong.*

Arun awoke filled with an unbounded energy and joy, knowing that he belonged in America and that all would eventually be well. Arun did not normally look to his dreams for guidance, but this energizing dream caught his attention. Simply having the dream changed him and his whole outlook on life. Just like in the dream, thereafter he felt refreshed, strong, and happy, confident that he would successfully create the life he longed for in America.

When things sometimes got rough, he remembered this dream and would feel its energy and comfort all over again. And within ten years his patience, goodwill, and hard work brought Arun the career, community, and friends that he had always hoped for, and he began to feel at home. He now felt as wonderful as he had in the dream. Arun had made it as a North American Indian!

When this energizing dream was discussed in a class on dreams, someone asked, "But what did the horse mean?" Everyone laughed. The answer was obvious. It didn't matter what the white horse symbolized, or what the beach or shoulder-length hair meant. Instead, the upliftment and energy of this energizing dream had instantly transformed Arun all by itself, putting him in touch with a deep current of purpose and rightness about himself and his future. Such an effect defines the energizing dreams.

2: Someone Is Energized to Experience Her Spirituality for the First Time

Valerie is a stunning beauty, a tall and lanky California blonde with an easygoing charm. She is a successful professional and is the epitome of the American dream—a young, beautiful go-getter. But most people do not know the long, hard road she traveled to achieve this. She had left an unhappy home at an early age, and had few memories of her childhood, which was mostly harsh, to draw upon for inner strength.

As an adult, she gained confidence, but occasionally parts of her youth bounced back and interfered with her happiness, leaving her feeling empty and alone. One of the things Valerie was never given as a child was a religious heritage of any kind, and she longed to find one. This was a hurdle Valerie very much wanted to jump over—to get a real sense of her own spirituality so that she could draw from its strength. She looked into spiritual groups and various religions, but God was still only a word to her, a deity who was distant and unsympathetic, to whom she felt no real connection. One day Valerie had an unusual dream:

I'm outside a reception hall with my friend Rosie, where a wedding is about to take place. We are standing in a grim concrete courtyard surrounded by tall buildings. Everything is gray and bleak. I see a sinister man on a nearby roof, who resembles a nasty giant in fairy tales. A small, fragile child sits on his shoulders, which worries me. A good guy suddenly appears on an adjoining roof, and at the speed of light he darts over and rescues the child. I'm relieved that the child is safe.

Suddenly the hero turns into an angel, translucent and dressed in white. Even at a distance I'm transfixed with awe at the sight of him. He disappears. But as I turn, I'm even more astonished to see another angel, just inches away. Though he has the face of a kindly old gentleman, he's definitely an angel, looking like the kind of father I would have liked, instead of the one I had, who molested me and abused me in his drunken states. This older angel is wearing a gown of white brocade with broad stripes of gold that glow with a brilliant light. He, too, is shimmering and translucent, and I'm mesmerized. He asks what my friend Rosie and I want most. Like meeting the genie from a magic lamp, we know we can make any wish and it will come true. Rosie asks to become witty and intelligent. He then looks at me with eyes filled with perfect love and understanding. With true sincerity I ask to be a channel of blessings to all I meet. I gaze at the angel, feeling completely loved. An incredible light emanates from him, and he becomes a vision of overwhelming beauty. Words cannot express the energy and joy which pours out of me, of a depth I have never felt before.

As Valerie woke up, she felt she had been touched and acknowledged by the Divine, to the very depths of her soul, and felt totally transformed. This energizing dream put her in touch with her inner self and her own divinity. It spiritually empowered her so that for the first time in her life, she felt able to relate to God and to her own spirituality. Valerie realized that God was that place within herself which inspired her to help others, a place where she felt in awe of life and filled with joy and love.

One could, as an intellectual exercise, interpret the symbols. The wedding as an opening scene can represent Valerie preparing to meet her "better half," the spiritual side of herself. The child on the giant's shoulders might be Valerie, chained to her past, unable to release her spiritual side. The child is held captive by the giant, an image of the enormous fears and bad experiences of her childhood. One could say all of this and more about the symbols of this dream and be correct. But with an energizing dream, none of this is necessary. The dream fulfilled its purpose simply by putting Valerie in touch with her own spirituality, and this needed no intellectual rumination or translation. It simply happened as a "new energy." This is the simple, spontaneous yet transforming magic that an energizing dream brings you, which you can then savor for the rest of your life.

IDENTIFYING FEATURES
OF ENERGIZING DREAMS

1. They Give You Energy

If you wake up filled with an energy you didn't have before because of a dream you just had, it is an energizing dream. You recognize it by its very effect on you, the effect of filling you with a new sense of life, a new energy, and a sense of wanting to get up and go in a way you were not able to yesterday. You are determined more than ever to accomplish whatever is on your agenda.

2. They Transform You

Somehow, just by having this dream, you feel different. This is the transformative quality of an energizing dream. It leaves you permanently changed from the inside out, so that you want to just bubble over with changes all at once. It brings a wonderful sense of renewal to your life. And you can take this energy and do just that—renew yourself and your life.

3. They Come at a Time of Need

Most often, you have this dream at a time when you feel very pressured. Or it may be a time of great confusion, so that you have questions that desperately need answers. The energizing dream does not necessarily provide an exact answer to a question, but it does give you such a sense of renewal that you sense the answer or know that the answer will soon be there. An energizing dream is a response to a need, and it acts to clear a path within you, thereby allowing the need to be fulfilled.

4. They Have Spiritual Qualities

Often the energy you receive has a deeply spiritual quality to it. It is as though you are given the precious gift of direct grace from the Divine. This feature is difficult to explain; you simply have to experience the effect of this "amazing grace" in order to understand it.

5. They Are Self-explanatory

An energizing dream is one of the types of dreams that is self-explanatory. You don't need to intellectually understand its symbols or themes in order to "get it." What you instantly get is the uplifting energy that comes automatically, so that it needs no explanation. However, the symbols may be striking and unusual, so if you want to explore their meaning, it's okay to do so, but it's not necessary to do so. Understanding the dream at an intellectual level is not important; the heart gets the message instantly and completely.

CHAPTER 14

Creativity Dreams: Dreams That Tap Your Creativity

In Nature's presence stood, as now I stand,
A sensitive being, a creative soul.
—WORDSWORTH

WHAT THEY DO

Many talented people have received creative inspiration from their dreams. The inventor of the Singer sewing machine originally put the machine's needle upward, trying to imitate how sewing is done by hand. But that didn't work. Then, in one dream he saw a bird pecking downward and in another, a row of knights in shining armor pointing their sharp lances downward toward the floor. These dreams gave him the idea to point the needle downward, and he invented the sewing machine as we know it today. In another example, the shape of the benzene molecule appeared to scientist Frederich Kekule in a dream. In addition, writers have often received the plot of entire stories. *Dr. Jekyll and Mr. Hyde* first appeared to author Robert Louis Stevenson in his dreams.

Dreams have always been a source of creativity. The unconscious seems to work like yeast in a dough, so that an inspiration slowly arises out of the dreamer's mass of thinking. These are just a few of the many well-documented stories of dreams enhancing the creativity of famous people, as well as of ordinary folk like you and me. In fact, the easiest way to get a creativity dream is to ask for one before you go to sleep. Take something you are working on, whether it's artwork or a project, or a work-related item that needs a breakthrough. Write down what the problem is, and some overall description of what you'd like as a result. For example, if you are looking for a way to solve a computer-programming puzzle, write down: "I would like the computer to be able to do such and such." Then ask for a dream that night that will shed light on the problem and offer a solution. Or, even without writing anything down (though that can help), just ask for a dream on that project or idea, and see what you get. You might surprise even yourself with a creative breakthrough.

EXAMPLES OF CREATIVITY DREAMS

1: An Artist's Painting Is Enhanced by a Dream

Marianne had been very close to her grandmother, who had lived with her family for many years, and she missed her greatly after she died. As an artist, Marianne wanted to honor her memory in some way, so she made a pencil sketch of her grandmother from a photograph. The sketch showed her grandmother as Marianne had often seen her and how she best remembered her—standing in her bedroom doorway wearing a white dressing gown and looking directly at her. Her grandmother's face was framed by silver-gray hair, and Marianne enhanced it by adding subtle and interesting contrasts of white and dark to her sketch.

She liked the sketch, but it felt incomplete. Unable to decide how to proceed, she put it aside, unfinished, and yet her heart often led her to think about it. Several months later she dreamed:

> I see my sketch and the photograph of my grandmother. It's very bland as a black and white pencil sketch and I realize it would look terrific as an oil painting. I go over the drawing, seeing where and how I need to

change it—which lines to darken, where to shade, and where to soften impressions. It is as though a teacher is standing beside me, so that I know exactly which shades I'll need to use to transpose it into a painting. White will remain the dominant color, and I'll use pale shades of sky blue for shading. I note, too, that a touch of red in her handkerchief and some red tones in her hands will add a perfect balance. I wake up knowing how to complete my picture and am so pleased. It will be a precious memory of my grandmother.

Can creative inspiration be any clearer? Marianne often saw her artwork in a dream and would receive clear direction, just as in the above creativity dream, on how to proceed further. Because she was a person who could relax and let go, Marianne had easy access to the deeper realms of the unconscious from which inspiration emerges. As a clever artist, she regularly watched for such creativity dreams, and therefore, often received them.

2: A Student's College Paper Is Helped by a Dream

Roger really loved his political science course in college, enjoying the class discussions about the ins and outs of U.S. politics. He wanted to hand in an especially interesting paper for this course. Having picked former president Nixon as his topic, he agonized on how to make it interesting. One night Roger dreamed:

I see President Nixon raising his arm at the end of a speech. People are responding to him, but it strikes me as a little authoritarian. I look back at the president and see him wearing the garments and headdress of the pope. Laughing, I wake up.

Because of this dream, Roger had the audacity to title his paper: "Nixon, the American Pope," and from there found some fascinating and original perspectives on his term of office which combined character insights with that president's political decisions. This approach brought out Roger's creativity and earned him a good grade. It worked, and his professor had no idea where that creative idea had originated. No doubt many a teacher has wondered whether less successful essays were inspired by a dream—a bad dream.

3: A Creativity Dream Shows an Author How to Organize a Book

The following creativity dream relates to the birth of this book, so I can't resist sharing it. As a child, I did not have artistic inclinations such as drawing or painting, but I loved to write. I played games of publishing a newspaper and gave my teachers offerings of childish plays and poems which they greeted with affectionate enthusiasm. As an adult, after learning to meditate and feeling generally relaxed and happy in life, shades of an artistic streak sometimes emerged, including being part of a tapestry-weaving group, which engaged me in hours of love and labor. Our work was eventually shown in museums as part of a national tour. Such creative flashes were just enough to keep me daydreaming about someday taking up painting or watercolors as a hobby, and I continue to love and admire all works of art.

My first love is still writing, but since painting is something about which I fantasize, it's not surprising that in dreams relating to my own creativity, I often see myself as an artist. One such creativity dream gave me the hint I needed for how to write this book. I didn't know how to organize the masses of information and insights I had collected over the years and wondered how to artfully weave complex ideas together. I dreamed:

> I'm at an exhibit in a quaint, simple art gallery. I see about two dozen canvases neatly arranged around the

walls in straight lines. The canvases, which are more or less of the same size, are detailed and colorful pictures of people involved in various activities. They're vibrant and show life in action with a depth and charm reminding me of something modern and yet very ancient. An art critic nearby has appraised them and rates them highly. I wonder who the artist is, then realize, with awe, that these are my paintings. I feel happy and yet humble that people like what I've done.

This creativity dream addressed several of my concerns. In terms of how to organize my thoughts, it hinted the information could be given in a colorful and interesting way that people and critics alike would enjoy. The scenes of people engaged in daily activities suggested that describing actual episodes of people's lives would be a viable approach. It occurred to me that including the dreams of many people would add color and interest. As I pondered this dream, the neat rows in which the paintings were arranged also struck me. I realized I wanted to separate my material neatly too, and could do so by giving each type of dream a separate chapter. And so, *The Bedside Guide to Dreams* was born— with the help of a dream, of course.

IDENTIFYING FEATURES
OF CREATIVITY DREAMS

1. Hobbies or Interests

If you have hobbies or interests, look for symbols and images containing them in your dreams. Such creativity dreams may come to help you directly with that hobby or interest, or they may be metaphors to help with some other talent you are trying to develop. Pay attention to any dream that shows you in a hobby, even if it's a hobby you don't have. It may represent budding creativity of that hobby, or something else.

2. Laughter or Feelings of Accomplishment

Watch for dreams that make you laugh, feel playful, or leave you with a sense of accomplishment. These are feelings often connected to the creative process, its development, and its use. A dream that brings out those feelings may well be a creativity dream that is giving you a nudge.

3. A Teacher or Apprentice

Watch for dreams that show a teacher giving you a lesson that you are greatly enjoying. Or look for scenes that cast you in the role of a student or an apprentice, where you are having a good time and are greatly absorbed in your task. These symbols and activities are often found in creativity dreams. The talent being developed may be a metaphor for something new you are about to develop, or it may be a talent you are already working on.

4. Dreams Point Out Creativity in All Areas of Life

Whether it is cooking, writing, sewing clothes, doing carpentry, playing tennis, or whatever, any interest can benefit from a creativity dream if you give it room to plug in to your inner self and into your unconscious. Some artists think that all of life is one great work of art that you yourself create. The way you dress, communicate, and relate to people are all ways of expressing yourself. Therefore, you can look for and use creativity dreams for every aspect of your life. Enhance your everyday life by adding the sparkle of a creativity dream's insight. Ask for ideas or a theme for your next party, or next meeting; such a polling of the unconscious can be fun. Remember, you are not obligated to take the suggestion of your dream. However, if you give your curiosity free rein, who knows what might turn up?

CHAPTER 15

◊

Practice Dreams: Dreams
That Are Practice Sessions

The child, the seed, the grain of corn,
The acorn on the hill,
Each for some separate end is born
In season fit, and still
Each must in strength arise to work
The Almighty Will.
——ROBERT LOUIS STEVENSON

WHAT THEY DO

Did you ever go to bed and wake up the next morning more tired than when you went to sleep? It could be that while you were sleeping, you were practicing something at an unconscious level. You may not remember any dreams, but if you did, they might be practice dreams. A practice dream rehearses whatever we're working on.

I used to teach evening classes, and there were many groups that were so enthusiastic, we would almost hate to finish the class. After such classes, I often dreamed that we would meet later that night and continue where we had left off, going over certain questions in more detail. Were we actually meeting at some soul level, and in our enthusiasm carrying on where we had left off? Knowing from my own dream experiences that we are capable of more than we know and understand, I think it's entirely possible.

Depending on what it is you are trying to learn, sometimes you need one or two practice sessions in order to learn it, and sometimes you need a year or more of practice. It is the same with practice dreams. Sometimes they appear as a series of dreams to help you learn something that is complex, such as a set of new skills or attitudes, and sometimes only one or two practice dreams are needed to get a handle on something simple.

EXAMPLES OF PRACTICE DREAMS

1: Practicing a Hobby

Even as a student in high school, Flo Ann had very clear dreams. Having an agile body, her mother had enrolled her in gymnastics and ballet from a very young age. By the time Flo Ann was in junior high, she was winning tournaments and had hopes of making the national Olympic team. Having high goals and great enthusiasm, Flo Ann gave gymnastics her all.

Her teachers and coach noticed how quickly Flo Ann learned new moves and routines. They didn't know that her nightly practice sessions via practice dreams played a key role. Each time a teacher introduced new and complicated moves and routines, Flo Ann would practice them in a dream later that night:

> I'm in the gym, trying out the new moves we learned today. I'm swinging on the bar, but at the same time I can see myself at a distance and I can feel every muscle moving. I see and imagine how each move should look and feel. I go through it and practice till it feels right.

Flo Ann would also experience this type of practice dream before a competition. It's no wonder Flo Ann won medals and trophies with ease. With the help of practice dreams, anything is possible!

2: Practicing How to End an Unsatisfactory Relationship

Kitty had been dating Rodney, an exuberant and flashy businessman, for months. She was a sweet young woman, and they had fun together. But Rodney could be very sarcastic and controlling. As the weeks went by, he became more and more aggressive, telling her how to do things and demanding that she do exactly as he asked. To avoid harassment and nagging, Kitty always agreed, but felt herself disappearing. She began to suspect they weren't right for each other and that she could be happier with someone less colorful but also less overbearing. But she found it hard to break the relationship off. One night Kitty dreamed:

> *I'm walking across a college campus, on my way to meet someone. I see three young men and confidently walk past them. As I walk past the first one, I flirt and say "hi." As I pass by the second man, I notice he is an old college friend who was like a big brother to me. He had always encouraged me to assert myself. I turn to him as though to ask a question, but realize I don't have to say a word because we understand each other just by looking into each other's eyes. We both know I already have the answer to the question I was about to ask. So I keep going and find that the third man is the man I've been dating. I ignore him and talk to the other two to demonstrate that I can lead my own life and don't care about what he says anymore. I wake up feeling good about my new independence.*

At an intellectual level, Kitty had already decided to end the relationship. She just had to muster the courage to make the break without fear of her boyfriend's reaction. This practice dream put Kitty in touch with what it would feel like to let him go, suggesting that it was just a matter of putting her attention elsewhere and ignoring her boyfriend's reaction. In fact, the dream reminded Kitty that flirting with others again would be fun! Finding an old school chum in the practice dream was a reminder that she needed to assert herself, just as he had always encouraged, and that she already knew how to do so. After this practice dream in which she practiced being independent and liked it, Kitty ended the relationship and never looked back.

3: A Practice Dream Helps Someone Overcome His Shyness

For a year and a half Ross had a series of dreams about climbing heights. As a teenager, he had been afraid of heights, but had gotten over it. Now, as a successful reporter, he was living the good life he had struggled to attain. Part of his new responsibilities included addressing groups, since he was often invited to speak about journalism at dinners and local high schools.

Because his girlfriend Lynn was into dreams, Ross recorded his dreams, and they often compared dreams over breakfast or while driving to work. At one point Lynn noticed that the climbing actions and images of heights were becoming a pattern in Ross's dreams. A typical dream was:

> I'm climbing a high ladder up to a window. My best friend is leading the way. I really don't want to go, but it's important to do so. Knowing my friend is there makes me feel better and I can't disappoint him, so I climb up after him. He's pleased. But when I get to the top, I freeze.

In a series of dreams, Ross had climbed a variety of heights such as staircases, a roller coaster, and buildings. Sometimes the stairs or ladders he climbed were firm and steady, sometimes they were shaky. Generally there was a loved one or friend nearby leading the way and giving him encouragement to keep climbing. And it was always urgent to continue to climb, as though some mission were being performed. The overall themes spoke of someone carrying out something fearful but urgent, something he didn't like but had to do anyway. At first neither Ross nor Lynn could figure out what this series of dreams meant.

Then Ross noticed that the people coaching him shared a common characteristic: They were all extroverts. Since this seemed to be important, he examined this trait in himself and estimated that although he was occasionally outgoing, mostly he was shy and kept to himself. So compared to the characters in the dream, Ross was an introvert. The following dream highlighted another common feature of those climbing dreams:

> *I'm a main speaker at a meeting. To get to the speaker's lounge, we have to climb two stories of pipes, hand over hand, which are situated along the outside wall of the room. I would have been afraid to climb over them, except that a blond older woman whom I respect and admire leads the way up the pipes. I'm amazed by her lack of fear, and taking strength from her example, I follow her up the pipes! Later during the conference I follow her up again, and even though I felt insecure, I am aware that we always arrive safely at our destination.*

From this dream Lynn noticed that besides the encouraging associate, there's generally a group involved that Ross is interacting with. Ross noticed, too, that as the series progressed, he was getting better and better at climbing. He began to ask himself the significance of groups in his life and what climbing and fear of heights could mean to him as a metaphor. Like laying out the pieces of a puzzle on a tabletop before putting it together, Ross and Lynn reviewed what they knew. There was always a group setting, an encouraging associate who set an example, and an unavoidable task.

Ross tried to relive the dream, often a good technique to get a sense of the meaning of a difficult dream. Letting the dream's emotions wash over him, Ross let himself re-feel what climbing felt like. By holding the feeling, lo and behold—it finally occurred to Ross that climbing the heights felt as scary to him as did public speaking—a new skill he had been trying to develop in the same year and a half that these dreams appeared. Despite Ross's shy and introverted streak, his work involved him with the public, and wanting success, he was determined to rise to the occasion. Thus, these were practice dreams in which Ross had been practicing overcoming his fear of public speaking. The last dream in his series showed how he conquered the last of his shyness forever:

I'm in a group. It's a beautiful summer day and we're at some sort of park, like water parks for children. We have to climb some high bars, like those on the sides of a roller coaster. I reach the top and am surprised to find myself at the highest starting point of a long, winding slide. The others are already sliding down and it looks like so much fun that I forget how high I am and begin to slide down, shouting "whee . . ." all the way down. I feel so young and free, and just let myself go.

Ross became less nervous giving speeches and, noticing a rapport with the audience, actually began to enjoy it. When he started looking forward to being invited, Ross knew, from the dream about the ride down a slide, that he had conquered his fear.

4: A Practice Dream Helps Someone to Stop Smoking

Carmela is a fun, young Italian woman, determined to have it all. Her life sometimes resembles a three-ring circus as she juggles caring for a young family, working, and finding time for the arts and crafts she enjoys so much. A modern young woman, looking after her health has always been a priority. But after having her two children, she no longer had time for exercise classes and hikes in the fresh air as she used to have as a single person. She regretted that she had gained some weight and had started to smoke. Feeling as though she had let herself go, Carmela nevertheless believed that one day she'd get back in shape. One December, Carmela began to dream:

> *I'm running through a forest. It's a perfect, warm summer day. I can feel the earth beneath my feet, and because I'm running without any clothes on, the wind feels natural and soothing against my body. I run long and hard, and my lungs feel full and exultant. I realize that is how a nonsmoker feels when running through a forest. I feel clean, strong, capable, and natural and the exultant feeling in my lungs is just wonderful.*

The first time Carmela had this dream, it grabbed her full attention. The message was very direct, saying: "This is how a nonsmoker feels." It felt so good in this practice dream to feel her lungs clear and clean, and filling with fresh air. She knew she would like to always feel this way, and because of this dream began to think about quitting smoking. During the first week Carmela had this dream once or twice, but in the weeks that followed, it began to appear almost nightly, interspersed with other dreams. It felt so good to run in the dream that Carmela began to look forward to going to sleep and having this practice dream. Carmela had other dreams, and many of them began:

> *I am a nonsmoker . . .*

And then the dream would continue. She began to say to herself in the dream, "What a good idea." This snatch continued as an opening line in her other dreams, alongside the running practice dream which continued to appear regularly. It was like listening to music by Bach where two main tunes interplay as point and counterpoint. And like listening to good music, Carmela was enjoying herself.

January and New Year's Day came along. Because smoking, or, rather, not smoking had been on her mind a lot during the past month, Carmela thought to herself, "Why not?" and decided that it was a good time to quit. She returned to work in the New Year and stopped smoking cold turkey! And though most people around her at work were smokers, strangely enough their smoking didn't bother her and she didn't feel at all enticed to have a puff. Neither did Carmela feel cranky and bothered. Furthermore, although many people gain weight when they stop smoking, she lost five pounds and felt extremely good. Thanks to her practice dreams, it was as though Carmela's mind and body were in such harmonious agreement to let go of smoking that it happened with complete ease.

Though she had stopped smoking, these dreams continued into February, and then trailed off. It had been so easy to stop smoking that Carmela felt proud and even a bit cocky about it, feeling very sure she had kicked her addiction. Oops. Just when we stop watching the road, we slip on a banana peel! At a party in early March, Carmela literally did not notice herself taking a cigarette that was offered to her, and smoking it. She was totally unaware of smoking it until, with horror, she noticed herself squashing the remnants of the butt in an ashtray. Once it was done, Carmela shrugged it off, deciding quitting was an easy thing to do—tomorrow. Naturally, by the next day she was hooked again.

Carmela realized she had become too sure of herself and regretted that she had taken the first puff. She smoked only one or two cigarettes a day for a few weeks, but then began to increase her intake. By the end of March she was back full circle to where she had started. Disappointed but realistic, Carmela forgave herself and resolved to deal with it again.

At the beginning of April her practice dreams began to reappear with the opening statement: "You are a nonsmoker . . ." And once again the running dreams appeared, which felt good. Carmela realized these dreams were a practice session for getting her mind and body ready to stop smoking. This time she was determined she would quit for good and not take another cigarette again, not even one puff. She had lost her momentum and now needed another wave on which to ride. So her practice dreams obliged her need. Like three different instruments in a band, a third practice dream began to interplay:

> *Someone is showing me what my health and body will be like when I stop smoking. It will be just as I've always wanted. I'll lose weight and it will be easy to maintain my weight. My health will be excellent rather than the ho-hum shape it's in now. And I'll be able to easily and naturally fit exercise and other healthy habits into my schedule. I know I will help myself tremendously by quitting smoking and I want to do it.*

This dream added one more impetus, increasing Carmela's resolve to go for it one more time. With each practice dream, she developed more and more motivation and strength to put her body on track again. As this resolve spilled over into her waking life, you can be sure Carmela successfully stopped smoking and regained the tip-top health and energy she had been wanting to reclaim.

By having such practice dreams, your psyche accesses the tremendous healing power of your unconscious, and channels it to you through your dreams to help you change or to learn new things. Why did such practice dreams keep coming to Carmela? As a tool, they take the pain and strain out of letting go of old habits and of developing new ones. I believe anyone can have such practice dreams because, like Aladdin, you have a magic lamp that will give you three wishes. To draw out the genie of your own lamp, you first have to want some change. Then your desire for the change acts like an instruction that feeds into your unconscious and lets it search for a starting point. Just like polishing a lamp, eventually you will get your wish, because if you keep wishing for it, the strength and tools you need will cross your path. This is what happened to Carmela. Even while smoking, Carmela harbored a secret but sincere wish to clear up her body's health and energy. So if you have a star to wish upon, keep wishing!

IDENTIFYING FEATURES
OF PRACTICE DREAMS

1. Repetitive Themes

Practice dreams are sometimes noticeable as repetitive action themes. One day you notice that you've had a dream with that story line before, and when you check your dream book, you notice you've had it several times. The scenes may differ, but the story line and actions are the same. Get a theme for the dream and match it to an area of your life where the theme may apply, and see if you can place what the practice may be about.

2. Repetitive Actions

A repetitive action may also be a sign of a practice dream. Notice what is being repeated, and translate it into a theme. If someone is singing, one may say it's a theme of self-expression. The practice dream may be about actual singing skills, or it may be some other form of self-expression you are working to develop. Trust your own instincts to discover what you are unconsciously practicing, because the more conscious you become, the sooner your talent will become ready for use in your waking life.

3. Something You Are Already Reaching For

A practice dream rarely initiates something new. Instead, it tends to work on a skill, an attitude, or an awareness that you are already reaching for. Take an inventory of what skills or new attitudes you are trying to develop. Then look at your dreams with this new perspective to see if some of the dreams are practice dreams. Better still, remember that you can dialogue with your psyche, so when you are ready, ask for practice dreams.

4. Priming the Unconscious

There is a lot of energy available in the unconscious that can be used for growth and healing, and we are just beginning to learn how to unleash it. Practice dreams are certainly one of the ways to access the hidden healing power of the unconscious.

5. Recognize Them by Reviewing Your Dream Journal

Because practice dreams may come in cycles and have repetitive themes or actions, you can recognize them if you review your dream journal once in a while. Or if you suspect a dream may be a practice dream, go ahead and review your dream journal. If you've never reviewed your journal before, you will discover that it results in a pleasant and fascinating peek at yourself—from a whole new angle.

PART IV

◊

Frightening Dreams

CHAPTER 16

Frightening Dreams

Let nothing disturb thee
Nothing affright thee;
All things are passing;
—St. Teresa of Avila

WHAT THEY DO

Having a dream is like having a conversation with a friend. Sometimes the topic is unpleasant, but that's what real friends do, talk about everything, both the good and the not-so-great aspects of your life. In the same way, your psyche sometimes talks to you about unpleasant matters, or issues that you would rather avoid. And like a child sticking his fingers in his ears and saying "I won't listen," you can try to push such dreams away. When you do, you mask your dream. Just as listening to something with your ears plugged sounds funny or distorted, so do your dreams become distorted if you try to push them away. This distortion can create frightening images of something that is not necessarily frightening. This is why I tend to say that there are no frightening dreams—only frightened dreamers. When you are afraid, you see your dreams through shaded glass, or through a fog. Anxieties and confusions distort straight and simple messages from the psyche, turning them into something frightening, but it's your own resistance that is making the message turn sour. If you had no tension or resistance in facing yourself or anything else in your life, you

189

would not have many frightening dreams. So what tint of glass you see dreams through depends on you.

But aside from the fact that you create most of them yourself, there are several kinds of frightening dreams. In the *first* kind, you face your actual fears. In the *second*, you deal with the pain and trauma in yourself and in your life. The *third* kind is the most common type of frightening dream and is reflected in the saying "I have met the enemy, and it is I." Here you meet a part of yourself that you prefer to pretend is not a problem. I may have a temper that gets triggered too quickly and easily, but feeling justified, I see my anger as righteous wrath. Someone else may drink too much, but he protests loudly if someone suggests he get help. All of us have a capacity for hiding what we don't like about ourselves, and when we meet this rejected portion of ourselves in a dream, it can be frightening.

When you dream of someone else doing something you dislike, you are likely seeing the rejected part of yourself, because it's easier to see in others what we disown in ourselves. In psychology this tendency is called projection, shown by the classic case of the impatient driver weaving recklessly in and out of traffic while swearing at how poorly other people drive.

When you are awake, your conscious mind neatly avoids the skeletons in your closet. But the conscious mind is no longer in charge during sleep, so your blind spots easily pop up to face you. At first a rejected part of ourselves can feel like a stranger; it shocks us so much that we try to disown it. Often this first encounter produces an explosive reaction in a dream because, not surprisingly, the dream came to you cloaked in fearful images. This is similar to what happened to Luke Skywalker in the movie *The Empire Strikes Back*. Luke enters a deep, dark cavern where he doesn't know that his archenemy, Darth Vader, a villain intent on enslaving the world to the dark force, is lurking. Like your own rejected parts, Darth Vader hides behind an awesome steel mask and a distorted voice. Turning a corner, Luke unexpectedly meets Darth Vader, and in a daring move cuts off Vader's head. He is shocked at his own daring, but even more astonished to discover that, as the helmet cracks open, it is his own face behind the mask. Luke's disbelief is very much like meeting a part of your own dark, secret personality, the unredeemed part of you that you hide so diligently from yourself and from others. It's natural to do so, because as human beings we all resist growing past our shortcomings.

There is a fourth but much rarer type of frightening dream, the kind that contains a literal warning about something in your present or in your future that could do you harm. A detailed description of how to recognize such actual warnings is given in the section on identifying features of frightening dreams. It's important to remember not to jump to conclusions: Make every effort to interpret a dream as though it is symbolic before deciding that it could be a literal warning, because most dreams are symbolic. However, if you can't interpret a frightening dream as a metaphor, watch for the following clues to see if it might be an actual warning. In an actual warning the dream tends to be unusually vivid, people look and act as they do in true life, and emotional reactions match the scenes portrayed (for example, you won't laugh at something frightening). Then and only then consider the dream's literal possibilities, but adopt a wait-and-see attitude.

In my experience, working consistently with dreams creates a rapport with the psyche. This rapport eventually opens up a sixth sense which helps you to recognize which dreams are improvement dreams and which ones are actual warnings. Because I have built such a rapport, I often wake up simply knowing what a dream refers to and I believe such an awareness comes to anyone who continues to regularly work with their dreams. Your psyche wants to communicate with you clearly, and therefore it will guide you in establishing full communication. If and when you're willing and ready, it will present you with new dream levels to notice. All it takes is patience and continued application.

EXAMPLES OF FRIGHTENING DREAMS

1: Facing a Fear of Upcoming Change

By appearing as a dream movie, a fear becomes something you can see outside yourself. It is easier to label the fear and deal with it in this way than when it was only a mass of undefined feelings. Rod's career was undergoing great change. He was a bit of a workaholic, but generally enjoyed life and spending time with family and friends. A calm fellow, it was easy for him to ignore the changes looming in his future, particularly a promotion he would likely get that would involve relocating from the small town he loved to the big city, which could drastically change his life. People admired him for not getting upset. However, Rod began to dream about his antique oak desk which he dearly loved. He had spent many happy hours using it as a student and as an adult. The desk had become synonymous with work he enjoyed, and a symbol of progress in his life and career. Ron began to get anxious and frightened when he dreamed:

> I've moved into an apartment with glass walls. I'm not home, but I can see thieves eyeing my desk through the windows and planning to take it. I wake up feeling vulnerable, afraid they'll take my most valuable possession.

Up until then Rod hadn't taken the time to think about his life. He had uneasy feelings about the career move in progress but had refused to think about it. However, ignoring your fears doesn't make them go away. So his psyche used the image of the possibility of losing his desk as a way to communicate: "You're feeling very vulnerable, and you do have fears of losing what's most precious to you." The threatening thieves and glass walls gave shape and form to Rod's unacknowledged fear that his upcoming promotion would be too uprooting. Thanks to this dream, Rod got in touch with the fact that the move was troubling to him and as a result managed to work it out, but this time from a real sense of knowing he was in control. He transformed his fear into an adventure, deciding to explore the exciting options of living in a big city, and thereby made room for fresh insight to replace old anxieties.

2: Facing the Fear of a Life Situation—A Threat from Another

Doris and her brother-in-law, Carl, had never been on good terms. She had tried to bury the hatchet, but he taunted her and was as overbearing as he could possibly be without incurring the family's wrath. By an unspoken agreement they avoided each other as much as possible but had to meet at certain family gatherings. After a family dinner where a few caustic words were aimed at her, Doris dreamed:

> I see a homeless street person, an old bag lady, walking toward me in the evening. The light is so dim that her face and features are vague. I can see she's old but she is very strong, and I see her arm muscle bulging. Her gray hair is long and matted; she looks unsavory and threatening. The bag lady begins to approach me, staring steadily into my eyes, which unnerves me. I'm afraid she intends to overpower me and steal my purse.
>
> As she gets to within a few feet, I become hysterical and shout: "Keep away from me, you old bag!" I almost attack, fearing she's about to attack me, but I hold back. She passes by, still looking at me intently but as she passes me I realize that she is actually harmless. I feel silly. She is strong, but now I know I'm stronger, and that she can't hurt me. I wake up genuinely terrified, suppressing the scream of shouting at her. But I feel relieved.

At the gathering Doris had resolved to ignore Carl's hatred and insults. She succeeded in backing off even though her pride had been wounded by his taunts. Thoughts of revenge and sharp retorts had begun to creep into her mind. Torn by

these conflicting emotions of trying to rise above the small-
ness of it all versus wanting to vent her anger and defend
herself, this frightening dream had appeared.

Who is the bag lady? She likely personified the threat
Doris felt from her brother-in-law, the vengeful part of herself that wanted to look mean and fearful in response to
him. In trying to help Doris deal with her conflict, her psyche put her fear into a visual picture so that she could have
a look at what she feared. As an image, the bag lady personified every fear and threat she could imagine from Carl.
Fearing that he would overwhelm her, Doris rightfully
wants to defend herself, and becomes hysterical. But the
bag lady isn't Carl—it's her own fear, anger, and vengeful
feelings toward him.

Because Doris worked regularly with her dreams, she was
able to quickly use her dream to mobilize the wiser part of
herself, allowing her to see that Carl was not really a threat
and she did not need to react so strongly toward him. The
only enemy Doris needed to face was her own fear, the
shadow in herself. she had not yet owned. As her fear
drained off, Doris managed to become civil to Carl, and
though they are not best friends, she now even gives him a
guarded peck on the cheek each New Year's Eve!

3: A Frightening Dream Enables Someone to Meet Her Own Disturbed Thoughts

A fashion-conscious single woman in her thirties, Sandy
was without a steady beau for a while. As a college friend
quipped over lunch, Sandy had miraculously managed to
get through two years without a man and still emerge sane
and in good humor. Sandy confided that it hadn't been easy,
relating the following episode as one of her more memorable ups and downs.

Sandy had only one rule while dating—no married men.
She hoped to have a home and family one day and believed
that a one-to-one commitment was special, and it was what
she wanted. Of course, married men didn't always know

this, like the coworker who began to try to get her under his spell. Hearing others boast about mistresses, he thought it would be fun to get Sandy interested. At first the man's attentions merely annoyed her, but being lonely and wondering whether she was taking her goals too seriously, Sandy began to contemplate an affair and let herself be somewhat beguiled. Yet each time she had the opportunity to actually get involved with him, something held her back. After several distressing months of going back and forth and changing her mind regularly, Sandy had this gruesome frightening dream:

> *I'm leaning over a basin, about to wash my hair. I part it through the center and see a bald strip in the mirror as though a shaver had cut a two-inch strip through the middle of my scalp. Looking up close, I see the shaved portion is covered with ugly, pus-filled sores. Disgusted, I suddenly know the rest of my scalp is in the same condition! I'm so completely revolted by the sight and desperately begin to wash my head, shaking it vigorously. Gobs of white stuff and blood shake off, spattering around the room. I realize I should have washed it out a long time ago and rinsed it down the drain.*

She woke up in horror at the memory of her scalp feeling as though it were really infected. Notice that the head is where we do our thinking, so images of the head, scalp, and hair in a dream are often a comment on what's going on in your thinking and attitudes. This dream was saying: "What you have on your mind is rash and ugly and you've let it sit so long that it's festering." Such a scene would give anyone a proper jolt! Sandy was meeting the frightening by-products of her own thoughts, that of contemplating this affair, which was contrary to her ideals.

Realizing she really didn't want to get involved in such a sordid mess, she accepted that the dream's unpleasant and scary images reflected the truth. When she really examined where she stood with the issue, she realized that just the thought of an affair made her feel guilty, dirty, and ugly, feelings superbly created and captured by the dream. Its ending suggested she could have rinsed the prospective affair down the drain a long time ago. Taking this as a cue, Sandy quickly put Casanova in his place forever with a few choice words, and cleaning up her own thoughts, put him permanently out of her mind.

4: A Frightening Dream Is a Literal Warning of Something to Fear

Babs liked dancing and tennis but wasn't much of a jogger. Yet as a junior in college, she often wore the trademark jeans and running shoes of her age group as she dashed from classes to her part-time evening job taking room service orders by telephone for a large hotel. Not fearful by nature, she thought nothing of walking the few blocks alone around midnight from her place of work to the bus stop. Turned on to dream analysis as a hobby by a friend, she was not too affected by this one snatch of a mildly frightening dream that had almost escaped her attention as she rushed to get up one morning:

I'm walking along a dark side-street late at night, rushing to get somewhere. I notice a shadowy figure across the street walking toward me, and as he crosses the street, heading straight toward me at a fast pace, I panic, realizing that he's out to get me. Terror-stricken, I freeze in my tracks, but then remember I'm wearing my running shoes, so I turn and run frantically. I reach the safety of a well-lit street with some people nearby.

Babs was in a rush that morning, too hurried to think about this vague dream. But on her way out the front door she chuckled as she noticed she had put on her running shoes, wryly thinking that dreams sometimes influence us more than we realize. The rest of the day was a mad whirl, and before she knew it, it was eleven-thirty P.M. and she was closing up the evening's room service receipts at the hotel. Babs was responsible for the final accounts and usually had no trouble balancing the accounting sheet to within a few pennies. Except for that night.

The totals were off and she couldn't find the error. Hotel policy dictated that as the person responsible, she had to stay and sort it out, yet every minute felt like ten because the last bus to take her home left at midnight. The bus stop was only three or four blocks away, so that when she finally found the error at eleven forty-five, Babs hurriedly handed in the receipts to the manager, and figured she could still catch her bus if she rushed. With only a few minutes to spare, Babs decided to take a shortcut down a dark and deserted side street she normally avoided.

As she walked at top speed, almost running, she noticed a man coming toward her on the opposite side who started to cross the street, heading for her. It all felt strangely familiar, and as she froze in her tracks, realizing she was in danger, Babs remembered her dream, now playing out before her very eyes. In all of two seconds she remembered she was wearing her running shoes and, as in the dream, turned around and ran for her life. Running despite a stabbing pain in her chest as she breathed, Babs reached the safety of a lighted thoroughfare, and saw that she was no longer being followed. This dream not only alerted her to save herself, but also increased her interest in dreams. Needless to say, Babs never took that side street home again.

IDENTIFYING FEATURES
OF FRIGHTENING DREAMS

1. Feeling Frightened

Frightening dreams are easy to recognize—they make you feel afraid! You can wake up feeling anything from mild fright to absolute terror.

2. Rejected Part of Yourself

You tend to hide the parts of yourself that you dislike, especially from yourself. So if you happen to meet a hidden part of yourself, sometimes called "your shadow," your natural reaction is to be frightened by it. Such meeting-of-yourself dreams is a common form of frightening dreams. And because you are only meeting yourself, you could almost say there are no frightening dreams—only frightened dreamers. If you accept this rejected part of yourself, work with it, and transform it into something likable again, you will be rewarded by feeling wonderful.

3. An Actual Fear

There are events, people, or parts of yourself to actually fear. A healthy fear is one where you are aware of a potential danger and take steps to deal with it without letting it overcome you or rule your life. Some frightening dreams are about actual fears. A frightening dream may point out an event, a person, a situation, or an attitude in yourself that could be destructive or dangerous.

4. Literal Warnings

There are frightening dreams that depict actual warnings. The following are some signs to watch for, to help you decide whether it might be a literal warning or not, but keep in mind that such dreams are rare. *First*, the overall effect of an actual warning creates a very vivid dream, more vivid than most dreams. *Second*, the emotional reactions within the dream match the reactions you would have if it were a real situation; in some dreams you might laugh at a frightening scene, but if it's an actual warning, you will feel appropriate fear. *Third*, a literal warning contains scenes that portray true-to-life details: a car looks like your actual car, the street like an actual street you know, and so on. Though most dreams, likely ninety-nine percent of them, are psychological and metaphorical portrayals of your own growth, these are the signs of the one percent or so that might be literal warnings. If all of these signs are present in a frightening dream, *and* you have made a genuine attempt to find an alternative, metaphorical meaning, consider the possibility that it might be a literal warning.

CHAPTER 17

Dreams About Death

It is in dying ... that we are born to eternal life.
—St. Francis of Assisi

WHAT THEY DO

Ninety-nine percent of the time, dreams about death are simply metaphors for major changes happening in your relationships, work, or personality. Because death and dying is the ultimate change we all experience, it is the perfect symbol for major changes, especially ones that frighten you. Death, as a symbol in a dream, represents a metamorphosis. Therefore, if you have a dream involving death, take heart. The only question you need to ask is: "What aspect of my life is undergoing change?" There are, of course, a small portion of dreams that may be actual warnings of death; guidelines for how to recognize them are provided later in the chapter.

Dreams of seeing a car accident are relatively common. Mostly these are symbolic because a car is a great metaphor for where you are going in life and how the journey is faring. Yet in real life, car accidents are a major cause of death and serious injury, so dreams that contain scenes of car crashes or death can hardly be taken lightly. As an example of their symbolic meaning, I once had a whole series of dreams about learning to drive, and often came close to crashing. Learning to drive was a symbol for practicing how to take charge of my life in my late teens, as I made the transition from a shy and insecure young person to a woman able to independently and confidently make decisions. Because we all tend to become too anxious about car-crash and accident scenes in dreams, it can't be said often enough: Most dreams, even ones about death or near death, are metaphors.

Yet there are a few dreams that are actually warnings that could help save a life. In one such case, Louis, who was an avid follower of his dreams, dreamed of a truck losing control on a hill and unexpectedly crashing into his car as he waited for a light to change at an intersection. A few days later the actual circumstance began to unfold, and he recognized it from the dream in a matter of seconds. Gambling that the dream was correct regarding what would come next, he drove into the ditch and averted what would have been a crash—exactly in the spot where his car had stood.

When we do have actual warnings of death, they come for two reasons. Sometimes it's time for someone, such as an elderly person, to die, so a dream comes to prepare us emotionally for this natural and inevitable event. Then there are deaths due to an accident or to carelessness. In this case, I believe warning dreams do appear to help us avoid something. In both cases, even though they scare us, dreams about death are helpful and kind messages.

EXAMPLES OF DREAMS ABOUT DEATH

1: A Dream About a Daughter's Near Death Is Actually About a Major Change

A recent dream greatly troubled Sue-Ellen. Though a stranger, she asked me to give an opinion of it during a conference because she thought it might be a literal warning about her daughter. She had dreamed:

> *I see my daughter Carolyn in her red car driving along the boulevard not far from her home. She's driving at normal speed, but as she turns a corner, she crashes into another car which she didn't see was coming. I'm distraught. An ambulance arrives and takes her away. I see Carolyn in the hospital, all bandaged up, but the doctor says she's fine and will be all right. I wake up frightened and badly shaken.*

This dream certainly had characteristics that could make it a literal warning. It had accurate, true-to-life details such as the red car just like the one Carolyn actually drives and it showed her driving along a street she normally takes. Secondly, the dream seemed more vivid than normal dreams. Furthermore, the feelings and reactions in the dream were appropriate to an accident. The good news, in case it was an actual warning of an accident, was that its ending confirmed that Carolyn would be fine.

But no matter how scary a dream is, the first rule for dream analysis is the hardest one—not to jump to conclusions. So despite this mother's natural distress, I asked her to bear with me and explore the dream as a possible metaphor. I asked Sue-Ellen, "Have there been any significant changes in your life recently, or are you on the verge of making some changes?" She thought for a second, then replied in the negative. This worried me. But taking nothing for granted, I refocused on her daughter, who was the central figure of this dream. Since dreams often tell you about your loved ones, I asked: "Was there any significant change in your daughter's life around the time you had this dream?"

Sue-Ellen's face froze for a second. She then laughed and said, "Why, yes." About the time of the dream, she had been shocked and upset by an announcement her daughter had made. Due to her husband's new job, her daughter and son-in-law would soon need to move thousands of miles away. Mother and daughter had never been separated before, and as her only child, this was a radical change for

Sue-Ellen. This news felt as sudden and as grievous to her as would a car crash, so to speak. Rather than being a warning about her daughter's driving, this dream was trying to prepare Sue-Ellen for the upcoming separation from her daughter.

Relieved, she confirmed that her feelings when receiving the news had matched those in the dream—a feeling of shock and helplessness. Such a "correspondence of feeling" is often an indicator that the right event has been related to the dream. Because this struck a chord of truth for Sue-Ellen, she no longer feared for her daughter's safety.

2: A Dream About a Daughter's Death Gives an Actual, Literal Warning

At a conference on dreams, Rose quietly shared with me the tragic experience that had brought her to the conference and to the study of dreams. Two years before, she had dreamed:

> I see my teenage daughter, Annie, getting into a car with two or three friends. They were out for the evening and are about to drive home along the highway, as they usually do. I see them in the car and notice they've been drinking. They're boisterous and happy, carrying on as teenagers do. An oncoming car comes by, veering out of control toward them, but it happens too fast for anyone to notice. They crash. I see my daughter, bloody and immobile with her head tipped backward, and I know she is dead.

Rose woke up in terror with the scene of her daughter's mangled body echoing in her memory. Rose felt very uneasy and thought about warning her daughter not to drive with those who had been drinking, but dismissed it as a foolish bad dream. Tragically, a year later her only daughter and three friends were killed in a car crash just as her dream described. Still in agony, she related the pain of losing her daughter. My heart broke as I listened to her wondering out loud whether, if she had taken the dream more seriously, she might have altered the ending. Only God knows the answer.

This dream did have the three clues linked to a potential, literal warning. First, the details were accurate: she saw the actual car, highway, and young people looking as they do in real life. Secondly, the dream was particularly vivid, as opposed to the foggy viewing-from-a-distance perspective that you often feel in a dream. This is because actual warnings likely come from the soul level and dreams from these deeper realms of consciousness impart a much more intense quality to a dream. And thirdly, the emotional level and reactions in the dream were appropriate.

I marveled at Rose's courage. Though nothing could change the past, she was determined to understand her dreams instead of fearing them. She reasoned that if such a warning came again, she might help someone. This was small consolation. But by learning to work with her dreams, Rose discovered that besides warnings, her dreams also helped her to get in touch with the strength and healing she needed after her loss. It is, however, a tragic way to discover that dreams can bring guidance and help, and the gracefulness with which Rose explored her dreams inspires me.

3: A Death Dream Prepares a Young Person Who Is About to Die for the Experience of Death

As a child, Christopher had been a healthy and happy lad. Yet when he turned thirteen, doctors diagnosed leukemia. For two years, bouts of leukemia and its painful treatment distressed and pained his entire family. With each remission, the family kept hoping the disease would remain dormant. But at age fifteen and a half, the illness had advanced too far, and the doctors could do no more for him. With the wisdom of youth, Chris accepted his situation. Trying to provide all the support they could, his family asked me to

visit with him. I was most impressed with the boy's courage, and a bond formed between us. Chris told me about a
dream he had at the time of his last attack, which he had
had while lying in a coma from which his doctors thought
he would not recover. Christopher had dreamed:

> It's a beautiful summer day. I'm on the banks of a
> grassy stream. Nearby is a simple wooden bridge and I
> start to walk across. I see a wise, kindly old man with a
> long, sparkling white beard coming toward me from the
> other side. On the other side of the bank, other elderly
> men are sitting on the grass, looking happy and peaceful.
> As I look into the old man's face, great love fills me, and
> I want to be with him. He extends a hand toward me and
> says, "Death is like crossing this bridge and lying down
> in the grassy banks beside this stream." I long to do so,
> but remember my father would miss me, so I run back.

Dreams such as this death dream were preparing Christopher for the time of his death, which was coming near. Its
theme of peace and love and the ease of death as simply
crossing a bridge were reassuring to him. Yet at a moment
when doctors thought he was not going to pull through, the
dream showed that his own concerns about those he loved
kept him from dying. This dream showed Christopher still
choosing to live, and will of the soul can keep even a weak
body hanging on. Yet it could only be a matter of time.

Not long after he and I had met, Chris had another attack
and lay helpless during a three-week coma. His father ver-
ified that he had been given huge doses of chemotherapy
that were very uncomfortable, and even painful. The father
sat by his son's bedside continuously and spoke to Chris in
his rare moments of lucidity. Perhaps because his soul was
close to death, even though he was in a coma, Christopher
needed to communicate with someone. Because I was
versed in dreams and soul communications through dreams,
and because we had recently established a bond of deep un-

derstanding, I was a good candidate. As a soul communication from Christopher, I dreamed:

> *I see Christopher sitting in the bleachers of a baseball
> field. It is pouring buckets of rain so thick and heavy that
> one can hardly see a foot ahead. He's wearing a fisher-
> man's raincoat, but the rainfall is so heavy and damp
> that he is suffering enormously. His teeth chatter and he
> feels so cold. He looks up at me, begging me to help him.*

My heart broke as I awoke from this dream, knowing that
despite being in a semi-coma, Christopher's soul and body
were torn, struggling between life and death. At some level
he wanted to be free from his body's pain, but he kept
hanging on to life so as not to grieve his father. From our
discussions I knew his anxiety for his family was an issue
of great concern to him. I couldn't help him directly, but
believing that his soul was communicating with me, I sent
him extra prayers to surround him with love and strength.
Again I felt great pain after a second dream communication, which put me directly in his shoes:

> *It's evening, around sunset. I've attended a conference
> all day, and people are going home. We're in a large,
> empty barn. An old professor whom I love and respect
> asks me to go out for supper, but I'm depressed and
> tired, so I decline. I go to my room, which is in one cor-
> ner of the barn. But as soon as I enter it, I regret not
> having gone to supper with him.*
> *I know I want to leave, because the room now seems
> scary with its long shadows falling in strange shapes
> across the room. I rush to put on a sweater that would
> make me look more presentable, and am in such a rush
> that I don't shout back to let him know I'm coming, tak-
> ing it for granted that I'll be only a second and that he'll
> wait. I rush to the door, but when I open it he's gone. I
> feel so alone, so totally alone. It's pitch black ahead of*

*me, and I'm terrified. I rush back into my room and slam
the door, screaming in panic and terror.*

I could feel Christopher's pain and terror, and awoke in a
cold sweat with a scream in my own throat. This dream
made it obvious to me that Christopher had changed his
mind and was ready to die. He now chose "to go with the
others," and leave the loneliness and darkness of his semi-
coma to which his illness had brought him. But because of
the chemotherapy, his body was hanging on despite itself.
Dangling between two worlds, one painful and one unknown, Christopher felt full and utter terror.

But miraculously, after three weeks in a coma, he recovered once more. Worn out but once again in remission from
the leukemia, Christopher was allowed to leave the hospital. It was summer, and he was overjoyed to sit in his beloved garden at home, resting in the sunlight. His family
hoped beyond hope that his condition would stabilize. But
I dreamed:

> *I see a room with four kittens running about, having a
> good time. I see a healthy one, brimming with fun and
> vitality. But looking more closely, I see the other three
> are thin and in poor health, with mangy, ragged hair. I
> know they are too weak to live. A voice says, "The body
> is not strong enough."*

With kittens as an image of the energies in Christopher's
body, this dream suggested that though the bout of leukemia was over, three-quarters of his body was too weakened
to see him through into a full recovery. Sure enough, within
days, and at home among loved ones, Chris finally crossed
the bridge, dying peacefully and quickly where he had
wanted to—in his beloved garden. I'd like to think that in
the end it was as easy for him to die as lying down in a
green pasture, just as his death dream had suggested.

One thing I learned from this experience was that death
dreams can prepare a soul for death. And a second thing I

learned is that we need to learn to let our loved ones go when their time arrives to pass on; holding on, even with motives of love, may only prolong a loved one's suffering.

4: A Sister Dreams of Her Twin's Death

Can a person's soul, aware it is about to depart from this earth to take the long journey through death's doors, take a detour to visit a loved one first? Common dream lore suggests the answer is yes. In parapsychology, such visits between souls during sleep are considered normal, requiring a relaxed, altered state of consciousness. Since you are relaxed and undistracted during sleep, you may be more open to such experiences when asleep than when awake. In my opinion, such visits are not really dreams, but actual experiences that we remember as dreams because dreams are the only vehicle of memory available during sleep.

Veronica and Alicia were twins, and as children they had been inseparable. Brimming with energy and enthusiasm, people remarked on their fiery, intelligent natures as well as on their striking appearance. By their adult years their tall regal bearing and jet-black hair pulled back into a French twist was a unique trademark.

Veronica and Alicia both married and each had her share of joys and sorrows. When Alicia's husband accepted a lucrative job offer and they moved to South America, the twins were sad to part ways. Losing each other's friendship, even as adults, was difficult to accept. They stayed in touch often by visits and correspondence, and although time and distance separated them for years, the bond between Veronica and Alicia remained strong. One night, shortly before their fiftieth birthday, Veronica, the twin who lived in America, dreamed:

> *I see my sister standing at my bedside. She gives me a hug and says, "Good-bye, don't be sad. We'll see each other again."*

The next day Veronica received news of her twin sister's sudden death. Relatives in Brazil described Alicia's recent words. She had been repeating often, "I want to see my sister just one more time before I die." Via this death dream visit, she did just that.

5: Someone Dreams of Her Own Death

If you have a dream about a funeral and feel happy, or at least you are unconcerned about it, you can instantly rule it out as a literal warning of death—unless, of course, you're looking forward to dying! Feelings in a dream are an important clue to their meaning, as it was for Linda. Linda had the Irish gift of the blarney. She enjoyed nothing better than telling an animated story, embellishing it according to the gleam in the listener's eye. A happy soul, one day she dreamed:

> I see myself lying in a coffin at my own funeral. My friends have gathered around my coffin, and instead of being unhappy, they're having a party. Music is playing and some are dancing a jig. Everyone's having a grand time. Watching from a distance, I'm pleased too, even though it's my own funeral.

Now, if someone announced you had six months to live, would you dance a jig? Hardly. Such news would be shattering. Yet the emotions in Linda's dream are that of much merrymaking. So the question here is: What change was coming into Linda's life that would give her cause for celebration? The answer came, as it should, in examining Linda's life. She had lived a decent and caring life, working, raising a family, and doing the best she could. Now in her middle years, Linda had discovered metaphysics and began to study the areas of dreams, ESP, and parapsychology. She discovered that these areas contained answers to the deep spiritual questions she had always had and she was overjoyed to find that her interests did not contradict the faith in which she was brought up.

These new areas of study and understanding brought Linda enormous peace and a quiet sense of joy. They made her feel as though she had found a part of herself that she had always searched for, like coming home after a long journey. It was a time of significant psychological change for Linda, and that was the real meaning of the death dream. It was a celebration of the death of her old self and a rebirth into a deeper spiritual phase, which was cause for much personal merrymaking.

IDENTIFYING FEATURES
OF DREAMS ABOUT DEATH

1. Images of Transition

Dreams about death often have images of transition and transformation. Common images are of crossing bridges, going on a long journey from which you don't expect to return, and scenes of funerals, accidents, or disasters.

2. Metaphors for Change

Instead of being predictions about an actual death, almost all dreams about death are metaphors for some major change. It can be a change in your life circumstances, relationships, work, attitudes, or changes in your personality. Even though we all know we are going to die someday, death is the biggest change any person expects to encounter and it always seems to come as a surprise. This is why death in a dream works well as a symbol of "more change than you thought you were ready for."

3. An Announcement

The rare dream about death that is a literal warning is usually an announcement that an elderly person has reached his or her time and will soon die a natural death. Generally, such a dream comes to those who love the person who is about to pass on, and its purpose is to gently prepare for the upcoming change. We all want to think those we love will be with us forever. Maybe they do live forever and wait for us in a heavenly realm!

4. Warning of Danger

On even rarer occasions, a dream about death can be a literal warning of the possibility of death involving a young or healthy person. Occasionally such warnings arrive in time to avert the danger; but sometimes, according to some unknown book of destiny, it is that person's time to go. In this case the dream comes to cushion the shock of those who survive.

5. A Good-Bye

Many families tell stories about someone who has died and come back to them, either as an apparition or in a dream, to say a final good-bye. There are those who believe the next level of life is not that far away and is very similar to life here on earth, just minus a body. If this is the case, it would not be unnatural for those who have died to want to come back and tell you they are fine. If a loved one who has just died appears in your dream, there's a good chance it may be an actual visit, remembered as a dream. If it has been a long time since he or she has passed on, the deceased may be passing on metaphoric values to you, or may simply be visiting. Only your heart knows for sure.

6. A Preparation for the Crossing

Mystics have always hinted that when people are about to die, a part of them knows it, which leads them to straighten out their affairs beforehand. Whether a person is suffering from a terminal illness or is approaching a sudden unexpected death (to the conscious mind, although the unconscious may be aware of it), dreams can be a preparation for death. Often a death dream preparing someone for dying shows a very loving, peaceful scene of the transition into death, like crossing a bridge or walking into another room, which helps the person lose her fears. If you have a loved one who is coming close to his or her time who remembers such a dream, let them share it with you. It may give both of you comfort to share such a preparation dream.

PART V

◊

Other People and Your Dreams

CHAPTER 18

Other-Person Dreams

For when the One Great Scorer comes to write
    against your name
He marks—not what you won or lost—but how
    you played the game.

—GRANTLAND RICE

WHAT THEY DO

Did you ever wonder what it would be like to see yourself as others see you? Did you ever want to know how someone else feels? If you want to be attuned to someone else, ask your psyche for an other-person dream. Psychiatrist Montague Ullman, a pioneer advocate of dream use for the general public, suggests that the social and other-person orientation of dreams is one of their most important features. It's a "beyond-the-person" component in dreams that coaxes us out of our usual self-centeredness and into an awareness of being kin to all mankind. A dream, says Dr. Ullman, has "a concern for connectedness . . . that monitors our ties to other human beings." If you look at dreams as a bridge between people, they evoke a sense of wonder about new vistas of understanding as reflected in other-person dreams.

EXAMPLES OF OTHER-PERSON DREAMS

1: An Other-Person Dream Shows how Others Perceive Someone Treated Badly by Her Boss

As a secretary in a large company, Crystal was a delicate creature who did top-notch work. Because she had mastered the art of cooperating with everyone, she was well liked. Her boss was a brilliant man and a well-known figure in his field. He was often charming and likable, but he could also be unpredictable and bad-tempered, subjecting anyone in close range to his acid tongue and dark scowl. As the nearest target, Crystal was often the victim of his unpredictable rages. Yet in order to keep the peace—and her job—she took it all with patience, albeit with pain.

Her faith and her dreams gave her strength, and other staff members understood her difficult position and lent her moral support. One of her associates was Jim, who was always nearby with a smile and a willing ear. Crystal often talked to him when days got rough. But despite such trials, she and others felt proud to work there, for the company's products and accomplishments helped many. Crystal bore her burden patiently but sometimes felt alone and vulnerable. During a week when her boss was particularly aggravating and demeaning, she dreamed:

> I'm near a pet shop. The owner has placed three pink flamingos outside the shop. He is outside beating them and shouting horrible things at them; two are already dead. I step forward to help the third one, but then decide my interference might make the tyrannical storekeeper retaliate more harshly when I leave. So, with revulsion, I walk on.

The dream's theme shows: "Someone watches mistreatment but knows they can't help." Taking this theme, Crystal asked herself two questions: Who was being mistreated, and who was watching and feeling repulsed but helpless?

She noted that verbal mistreatment occurred at work, from her boss, so she was the one mistreated. The pink flamingos symbolized female employees in a vulnerable position, women like herself. The dead flamingos represented other women who had decided enough was enough and had already quit; she, as the third woman who worked for him, had stayed on. The shop owner was obviously her boss, while Jim, her friend and ally at work, was the helpless onlooker who was watching in disgust.

The dream summarized Crystal's predicament. But more important, it put Crystal in Jim's shoes, showing her how horrified he was by what was going on and how he sincerely shared her pain and embarrassment. It put her in touch with his motives for not interfering—he did not want to aggravate her boss and precipitate further verbal abuse. Just knowing at a deep inner level how much he shared her pain gave Crystal strength, and deepened her respect and trust for him. This made her feel stronger and less vulnerable at work, which was the effect the other-person dream wanted to create. It was telling her: "You are not alone; others do care."

2: An Other-Person Dream Shows how Someone Perceives a Friend in Pain

As an observant person, Janet was usually aware of the moods and sensitivities of the people around her. But like many, when she becomes despondent, she shuts others out. At one time when she was feeling down, she dreamed:

> I'm on a street corner standing under a large umbrella with a friend nearby. It's dark outside and pouring rain. We've been attending a conference and are now waiting for a bus to take us home. I don't understand why, but my friend prefers to stand alone in the rain rather than under my umbrella, even though it's big enough for both of us.

The dream describes someone who refuses an offer of taking shelter. So Janet, who works with her dreams regularly, asked herself, "Who's feeling vulnerable, like an orphan in the rain, and seems inconsolable these days, and is refusing help?" She soon recognized herself as the sorrowful lady, since she had been dealing with a bout of the blues brought on by the end of a relationship. But if she were the inconsolable person standing out in the rain, who was the person standing by, watching her and trying to help her?

Janet realized that her best friend, Miriam, had noticed her dampened spirits a few days before and had tried to comfort her. Miriam had cheerfully tried to get her to go to a movie, but steeped in self-misery, Janet had brushed her friend off, abruptly ending their conversation. Janet later felt guilty about this because she and Miriam were good friends and in tune with each other. The other-person dream had appeared to resensitize Janet to Miriam, showing her how her self-pity had made her reject her friend and be unwilling to accept her comfort. It put Janet in touch with Miriam's genuine caring, and in the process eased her heart and deepened their friendship. Thanks to this other-person dream, she not only emerged out of her self-absorption but also quickly renewed her friendship.

3: An Other-Person Dream Puts Someone in Touch with Another's Need for Attention

Paula is a minister's wife, and a good listener. People relate to her warm and calm manner and come to her when they need someone to talk to. Discovering that she could derive insight from her dreams was exciting for Paula. Rather than contradicting her strong faith, she found that working with her dreams deepened her spiritual understanding. Having experienced what dreams can do, Paula believes they come as guidance from the soul and are one of many tools for understanding life that the Creator provided. One day she dreamed:

I'm with our church group, working and helping out. All of us who are workers are in one area, separated from others. I know there's a small child down the hall whom I love dearly. She's being taken care of, but I intuitively know she needs more attention than she's been getting. I feel her aloneness and her hunger for attention, and I want to go to her and be with her. It feels important, so I make time to do so, and it feels good.

At the time, Paula was involved in church projects that took up most of her time. With a busier schedule than usual, she had less time for friendly chats over tea, which often allowed parishioners and friends to unburden themselves to her kind ear. This dream suggested that someone she knew needed her attention, just as a beautiful, neglected child would. She searched her mind to figure out who that could be, and then it clicked. There was a young woman with many cares and heartaches who had recently taken a shine to Paula and often dropped by.

Paula had grown fond of her, and realized that she hadn't seen her new friend for a few weeks. Taking this other-person dream to heart, she called the young woman and invited her to tea. As the dream hinted, the invitation was timely. The young mother admitted she had been feeling especially in need of solace lately, and had no one else to turn to. Because this other-person dream had tuned Paula into her plight, the despondent young woman got the attention she sorely needed.

IDENTIFYING FEATURES OF OTHER-PERSON DREAMS

1. From Someone Else's Point of View

The other-person dream acts like an antenna to put you in touch with how another person is feeling. It increases your understanding of that person, and the role you play in his

or her life or that he or she plays in yours, and thus
strengthens or clarifies something in the relationship. Seeing and actually feeling the other person's point of view can
heal you or help you heal him. These are very special
dreams, a true gift from the soul that binds you closer to
another person in a way that words cannot describe.

2. It Provides Hints

An other-person dream always contains some helpful insight for you about the other person. It can be a hint about
how she views you, how you view her, or where she is behind the mask she normally wears. It can show you how to
help her, or just to understand her better. Or it can inspire
love or healing, sympathy or caring.

3. Identifying One Is Tricky

The other-person dream is a subtle dream type, making it
difficult to identify. When you begin to notice your dreams
regularly, you may not see many of these at first, but in
time you will notice them, and they will become easier to
identify. The clearest cue often comes from putting a theme
together well (the action one-liner), and then deciphering
the area of life to which it belongs. Such a theme-to-life
match, when done successfully, helps to spark the insight
regarding the meaning of the dream and to identify what
dream type it is. If all else fails, ask the question: "Suppose
this is some else looking at me, or me looking through the
eyes of someone else?" Once you decipher your first other-
person dream, others are easier to recognize.

CHAPTER 19

◊

Counseling Dreams: Dreams Helpful to Therapists and Counselors

We took sweet counsel together . . .
—ROBERT BROWNING

WHAT THEY DO

Psychology's founding father, Sigmund Freud, wrote an article recording telepathic exchanges between a patient and himself; he noted that such exchanges were common in the dreams of his patients. Counseling dreams are likely a part of the same phenomenon noted by Freud, a phenomenon also noted by therapists in recent years.

But a counseling dream does more than transmit thoughts and feelings between therapist and patient. As an added step, it also provides insights regarding the causes of the person's problem and supplies hints for the direction of therapy and how to time it. As such, the counseling dream has the potential to dramatically enhance a therapist's ability to foster healing.

EXAMPLES OF COUNSELING DREAMS

1: A Dream Puts a Therapist in Touch with Something That the Client Is Too Afraid to Express

It was my first session with Marie, an attractive, well-dressed woman in her late thirties. She was unhappy in her marriage but spoke about it only in vague, general terms. She seemed to be holding back, as if it were a strain to communicate. She spoke in a barely audible monotone, and her slender face, with its high cheekbones, remained motionless. Obviously, it was almost impossible for her to talk about what was troubling her. Thus, after the first half hour, I still had no sense of why she was coming for counseling. But it was obvious that she felt very much alone. Finally, she began to reveal that she was having an affair. She felt extremely guilty deceiving her husband, but was not prepared to end the affair. However, the tension of her feelings were crippling her, and Marie didn't know what to do.

I tried to discover why the relationship with her husband was unsatisfactory but made no headway. Marie described her husband as a good man, kind and generous, who loved her dearly. They could communicate well, he was faithful and supportive of her career. In the end she kept insisting that she really loved him. He sounded like such a good husband, I wondered what she was gaining from the second man. Why was the heavy guilt and tension of having the affair a price she was willing to pay, even though it was obviously tearing her apart?

I felt her pain and loneliness yet knew that some important piece of the puzzle was missing. Then something struck me. I suddenly noticed that the feelings of pain and frustration I saw in Marie seemed vaguely familiar. I remembered a dream I had just had the night before that contained the same themes of loneliness, isolation, deep pain, sorrow, and suffering in silence. I then wondered whether my dream might relate to Marie's plight. I had dreamed:

> *I'm in a women's dorm, feeling very alone. It's the middle of the night, but I'm just going to bed as if I've come back from somewhere and I must be very quiet. I turn and know someone is behind me. Sure enough, there's a dirty old man in a dark corner who looks like a decrepit street person. His rags are filthy and I recoil as I notice he has no legs, only bloody stumps where his legs should be. I freeze, hoping he won't bother me; perhaps he hasn't even seen me. But it's too late. His cold hand reaches out toward me and I know he wants me in bed with him. I feel revolted yet know I'll get through this somehow. To my great relief, his hand just misses me and I escape and go to my room, which is safe. Later, I'm telling someone about what this feels like.*

The dream's emotions of aloneness, apprehension, guilt, and furtiveness were the same ones I sensed in Marie. Like striking a familiar chord on a harp, there can be such a correspondence of feeling linking a dream to a specific event. In this instance, an emotion acts as a label to identify the event to which it belongs. I quickly mulled over the dream's images as Marie continued to speak. What struck me most was the feeling of shock and loathing toward the old man, partly due to his bloody and dirty appearance, and partly because he had no legs. Knowing dreams sometimes provide a lot of literal information, I dared to wonder whether Marie's husband was actually an invalid in a wheelchair.

If this were so, the dream furthermore suggested that she was repulsed by his disability, perhaps more deeply than she was able to admit even to herself. Yet she did love her husband, and such contradictory feelings of love versus revulsion would be enough to tie someone up in knots, as she was. His disability might also be enough to drive her to have an affair to meet her sexual needs, which would further add to her guilt and distress.

This was, so far, all speculation on my part, and it seemed to be farfetched at that. But because Marie appeared to be unable to describe the place of pain in her that desperately needed attention, I decided to cautiously test out my suspicions. I confronted her with the fact that I wasn't clear as to what the real problem was. This brought a look of recognition and relief to her face, as though she were glad that I could see beyond her limited communications. "You're right," she replied, giving me permission to proceed. I then told her that perhaps I could guess what the problem might be. She was guarded but interested and asked me to go ahead. So I continued. "Could it be," I ventured, "that your husband is an invalid in a wheelchair?"

A look of shock crossed her face, followed by the first relaxed expression I had seen in the entire hour. She must have felt horrible admitting that she was cheating on an invalid husband, but, confronted with the truth, she was relieved to have it out in the open. Now she could begin to discuss her situation and feelings more freely. Although it would still take a lot of work to sort out her feelings and decisions, this counseling dream uncorked her bottled-up emotions and provided the needed first step toward healing—that of opening up her ability to communicate.

A skilled therapist could have helped Marie without the benefit of the dream, but it would have taken much longer for the process to begin. As in this example, counseling dreams can provide invaluable insights, allowing a therapist to step into the person's shoes and tune in directly to her feelings and problems. It allows a counselor to directly feel the patient's pain in a way that words cannot describe, and thus creates more understanding in the therapist. A therapist can get along without counseling dreams, but after getting your first car, would you choose not to use it and take a bus? In the same way, a counseling dream provides a vehicle that gets a therapist where she needs to go in a way that is faster and more convenient.

2: A Dream Puts a Therapist in Touch with a Client's Temporary State of Mind

Nan had been in therapy a long time. She had already worked out difficult issues and was finding strength and self-assurance. As in life, therapy has its times of progress and plateaus. On the morning of Nan's regular appointment, I had this dream and it was easy to guess the state of mind she would be in that day. I dreamed:

> *A lighthearted, happy teacher is showing a girl how to garden and get "delights" from the garden. There are violet and pink colors in the background sky, which is creating a soft and pretty scene. It's spring, yet there's still some snow on the ground nearby. The girl is downhearted. She tries to follow instructions and wants to plant flowers and pull weeds correctly but can't get past her pessimistic, heavyhearted feelings. But it's all right that she can't. The teacher knows it's a temporary stage she has to go through.*

Sometimes emotions from past traumas ambush us. They take over and color our moods as surely as does a bout of flu. The person may not know why or how they caught the flu, they just know they feel miserable. This sometimes happens while in therapy. Some event triggers a negative memory and opens a floodgate of emotional leftovers that change the client's mood even though they don't know why.

Honoring the counseling dream's suggestion that it was okay for Nan to go through her depressed mood, I did not try to draw her out of it. Sometimes you must relive the pain of the past before you can let go. Sure enough, as a few weeks passed, it turned out to be an important and fruitful phase that led Nan to finally let go of some painful childhood memories. Thanks to this counseling dream, I put her state of mind into perspective, and, like an unfolding flower, let it take its own course toward healing.

3: A Dream Counsels Someone Regarding a Child's State of Mind

Sandra was a counselor who took dreams seriously—her own and those of her clients. She knew the value of interpreting her own dreams and began to watch for ones that referred to others. Sandra was close to her family and they knew they could always count on a sympathetic and intelligent ear from her. So it was no surprise when her cousin called, wanting to discuss a decision she had to make about her fourteen-year-old daughter.

The oldest child, Lily, was going through a period of feeling alienated. She had a younger, prettier sister who easily charmed others, whereas Lily, though nice-looking, was generally shy and awkward with people, a contrast that sometimes led Lily to feel a lack of confidence. Despite supportive efforts and advice from her mother and others to just be herself, Lily was having a rough time. The school year had ended, and because she was indecisive about whether or not to attend summer camp, her mother wisely did not force the issue. In the end Lily decided to attend camp, but now, after only a few days there, Lily was calling and asking to come home. Wanting to clear her thoughts with someone about the best course of action, Lily's mother called Sandra.

Sandra was close to her cousin's family and knew the difficult stage Lily was going through. Was it best to encourage her to stay at camp so that she'd become more independent or was it better to bring her home? While talking to her cousin, Sandra suddenly remembered a troubling dream she had had the night before. In the light of her cousin's phone call, the dream suddenly made sense:

> *I'm with the family and we are all on the way home from a picnic. There's a lighthouse and everyone has gone inside to explore it, but I feel left out and stay outside by the entrance. I decide not to wait for everyone*

*else and start to walk, but then I change my mind and try
to enjoy being with the group.*

*My playmates decide to explore the cliffs nearby. We
climb a bridge that's alongside a cliff. There are huge
boulders and water with a dam below and a railing
along the edge surrounding the dam. The others scram-
ble forward at a fast pace, but the slippery rocks scare
me. I don't find it fun and I don't feel part of the group
anymore. I lose sight of them because they are so quick,
and suddenly I feel stuck. I don't know whether to climb
up and follow them or go back down the hill. Then I notice the rail I'm holding on to is covered with ice and it's
hard to hold on to, and the ground is very slippery. I feel
very alone, cut off and frightened, and freeze in my
tracks, afraid of the strong currents in the deep water below, where I could fall. I'm terrified.*

The theme describes someone who starts out on what
seems to be a pleasant jaunt, then finds herself cut off and
stuck in a scary and dangerous spot. Talking to her cousin,
Sandra recognized that this was a counseling dream that put
her into Lily's shoes. Because the counseling dream had let
her feel the fear and desperation that Lily was going
through, Sandra knew the advice she would heartily en-
dorse: Let her come home and welcome her without giving
her any guilt trips about changing her mind or being a baby.
A sensitive child, Lily obviously needed to feel the protec-
tiveness of home longer than others. Sandra's cousin took
this advice and, as expected, in good time Lily outgrew her
fears and became a confident young woman.

As in this example, counseling dreams help provide insight for loved ones as well as for strangers. They often appear before you face a situation, as if the psyche, from a
vantage point of drawing on ESP levels, already knows the
problem will appear at your doorstep and prepares you with
the tools to deal with it.

Even if you are a counselor or therapist, learn to understand your own dreams before tackling those of clients or

patients. The two founding fathers of psychology, Freud and Jung, worked with their own dreams on a daily basis before looking at their patients' dreams. I don't believe it is possible to deal adequately with someone else's dreams unless you also regularly work with your own. Having personal experience is necessary for a deep knowledge and understanding of dreams. Knowing only the theory won't cut it.

IDENTIFYING FEATURES OF COUNSELING DREAMS

1. Summarizes a Problem or Situation

A counseling dream can summarize a specific situation or provide an overall perspective about the client that is useful in the therapy process. It can point out sources or causes of an issue and can accurately provide insights as steps toward healing. It is a powerful tool for therapy.

2. Empathy

Another major purpose of a counseling dream is to create an empathy between the therapist and counselor. A scientific study examined what determines whether or not a patient will improve during one-on-one therapy, and discovered that it is the level of empathy that the patient perceives from the therapist. Because a counseling dream provides not only intellectual insights about a problem, but allows the therapist to directly and actually "feel" the pain or struggle or emotions of the client, it can't help but increase empathy and rapport. This is a very important part of creating healing.

3. Provides Parallels

Watch for dream themes that parallel a client's basic problems, feelings, or style of communication. This is a way of finding a match-to-life effect that tells you it's a counseling dream. Once you discover that one of your dreams is a counseling dream, the category will be increasingly easier to recognize.

4. Speeds Up the Healing

Therapists who use dreams in counseling testify to the fact that dreams are a most helpful part of the healing process. The counseling dream does not eliminate the therapist's work, it merely speeds up the healing by providing some insights that could have taken a long time to uncover using the traditional tools of listening, careful questioning, and observation. The accurate insights of a counseling dream can save both client and therapist time, suffering, and wear and tear.

5. Is Brought By a Sincere Desire to Help

Counseling dreams are evoked by a therapist's sincere desire to help someone. It is as though your psyche says, "Because you really care, I'll give you all the help I can from the unconscious." If you are a therapist, it's a tool well worth exploring.

PART VI

◊

Infinite Harmonies: Divine Graces That Come Directly Through Dreams

CHAPTER 20

Healing Dreams: Dreams That Heal or Lead to Healing

> To you that fear my name shall the Son of
> righteousness arise with healing in his wings.
> —MALACHI

WHAT THEY DO

Is it possible to go to sleep sick and wake up partially or totally healed? Yes! The healing dream is different from other dreams. It does not come merely to give you information. Instead, the healing dream brings you out of a state of disease and into a state of harmony and ease. It thus creates a state of health and healing. When there is harmony between body, mind, and the spirit, wholeness and health occur. Dis-harmony and Dis-ease lead to ill health, and realignment restores health. Such a realignment is often easier to achieve when you are asleep because cares and worries have been set aside.

The healing dream is a rare dream type, but over the years authors like Janice Baylis, Elsie Sechrist, and Harmon Bro have consistently described them. A healing dream can heal a physical, mental, or emotional state. I asked for a healing dream only once, and to my astonishment I received one. There are no guarantees, but those who have had a healing dream know it's available for the asking.

EXAMPLES OF HEALING DREAMS

1: A Dream Heals a Past Trauma

Born with a debilitating disease, Diana's first child, a baby girl, did not live to see her first birthday. Not able to contain his pain, her husband reacted by blaming Diana rather than supporting her, which led to their divorce. These events, especially the loss of her child, left Diana with many conflicting emotions, including a desire to have another child, but her desire was tempered with fear. Determined to go on with her life, she picked up the pieces and established a successful business. A few years later Diana began to date someone who was loving and supportive.

Meanwhile, Diana was renewing her strength with the help of a counselor. She had progressed a great deal but had not yet dealt with the trauma of losing her child because the issue was still too painful for her. But life sometimes presents ironic twists of fate, and as things turned out, one day Diana's business required that she schedule a meeting in the very wing of the hospital in which she had lost her child. Just the thought of going there filled her with dread. But through the years, her counselor had encouraged her to use her dreams and trust her inner self to provide the response she would need. As the day approached, however, Diana felt extremely apprehensive. The night before the meeting, she dreamed:

> I've been working very late on a publication with an associate, and suddenly I'm very tired. Strangely, I tell her I have to leave now to go to the hospital to have my stomach cut open. I'm scared it might hurt, but not too scared. At the hospital I notice that the doctor who will carry out this surgery is my gynecologist, the same one who was involved when I lost my baby. This shakes me up, but I have confidence in him. Someone in the waiting room asks me why I am having my stomach cut open. I reply firmly: "I want the sun and moon to shine inside."

Then I am wheeled into the operating room, fully conscious. The operation is done very fast and I feel no pain.

Suddenly I'm back in the doctor's office, fully dressed. My mother is waiting there for me; she reassures me and drives me home. A sense of relief washes over me and I wake up feeling healthy and overjoyed. I think of my lost baby but no longer feel the terrible pain, knowing she is somewhere where the sun and moon always shine. I feel an exquisite sense of release.

Diana went to sleep the night before the meeting, still caught up in the agony of her baby's loss, but thanks to this healing dream, she woke up feeling at peace and fully resolved about it. That day she was able to attend the meeting without fear and face the hospital ward where it had all happened without any apprehension. How did this healing dream manage to transform her?

Diana had fallen asleep feeling quite anxious. In the dream, her psyche presents an opportunity, in the image of the operation, for dealing with her trauma. Diana must choose whether to have the operation and then does agree to it, admitting that she is afraid of being cut open—that is, afraid of touching the pain at the heart of her trauma. But she decides to trust her doctor, thus trusting in the healing process her soul wants to provide. At some unconscious level you understand the symbols of your dreams even as you are dreaming them. This attitude of acceptance prepared the stage for Diana's healing.

Next she must finally let go of all barriers and fears, as shown in the dream by someone asking her why she is going through with this operation. Confronted with her own fears one more time, she overcomes them by providing a positive reason for going ahead, stated in poetic terms as "I want the sun and moon to shine inside." The sun and moon suggest life's regular rhythms of day and night, light and shadow, joy and sorrow. With this statement Diana dissolves her last barrier and the healing happens in a flash.

Before she knows it, it's all over, and she has the consolation of her mother at her side to take her home, which symbolically reinstates her own ability to be a mother again.

On awakening, Diana felt "an exquisite sense of release." She was healed. She had let go of the past, finally and completely. Three years later she remarried and without fear had another child. Diana is now the delighted mother of a healthy red-haired boy.

2: A Healing Dream Creates a Playful Attitude of Joy Which Then Allows Physical Healing to Take Place

In over twenty years of working with dreams, I've had only one full-fledged healing dream, but it was unforgettable. I had heard of this dream type but had never experienced one. Until . . . At one point during a year I had several operations to repair facial bones injured in a childhood accident. Although the third was minor surgery for which I did not even stay overnight, it had been a busy year and a very active month, and my body was run down. Returning home from the hospital, my breathing was hampered by my bandaged face and I felt so tired that it felt as though I had one foot in the grave. I was too tired to even recuperate.

That night I was in great discomfort. I addressed God as the source of all healing, saying sincerely though nonchalantly: "Lord, if I ever needed a healing dream—this is the night!" Then I fell into a numb sleep. My own laughter woke me up around dawn. Emerging from a deep sleep, I remembered this dream:

> *I see a huge Mayan dragon. It is placed within a square with rounded corners and its body is curled up into perfect concentric circles. I am totally mesmerized by its eyes which hold the wisdom of the ages, but also all-encompassing love, so much love that I feel almost overwhelmed. My eyes move to its body. The lines of its body follow the path of a circle going out from the cen-*

*ter, forming more and more perfect circles. Yet the lines
of the circle are not lines. They are dots—perfect circular
dots like pale peach-colored pills more perfect in shape
and symmetry than anything I've ever seen. These tiny
circles line up to form lines of concentric circles which
lead into the center of the dragon, and, paradoxically,
out again.*

*My gaze is hypnotized by one of these paths. I follow
it and notice that the pills are moving forward one at a
time at the rate of a pulsebeat. The pulsebeat is silent yet
resounds like the rhythm of life itself. The pills move
clockwise until they get to the outermost point of the
dragon's tail. There, to my amazement, the tail has come
full circle back to the dragon's majestic head. And at
each pulsation a pill drops from its tail into the dragon's
mouth as though it's the most natural thing in the world
to do. I see this dragon can feed itself forever, for its supply of pills is unlimited.*

*I gaze wide-eyed. It's the most solemn, special, and yet
amusing thing I've ever seen. I feel like a schoolgirl who
knows she should take something very seriously but her
playfulness overcomes her, so she laughs instead. A feeling of mirth wells up in me beyond my control as I delight in this strange creature, and my joy fills me with
energy. As I wake up, I feel this energy flowing through
me, and I feel very happy.*

I awoke from this healing dream with a sense of wonderment, jotting it down at about five A.M., then going back to
sleep. I nicknamed my energizing friend the Mayan regen-
eration dragon. That day and for many days afterward, each
time I thought of my dream, it filled me with a joyous energy. I would relax and literally laugh out loud remembering its outrageous yet enormously peaceful images, and the
eyes that held the wisdom of the ages and all of the love
contained in the universe. I recovered quickly, resuming a
busy schedule almost immediately, and feeling bathed in
some eternal love.

That wasn't the end of my Mayan dragon story. Its images came back to amaze me even more a few months later. While reading a book about ancient symbols, I was surprised to discover that the image of a dragon swallowing its own tail was an ancient archetypal symbol used by medieval alchemists and other mystics. They called it the Oroburus and regarded it as the ultimate symbol of the "life force" itself. I did not know this at the time of my dream, yet my Mayan dragon was every inch a life-force energy. I had even described it in my dream diary as an image of the very pulse of life itself.

It continues to astonish me that though it was a mere dream symbol, this tail-swallowing dragon could produce a well of energy from which I could draw actual physical strength. I'm still energized by it as I recall its tremendous force, and yet its utter peace and gentleness. As my experience proved, the dragon swallowing its own tail is indeed more than a mere symbol. Somehow, it is related to the essence of life itself—some mystical connection we all have with the universe. Despite my ignorance, my soul was able to link me up to it to provide an unusual healing experience. If it can happen to me, it can happen to anyone. The healing dream is definitely one of life's mysterious and unexplored horizons.

3: A Healing Dream Revives Someone's Emotional Strength

Albert had been in a dream group and kept an eye on his dreams to help him through life. He was in a career that could be very demanding in both time and stress, but was managing to do it well. However, during an especially challenging time of juggling difficult people, deadlines, and the stress of important deals, he felt totally worn out. He wondered how he would face another week at work without a vacation or a change of pace. That night he dreamed:

I am totally exhausted and drained. It's time to go to work and I'm looking for certain pieces of clothing that I want to wear that will make me feel good. I know they are in my closet, but I can't find them, and I'm getting more and more frustrated and feel overwhelmed, as if this is the straw that breaks the camel's back. Suddenly I hear a voice behind me that says in a powerful tone, "Look deeper." Sure enough, I look deeper into the closet and find what I am looking for. I wake up feeling an enormous sense of peace. It gives me a feeling of renewed energy and a new outlook on life.

Albert went to sleep feeling exhausted and overwhelmed in many ways. Thanks to a healing dream, he awoke with a sense of peace, energy, and an attitude that he could handle anything. That is the power and the blessing of a healing dream.

4: A Dream Heals the Body's Stress, Which Then Heals Everything Else

Marilena is a determined young woman with a good head on her shoulders, a lovely way with people, and a winsome smile. It took her a long time to break into the field of public relations, but, determined to do so, she had persevered against all odds. One of her first jobs in the field enabled her to learn a great deal from a woman who was her immediate superior, and she loved her work. However, the man who ran the company was, in her own words, a sleaze and a bully—and that was supposedly a kind description of him.

Thus, after she had worked there for less than a year, when Marilena was told in confidence by her boss that she was leaving, she was devastated. However, because Marilena had apprenticed so well, she was also advised that she would be offered the managerial level position that would soon open up. That of course meant that she would need to work closely with Mr. Sleaze, which was not an option she cared to take. However, after further discussion with her mentor who was about to leave, Marilena saw that the position was a great opportunity to gain needed experience, and as a newcomer to the field, she would be unwise to refuse it.

Marilena had a month or so in which to make up her mind and took a vacation to think things over. During her time off, she decided to take the promotion, swallow her pride, and work for a man for whom she had no respect. On the last day of her vacation, Marilena felt torn apart, knowing she would return to a job she would now hate and was beside herself with rage and confusion. That night, Marilena dreamed:

> I am feeling totally exhausted in body, mind, and spirit and am filled with unhappiness and tension. Suddenly a handsome man with rippling muscles walks into my bedroom. He is perfectly charming but not making sexual advances. Instead, he proceeds to give me a full-body massage. Starting from my arms and hands and working down to my feet and legs and back up again to my back and neck, I can feel every touch of his hands, first drawing each muscle tight and taunt, then releasing it into a full relaxation. It feels blissful, like a total, actual massage. He finishes and gives my temples and head a gentle massage, and I feel completely healed and relaxed. As I continue to lie in bed, I experience feelings of complete love and total peace. He leaves as quickly and gently as he had arrived. I awake feeling supremely relaxed and am at peace with myself and with the whole world. I think I have actually had a massage, it felt so real.

Marilena went to sleep contemplating a job she was dreading and one that had tied her up in knots of anxiety that she had never before experienced. But she awoke with none of those feelings and reactions. The healing dream used the image of a physical experience of massage to relax her and bring her a sense of love and peace and, in its wake, symbolically created an emotional healing.

The following day, Marilena went to work floating on air

and enveloped in a sense of love, peace, and harmony, blissful feelings that continued for three days. On the third day, without planning it, her sense of peace had produced such a sense of empowerment that she decided to confront her new boss, the man whom she despised and dreaded. She spoke to him confidently, openly, and directly. Marilena honestly expressed her reservations about working for him and let him know that there were certain behaviors and attitudes that she would not tolerate, even though her former boss had done so. She admitted that she did not like him very much but, knowing that he was good at his job, told him she was willing to work with him and give good service, as long as he did not cross the line in his behavior toward her. To her amazement, rather than fire her, he accepted her boldness with respect, and they worked out an arrangement for working together. Thanks to her healing dream, Marilena put her cards on the table and was able to stay in her job while retaining her integrity and honesty. This experience convinced her of the power of dreams, and she continues to work with them.

IDENTIFYING FEATURES OF HEALING DREAMS

1. Instant Healing

A healing dream can create an experience that provides healing. Thanks to a healing dream, you can go to sleep needing an emotional, mental, or physical healing, and awaken healed. Though this occurs more frequently for emotional and mental types of healing, it does also occur for physical healing as well.

2. A Soul Experience

Although you remember it as a dream, a healing dream is actually a "soul experience" rather than a dream. Because of some need or request for healing, the soul mobilizes special energies from itself and from the universal light, to interact with your conscious and unconscious mind and body, in order to create a healing. This interaction becomes a healing, which you remember as a dream.

3. Types of Healing Dreams

A healing dream can create a physical healing or an emotional or mental healing. It can heal past traumas, although using dreams to heal traumas is best done under the supervision of a skilled therapist who knows dream processes. Healing dreams may create instant healing, and they often do. At times they create healing in stages, depending on the need and readiness of the dreamer.

4. You Need to Ask for One

Although it may occur spontaneously, healing dreams generally come after a person requests one. I believe the healing dream is one of your direct links to the Divine. It represents unusual and unexplained soul and energy resources available to all for the asking. So if you need one, go ahead and ask for one.

CHAPTER 21

Integration Dreams:
Integration of the Self
Achieved Through Dreams

I held it truth, with him who sings
To one clear harp in divers tones
That men may rise on stepping stones
Of their dead selves to higher things
—TENNYSON

WHAT THEY DO

If you've been with me so far, you may think I'm pulling your leg with this next revelation about an integration dream. Believe it or not, you can go to sleep as Jane Smith or John Harris and like a new, improved version of a detergent, you can wake up as Jane Smith Plus or John Harris Plus. If you experience an integration dream, you'll never be the same again because it leaves you feeling more whole, more alive, more confident, and stronger— permanently. It's as though you find a piece of yourself that was missing, whether you knew it or not, but now that you've found it, you feel a new sense of wholeness. All of that from a mere dream!

Common images in integration dreams are scenes of mountaintops, perfect circles which are metaphors for eternity, images that radiate light and beauty, and the wise old man, among others. Seven, which is thought to be a mystical number, also often appears in integration dreams.

An integration dream is one of the extra special spiritual experiences you can have while dreaming. It attunes you to the Infinite Harmony. Dreams are not the only way you trigger an integration in yourself, but it may be the simplest way. Integration dreams change you, but it's impossible to understand their effect until you experience it for yourself. You can describe music as black dots with lines on paper and you can say that it makes noise that is very pleasing; but until you actually hear Mozart or Bach, you don't know what music is. Listen for the music.

EXAMPLES OF INTEGRATION DREAMS

1: An Integration Dream Puts Someone in Touch with Her Spiritual Growth

In an unexpected dream, Madelaine saw:

> There's a jade figure of Buddha sitting on a beautiful shelf in front of me. The figure is large and full and fills me with wonder. Then I see six more Buddha statues, each in jade. Each is identical to the first, and each is smaller than the last, like a set of seven dolls in descending order of size. I'm filled with a sense of peace. The scene leaves me feeling strong and confident.

Madelaine had been struggling to grow spiritually for several years and monitored her dreams regularly. This integration dream made her feel as though she had received a special grace that put her in touch with her spiritual qualities. She was amazed to find that it left her permanently changed, as though some of the qualities she felt in the dream permanently seeped into her system. Her state of consciousness was permanently and positively altered by a new sense of peace and strength. And yet, she explained, these words don't do justice to the change she actually felt.

2: An Integration Dream Brings Upliftment, Energy, and Strength

Mark was a spiritual seeker trying to live a sincere life of service. One night he dreamed:

> *I'm flipping through my small phone book, looking for a number. Suddenly I find it, and it is so unusual that it instantly strikes me. It reads: 777-7777. As the numbers register in my brain I'm fulled with an incredible joy and feeling of lightness, as if I've been given the most special message of my entire life.*

As joy and a feeling of lightness filled him, Mark awoke changed. The dream's effects created an amazing feeling of energy and strength whose peak continued for days, and a feeling of upliftment that defied words. There was nothing logical to this dream; it just left him with a permanent boost of confidence that launched Mark into a new and happier dimension of himself. Each dreamer has his or her own mystical, uplifting symbols that find their way into integration dreams.

3: An Integration Dream Brings a Spiritual Strength That Alters Shyness into Confidence

In my younger days I was shy and timid. Over the years integration dreams have repeatedly created harmony, strength, and sureness in me. While learning to meditate and sincerely seeking to be a channel of blessings, one such dream banished the mousy me forever. I dreamed:

> *I see famous psychic Jeane Dixon, whom I greatly admire, pouring her heart out to her husband, telling him of her own shortcomings as if reading off a grocery list. Her husband listens fully, then takes her in his arms and holds her tenderly. They fuse and become as one, blending in love within a circle of light. Three small circles of*

light appear at the top of his forehead, in a line rising upward. As Jeane Dixon moves away from him, I see she also has the circles of light on her forehead. Her husband says to her gently but with great force: "Now you have all that you need."

This integration dream stemmed from the deepest part of my soul, bringing me the wisdom and sincerity that I admire in Jeane Dixon. It left me feeling more uplifted and at peace than I thought was possible. As the dream begins, someone is acknowledging her shortcomings, hinting that an attitude of humility and honesty may help create the attunement necessary to plug in to such dream realms of grace. Mulling over the dream, I began to recall the sequence of thoughts and feelings that may have brought this dream to me.

A short time before having this dream, I had realized that I had a lot to learn in order to become a committed, useful, and loving human being. For the first time in my life I took a good look at myself without fear and accepted my faults and shortcomings instead of denying them. It made me sad to admit that I was not as great as I used to pretend I was, but I resolved to work with my limitations rather than feel sorry for myself. Years later, many of the same faults are still with me and I've even accumulated some new ones; but some old ones have slowly dissolved. Does such honesty work like a magnet to attract growth experiences? It's possible.

IDENTIFYING FEATURES
OF INTEGRATION DREAMS

1. Common Images

Common images of an integration dream include the wise old man, circles of any kind, radiating light, high mountains, and, for some reason, the number se en, which is believed to be related to things mystical.

2. Unexpected

Although you can ask for an integration dream, it tends to come unexpectedly, like a surprise "well done" or a pat on the back from the Divine. It leaves you feeling wonderful.

3. Striving

An integration dream tends to appear during or just at the end of a period of genuine striving toward growth. But there is no guarantee you will get one, even if you are striving. If you look for a reward, it seems to elude you. But just by being sincere and doing what you genuinely believe in, an integration dream can appear. It is like catching a butterfly—you need to sit still and wait for it to come to you.

4. Emerge from the Soul

Integration dreams come from the soul level, attuning you to a grace and energy that surpasses explanation. It leaves you feeling transformed, more alive, confident, and stronger than ever before, and the effects are lasting. The greatest gift it gives you is a new sense of wholeness; you never knew you were missing some part of yourself until an integration dream comes along and fills in that unexpressed, empty space. It's like finding a new friend who makes you realize that you were lonely before and didn't even know it.

5. It Gives a Wholeness That Has to Be Experienced

Some dream types can be described, and whether you have one or not, you can understand what it's about. But you have to actually have an integration dream to fully understand the change in wholeness in yourself that it creates.

PART VII

◊

New Horizons: Exploring Spiritual Unknowns Through Dreams

CHAPTER 22

Dreams That Cross
Death's Threshold

Like pilgrims to the appointed place we tend;
The world's an inn, and death the journey's end.
                                    —DRYDEN

WHAT THEY DO

According to mystics from all cultures, dying is like walking through a door into another room—minus your body. Death's door is a revolving one because the next realm of life we enter isn't that far away or that different from life here on earth. Those who study parapsychology know this is the case from accounts of people who have come close to death, or from those who have actually died and then miraculously revived and lived to tell us what they saw.

From this point of view, loved ones who have died can sometimes choose to come back to visit now and again. Love does not die, so why shouldn't a grandfather want to return to see how his grandchildren are growing up, or a mother look in on the children she left behind? Most religious traditions describe a hereafter, so why should it sound strange that loved ones go to a place not too far away, where they continue to work, study, and play and even have time to visit their old neighborhood—right here? This version sounds more plausible to me than sitting on a cloud, playing a harp for eternity!

When loved ones do visit from the next realm, we remember the visit as a dream. Free of distractions as we sleep, we're more able to tune in to those who have passed on and more able to allow these soul-to-soul visits and communications to take place. Taking a deep breath, let's see what some have experienced with this dream category. But keep in mind that this is not a dream, but more likely an experience remembered as a dream, and the dream format is the device used by your unconscious mind to remember it.

EXAMPLES OF DREAMS FROM THOSE WHO HAVE CROSSED DEATH'S THRESHOLD

1: A Loved One Visits on a Special Anniversary, Which Is Remembered as a Dream

Mabel was very close to her husband, Don. In their many years of marriage, they had become true friends and lovers as well as mates, so she grieved deeply when he died, but knew it was best to get on with her life. But on the evening before her first Valentine's Day alone, she dreamed:

> *I see Don standing in front of me. He smiles at me with the smile I've always loved, glowing, simple, and sincere, and hands me a dozen red roses. I feel so cherished.*

Don had always given Mabel red roses on Valentine's Day, a tradition he had started early in their marriage. So roses were a special reminder of their love. Was this a dream or an actual visit by Don from outer spiritual realms, a visit just to say "I still love you"? In the eternal scheme of things, it seems entirely possible that Don did really come back to confirm his love on Valentine's Day, since it was an anniversary he had always kept. After all, no matter on which side of life's thin veil we live, who can forget thirty-two good years of marriage?

2: A Father Returns to Reassure His Son

When Kevin's mother was widowed, he stayed with her a few weeks to lend support. Shortly after the funeral he dreamed:

> *I see my father outside my bedroom. He quietly comes in and hands me a bouquet of flowers to give to Mother. They're white and yellow flowers with a few violet ones mixed in, just the kind he used to grow. He's pleased to be visiting and looks happy, and tells me he's glad Mother is being looked after. I wake up feeling he was actually there.*

Kevin isn't gullible. He just understands that there is more to life than meets the eye, so he accepted this as a natural visit from his father. Kevin felt reassured, which is a common reason loved ones visit. Months later Kevin wondered how his father was doing in his new home in the sky. He dreamed:

> *Dad comes into my room holding giant-sized cutlery—a table knife, a fork, and a spoon—all of which are as big as his hand. They remind me of a child who holds a spoon that's too large for him, but needs to begin to practice using it. Dad shows me how he's learning to use these items and I then know he likes it. He always did enjoy new gadgets while alive. I know he's well and happy.*

Responding to Kevin's love and curiosity, his father came back to try to describe his new activities. The giant knives and forks were merely symbols for new tools and talents that his father was striving to learn in the afterlife, serving to get the idea across to Kevin that his father was adjusting to his new life. This dream visit did the trick for Kevin, reassuring him that he no longer needed to worry about his father. He knew that if his father had tools to use and work with, he would be happy anywhere!

Sometimes if you lose a loved one, there can be a tendency to hold on to the memory too tightly. A period of grief is necessary and unavoidable, but if you refuse to get on with your own life, you can also hold back the loved one, who is still too much in your memory, from getting on with his or her new life. Life must go on, from both sides of the veil.

3: A Daughter Stays in Touch with Her Deceased Father Through Her Dreams

Early during one Christmas season, Martin, an active man in his forties, complained of headaches, dizziness, and feeling weak. Within a month he was dead of a brain tumor, leaving a shocked widow and seven children behind. Kira, his youngest child, had been closest to him, and in retrospect realized she had dreams that had hinted at his sudden demise. As a teacher and counselor who worked with dreams, her mother encouraged Kira to continue to watch her dreams. The family grieved, stunned by how quickly his illness and death had taken place, and they turned to one another for solace. Kira shared her father's musical talent; just before he had died, he had been so proud of her singing lessons. He obviously continued to be, as a month or so after his passing she dreamed:

> Dad walks into my bedroom. He tells me he loves me and wants me to continue my singing lessons. I promise to do so. I ask him whether he's seen Uncle Chris, who had died the year before, and he replies that he has. We talk for a while. Then I ask if he's seen God. He pauses for a second and says God is very real there, but it's not the way we think. I ask more questions. Before he leaves, he again implores me to continue with my singing. I wake up knowing he's well and comfortable in his new life.

Not yet brainwashed by the world's skepticism, Kira naturally accepted that her father had continued to live elsewhere, in some new realm. Her father visited her a few times more, which she remembered as dreams, reassuring her and the family of his love and interest in their lives. Her brothers and sisters welcomed these episodes, supporting her in the belief that these were actual visitations from their dad.

Events took a startling and hilarious turn. A few years later, having blossomed into a beautiful young woman, Kira became engaged to a handsome young financier and left home to live with him in a neighboring town. The family liked Burton, her husband-to-be, and approved of their plans to save their money for a year, then marry and purchase a home and settle down. He was stable and good-natured, so they knew he could be counted on to provide Kira with the roses-and-picket-fence life that she wanted. Burton was good-hearted and pragmatic, but completely skeptical about dream experiences and the hereafter. That is . . . until he dreamed:

> Kira's father walks into our bedroom and wants to have a serious talk with me. He tells me he loves Kira very much, and says to me sternly, "I want you to take good care of my little girl. Promise me that you'll take good care of her." Flabbergasted because it feels so real, I agree to do so. But I obviously don't sound very convincing because he motions to me, sits me down in a chair, and repeats: "Now, Burton, you must swear to me—swear—that you'll take good care of her!" Sensing how immensely important this is to him, I take a solemn oath to protect her and care for her. I wake up completely unnerved, totally convinced that I've just spoken to Kira's father.

Needless to say, Kira's father made Burton believe that the hereafter is very real. Burton loves Kira deeply and knowing that her dad still keeps a watchful eye, he now takes his responsibility twice as seriously.

4: A Near-Death Experience Is Remembered as a Dream

Sylvie didn't die and return from the dead, but she came pretty close. While playing on the sidewalk with friends as a child of about age three, something she said made another child, Clive, cry. When Clive stopped crying, he grabbed a large rock nearby, stormed up behind Sylvie, and gave her skull an almost fatal blow. Sylvie has no memory of being struck; her next memory is of watching herself in the hospital in the operating room. Doctors verify that she was near death and in a coma, yet Sylvie remembers:

> I watch myself being wheeled down a hallway in a hospital as if I'm up on the ceiling, looking down. My head is bandaged and I'm taken to a room with trays of shiny instruments. The doctors work over me.
>
> Later a doctor walks out into the hallway and approaches my mother. He tells her it looks pretty bad and thinks that I may not pull through. Mother begins to sob uncontrollably and I feel her deep pain. She grieves so badly at the thought of losing me that I can't stand it. I rush to comfort her and want to put my arms around her. The next thing I remember is that I feel heavy and surrounded by blackness, as if I'm lying in my bed with my eyes closed. I feel groggy.

The soul continually makes choices. By sympathizing with her mother's pain, though at the brink of death's door, Sylvie's soul made the choice as a child to return to its body. She turned back and revived. This is not quite a visit from the dead, but a scene of someone who took a step toward it, and was in the in-between state between life and death. It shows that the choice to live is still possible, even at death's threshold. It is remembered as if it is a dream because the memory has only the dream context as a device to retain the experience.

IDENTIFYING FEATURES OF DREAMS THAT CROSS DEATH'S THRESHOLD

1. They Have a Literal Quality

You experience a visit from a loved one who has died as a very real experience, even though you remember it as a dream. The visitors look like themselves, and they talk and behave as they did in life. That is because it likely is a real experience, but dreams are the only mechanism of awareness and memory that you have during sleep.

2. A Simple Exchange

An actual visit from a loved one is not an easy connection to achieve, from either side of the veil. Therefore, when it actually happens, the exchange tends to be a simple one. There may be few words spoken or a brief conversation, but just as often the loved one will merely look at you in a reassuring way. It's difficult to bridge these two dimensions, especially when many people here are unaware that it can be bridged.

3. Just to Let You Know

Most often, the purpose of a visit from a loved one who has died is to reassure you that they are all right and that they still care. If life is eternal, then so is love, and they want you to know that. Though it's a strange thought to some people, life does continue at some other level, not too far away and not too different from here.

CHAPTER 23

Dream Visits to Other Realms

Praised be the fathomless universe
—WALT WHITMAN

WHAT THEY DO

Did you ever wake up feeling more tired than when you went to sleep? Or did you ever wake up feeling disoriented? If so, you may have been journeying to other realms in eternity while asleep and didn't even know it. At night the soul can literally lift out of the body and explore other environs. In the last chapter we noted how departed loved ones come back for a visit. In this chapter we examine how our own souls can leave the body at night, a phenomenon called astral travel. As we journey far and near at night, mystics tell us the soul's contact with the body is maintained by a silver cord, ready to spring back at a split second's notice.

You may unconsciously, at some soul level, choose to visit loved ones next door or in a neighboring city. You can visit those who are sick or in need, in order to console them a while with your presence. Or you can visit another part of the world—saving considerably on plane fare. And on very rare occasions souls have been known to visit other planes of life, realms where departed loved ones, angels, and who knows what else, reside. You need to distinguish such episodes from regular dreams, because such night visits are actual experiences but are remembered as dreams because dreams are your only mechanism of awareness and memory during sleep.

Speaking of dreams and night journeys, mystics have intriguing things to say about how dreams relate to your life, the afterlife, and to your growth in eternity. Dreams take the thoughts, actions, and energies you generate during the day and play them back to you so that you can view, confront, and assess whatever you are daily creating in life. Mystics tell us this is the closest preparation we have for the next level of life—the fourth dimension which we call death. If that doesn't boggle your mind—nothing will.

EXAMPLES OF OTHER-REALM DREAMS

1: Journey to a City of Light in the Sky

As a child, I loved to go to sleep, so it was never difficult to send me to bed. As an adult, I now understand why I was eager to go to sleep. This is what would happen as I would drift off to sleep:

> When I went to sleep as a young child, I would feel a rush of energy, as though I were on my way somewhere. I could feel myself flying through the air and always knew my destination—a city of light in the sky. I would fly there and see it as I approached from a distance. Some buildings looked round and flat, others were tall, but all were beautiful and brightly lit. I loved the lights. There were parks and trees all around too. I don't remember what I did once I arrived, but I longed to go there every night. It felt wonderful to be there.

Was I actually visiting a city of light in the sky every night? Considering it was a clear and regular recollection, I think it's entirely likely, especially because regular dreams have a less distinct and far-removed quality about them. In cases like this, your own impressions are the best direct clues as to what's going on. By the same token, many recent writers of their experiences of dying and returning from death include descriptions of such a city of light in the afterlife. Those who have died and revived describe cities of light in the sky, as well as other mysterious vistas. And though it does not happen often, some little ones retain a strong connection to such in-between realms, and as toddlers they have vivid experiences related to them, as I did.

2: An Astral Night Journey to Another Continent

Terry loves to mine her dreams for golden insights and often calls a fellow dream enthusiast to share her experiences. As a dream veteran, she accepts a lot as commonplace that would astonish others, but the following experience amazed even her. For three nights in a row Terry went to sleep feeling as though she were concentrating intensely on something. Then she would wake up more tired than she had been when she went to sleep. The first two nights she dreamed of confusing, vague scenes of long roads and shadowy pastures, but had no clear dream recollections. But on the third night Terry dreamed:

> *I see myself whizzing through the air. I don't know where I am, but know I'm in a foreign land. I'm high up and looking down as though I'm trying to get my bearings from one hundred feet above the ground, and feel I've been following a map or a guide to get somewhere. Suddenly I notice the bank of a river and recognize it as the Ganges in India. I know I've arrived at where I wanted to go. Next thing I know, I'm with my Indian friend Kiran and her husband. She has been away, and it's so good to see her. We embrace briefly and say something profound to each other. It was important to talk to her and I feel good about it.*

Terry woke up feeling as though she had really spoken to Kiran. As she emerged from sleep's grogginess into a wakeful awareness, she toyed with the possibility that it was an actual visit. After all, Kiran and her husband had indeed left a few weeks earlier for a month's stay in India to visit relatives, and Terry did miss her a lot. In fact, she thought about her friends often and wished she could touch base with Kiran. As a response to this wish, it looked as though her tiring nights were attempts to do so.

Undaunted by two unsuccessful attempts, on the third night Terry made it. Impossible, you say? Even if she reached the shores of the Ganges, how would she find her friend among millions? Perhaps no one knows how, but dream experiences do hint that our mind and soul are capable of much more than we imagine. This easily includes the ability to find each other as individual souls, night or day, as though soul fingerprints can be matched and traced by some giant computer in the sky to which we all have access. If a computer can do it, so can the multifaceted, and as yet unexplored realms of mind and soul.

3: A Dreamer Notices That She Is Astral Traveling

Whether you remember them or not, short astral travel jaunts at night are common, such as the one Dawn remembered:

> I've been somewhere and am on my way back. I see myself traveling, flying swiftly through the air. Suddenly I realize I'm dreaming. I notice I'm about six blocks from home, having a great time flying over Grand Street and noticing the city is deserted at night. I realize it's time to get home and become concerned that my body's been left alone too long. I awake up with a start, as though I've landed with a thud back into my body.

Dawn remembers this as a clear experience of traveling while asleep. Along the way she notices that she's dreaming and that she has to return to her body. This is a typical illustration of how astral travel is distinguished from a dream by the dreamer herself, while dreaming. Dreamers typically gain some awareness of being in the air, then look down and see details that match what they would see when awake.

4: An Accidental Visit to a Frightening Realm

I had heard many tales of cities of light beyond death, as well as other places not quite so bright or positive in nature. Keep in mind that theory has it that someone who has just died still has the same habits, desires, and thoughts as when he or she was alive. Thus, simply dying does not turn anyone into a saint; it just leaves you as you, minus a body. So just as when they were alive, some souls continue to be caught up in perversions and obsessions such as alcohol, drugs, and illicit sexual desires. Like a magnet's pull, such tortured souls gather into a separate place until they can release themselves from depravities. There they writhe in the pain of their own unfulfilled desires, staying in this heavenly drying-out station until they choose to let go of harmful desires (though it is said that they are watched over by caring angels the whole time). So in addition to cities of light, there are stations of distortion, pain, and misery akin to those described in Dante's Inferno somewhere just beyond our vision.

There are accounts now and again of people who accidentally wander into some such heavenly realm. I pondered how close I came to such a place of mystery after this astral travel dream remnant:

I realize I'm dreaming and that I'm hurtling through the air, but I feel nonchalant and adventurous about it. I know I'm very far away from home. I approach a "dark area," as though viewing a very menacing sky, and just barely glimpse a black figure as though in a monk's robe, whose face is a deep shadow. Before I know it, I've zoomed close to it without intending to, as if accidentally

*turning a corner and suddenly seeing someone where
you didn't expect to find him. In a flash, like a strong
bolt of lightning, I hear a sharp voice behind me, a voice
I recognize as that of a friend and a teacher ordering me
to "get away from there—fast!" I instantly wake up startled and genuinely frightened, knowing I came close to
something unsavory and dangerous, and never wanting
to go back. I jerk into an awake state, and I shudder.*

I felt as though I had accidentally reached out a hand
toward an electric fence, yet was saved from touching it in
the nick of time. This kind of an experience is extremely
rare during the dream and sleep period. Nevertheless,
knowing myself to be adventurous both by night and by
day, I pray each night to be protected in the Creator's love.
That night I was especially glad I had done so! I was also
grateful for my unseen guardian, possibly a teacher or an
angel from some other plane who regularly travels with me,
even on rare and exotic explorations.

Such night travels to other realms or places are a part of
life's yet uncharted territory. If you even remember them,
you tend to remember them as dreams because dreams are
the only vehicle of memory that you have during the night.

IDENTIFYING FEATURES OF
DREAM VISITS TO OTHER REALMS

1. Scenes of Flying

Though some dreams about flying are metaphors for feeling
free or progressing in an area of your life, there are flying
dreams that reflect actual flights your soul takes at night.
This is called astral traveling, and is reported by many. You
can tell you are astral traveling because there tend to be
some literal, recognizable details such as a street or place
that you actually know.

2. Recollections of Distant Places

Some astral travels are to other cities, or even other countries. If you wake up with a feeling of tiredness and recall scenes of distant places, you may have been visiting some far shore.

3. Body Gives a Jolt as Your Wake Up

If your body gives you a jolt when you wake up, your soul may be returning and landing with a thud into your body after some night travels.

CHAPTER 24

ESP Dreams

The Past, Present, Future, all are One
Forged by the link of God's own hand,
The Mother/Father God who binds all souls
To one another's spirit.

—JOEY CRINITA

WHAT THEY DO

ESP (extra-sensory perception) dreams tell you about your future. Mystics say we pre-dream everything of importance that happens to us. An ESP dream can act as a warning, a reassurance, or it can simply be a preview of what is around the corner. It is as though a part of you can see from a higher view, like someone standing on a mountaintop who can see the traffic below, and thus can report how it is shaping up. The ESP dream comes to encourage and help you, not to scare you. It does not give you extraordinary powers. Instead, ESP dreams are experiences natural to everyone, but most people don't pay attention long enough to notice them. Keeping an accurate dream journal is an important part of noticing and confirming such glimpses. Accurate parallels between dreams and real-life experiences are too numerous to ignore or to chalk up to mere chance.

All types of dreams often contain hints of ESP, like a dash of spice that adds flavor to many dishes. Maybe one reason this is possible is that our psyche, through some soul dynamic, can plug in to the collective unconscious described by psychologist and dream expert Carl Jung. Mystics tell us that the subconscious mind experiences everything as if it were in the present. Thus the unconscious simply advises us, through dreams, of conditions building up, like describing a ball rolling down a hill and where it might land as if it is happening now. ESP dreams show us that the psyche is capable of a wide range of psychic dynamics.

EXAMPLES OF ESP DREAMS

1: An ESP Dream Allows Someone to Experience Her Sister's Wedding

My mother was an immigrant who came to America just after World War II. She often described how she and my father ran across Europe during the war to escape the Nazis, finally finding their way to a refugee camp and safety. Because all telephone and mail service was cut off in war-torn countries for several years, she was not in touch with her large family of five brothers and sisters. One night she awoke startled by a dream which was "so real" that it left her crying:

> *I see myself by the door outside my childhood home. People are going in, dressed up for a special occasion. My favorite younger sister comes to the door and invites me to come in for her wedding. I am so happy for her, and desperately want to go to the wedding. But for some reason I can't cross the door's threshold. This makes me very sad, and I wake up crying.*

When my mother woke up, for some reason she marked the date and time of her dream on a piece of paper. Though she was sad, the dream was also strangely comforting. Several years later, when mail service was restored and she received a letter from her sister, she was amazed to find the ESP dream had come to her exactly on the day of her sister's wedding! It now made her happy to know that in some strange way, she had been a part of her dear sister's wedding, even if only in spirit.

2: A Single Woman Dreams of Her Future Husband and Wedding

Maria is one in a million. She is striking to look at, intelligent, hardworking, and fun to be with, and she loves teaching her grade-school youngsters. Maria is always at the center of the action. Everyone loved her practical yet dynamic and caring ways and thought she would someday make someone a wonderful wife. Maria thought so too, and secretly longed to share her life with a good man. Yet despite her vibrant lifestyle and personality, few know that she suffers from multiple sclerosis, an illness which, like thorns around a beautiful rose, had deterred many a suitor. By her early thirties and after several disappointing romances, Maria resigned herself to a life alone. Yet one autumn in September she dreamed:

From the back of a church I watch myself walking down the aisle in a beautiful white dress. It's my wedding day. There's a man beside me with reddish-blond hair and a bald spot; I don't recognize who he is.

This dream made no sense to her, so she shrugged it off as wishful thinking. Then in November she had another dream which she thought reflected her very busy and hectic life:

I'm moving. Men are taking my furniture from the tenth floor of my high-rise apartment building and bringing things up to a new sixteenth-floor apartment. I watch that they don't scratch anything as it goes in and out of the elevators.

In December Maria, tired from her illness, heaved a hearty sigh of relief when the three-week Christmas break finally arrived. Besides cozy holiday gatherings, she took the opportunity to refresh herself by watching an occasional comedy movie on her VCR and from time to time sleeping late. One morning she woke up with this delicious dream:

> *I'm decorating a beautiful wedding cake, spreading thick white creamy icing carefully into lovely swirls all over it. Then I use silver decorations, and afterward an array of colorful dried fruits, taking great pains to arrange them in unusual, striking patterns. I'm having such fun, and it turns out to be the most beautiful cake I've ever seen.*

Maria was involved in several new projects for her school. Having learned some basics about dreams from a friend who worked regularly with them, she guessed that this dream mirrored the great joy and pain she was getting from her young pupils. Wrong! It turned out to be a full ESP dream. Just after New Year's, Maria was in her building's penthouse laundry room and began to chat with a fellow tenant. They made each other laugh so hard, each imitating some laundry commercials, that they decided to continue the conversation over tea in a nearby restaurant. Three hours later her new friend, Peter, invited her to dinner.

Besides an easy rapport, they had much in common. Showing what a small world it was, it turned out that Maria had known Peter's mother, now deceased, whom he had adored. And when she mentioned her illness, unlike other men she had known, Peter did not bat an eyelash. He had dated a girl with multiple sclerosis and knew it was possible for someone with this illness to lead a relatively normal life. Maria was impressed by his understanding, and when she noticed his receding hairline, it reminded her of her dream about the man with the bald spot.

They began to spend a lot of time together. The first morning they had breakfast together in her apartment was a memorably romantic* one. By February Peter confessed that he had been drawn to her for two years but had been too shy to approach her. Her family adored his solid ways and loving, gentle personality. On Valentine's Day he proposed. By June they were living together, and wouldn't you know it, they needed a larger apartment to share, so Maria moved from her tenth floor apartment to one on the sixteenth floor, just as she had dreamed.

A year later Maria walked down the aisle in a beautiful white dress with Peter at her side. It was a perfect wedding, and to this day, their marriage stands as one of the happiest around. The wedding cake in her ESP dream was a great symbol for the meticulous planning she had put into creating her wedding day to make it an unforgettable and beautiful experience.

Mystics tell us that you pre-dream every major event, good or bad, that will cross your path. ESP dreams are simply a road map, and sometimes it's useful to see what's coming down the road.

3: An ESP Dream Warns a Woman of Impending Bad News

Dolores holds an executive position in a large hospital of a major city, where her determination to see that things are carried out properly has won her the respect of many. Her friendly personality, sincerity, and warmth also make her popular with everyone, and greatly loved as a friend and an associate. While away on vacation late one summer, she took the opportunity to totally escape from the world and relax, and did not bother to read newspapers, listen to the radio, or watch any television. But one night she had a strange dream that left her feeling unsettled for a long time:

> I am in a work environment. It seems familiar but at the same time it feels unfamiliar and is not where I currently work. A close friend is also in the dream. I watch her send me large brown envelopes containing obscene

scenes; it is information she has been clipping and is sending to me through the internal mail system at work and asking me to pass this information on to other members of the department. Sending such material is not typical of her behavior, and it leaves me perplexed and upset because it is so out of character for her to deal with obscenities. I wake up with a sense that something terrible has happened or is about to happen. I feel heavyhearted and uneasy throughout the day.

Two days later Dolores arrived home from her vacation. Checking her telephone answering machine, she noticed a message from the friend who had been in the dream, urgently asking her to call as soon as she returned. Immediately returning the call, the friend told Dolores about a recent tragic slaying of a professor with whom she had once worked, someone whom Dolores had greatly admired and cherished as a friend. Astonished, Dolores recounted her strange dream to her girlfriend, and was further shocked to hear that her friend had been clipping every news story about the slaying for Dolores to read, and had actually placed them into a large brown envelope and mailed them to her through the internal hospital mail system, just as Dolores had seen in her dream. The friend knew that Dolores would want to know all the tragic details.

Dolores realized that she had had an ESP dream preparing her for the terrible news she would receive via her friend. The dream's details were accurate, showing a familiar environment where she had worked with the professor some years back, and yet it was not where she worked now. The obscenities related to the fact that her former associate was murdered, hinting that he had died in an obscene manner at the hands of a raging madman. Dolores was saddened by it all, and yet realized that her psyche, as a kindness from the soul, had tried to prepare her for the shock during her vacation, softening the blow of the news via an ESP dream.

4: A Dream Tells a Teacher Her School Will Have a New Principal

Meryl took a one-year leave of absence as a high school teacher to complete her master's degree in another city. A year later, with the degree she had earned tucked under her arm, she was preparing to return to her hometown. Before she had left to get her higher degree, the principal of the school where Meryl taught had been very supportive of her studies and had acted as a fine supervisor and a special friend. She looked forward to again taking up her position as a schoolteacher under his supervision. But just before returning home, Meryl was jolted by this dream:

> *I see myself entering my old school with enthusiasm, so glad to be back. I go to speak to my principal, eager to say hello to him and catch up on the news. But rather than responding in his usual warm manner, I'm taken aback because he's very solemn and says, "I'm leaving and there's no job here for you anymore. You'll have to teach at Mount Vernon instead."*

Meryl woke up very troubled. Metaphorically the dream would have suggested she felt rejected by someone, but that didn't fit the actual circumstances or emotions in her life at the time. So a friend who studied dreams suggested this could be an ESP dream. Not having spoken to her principal in months, Meryl had taken it for granted that her old job would be waiting for her as they had planned. It seemed unbelievable to her that her principal would have left and that her job would be gone.

Meryl arrived home to discover that the dream had described exactly what awaited her. To her distress, her former principal had left the school and her position as a high school teacher was no longer available. As her dream had implied, Meryl found a new position in Mount Vernon, in a larger and more modern school, but one that lacked the grace and charm of her previous environment. Initially this change shook her up. But since her ESP dream had prepared her somewhat for the shock, her chagrin did not last, and within a few years she had become a department head at her new school.

5: A Sports Fanatic Dreams the Outcome of the Final Game of the Stanley Cup Hockey Playoffs

A handsome French-Canadian, Bernard lives in Montreal, home of the Montreal Canadien's hockey team. In the spring, when the playoffs begin and Stanley Cup fever takes over, Bernard and all the other red-blooded Montreal males go to the Forum Stadium to watch the game live in the arena, or they stay glued to the television set, especially if "Les Canadiens" are in the finals.

A successful entrepreneur, Bernard's business often requires him to work long hours. Late one night, exhausted but nevertheless watching one of the hockey season's critical games, much to his dismay Bernard fell asleep toward the end of the game. Just before he fell asleep, the score was tied, and when he awoke, the game had ended. He wanted to kick himself for missing the ending of such an important game of the series. But too tired to dwell on his misfortune, he let his body find the familiar grooves of his bed and fell into a deep sleep.

Waking up early the next morning, Bernard asked himself the score of the previous night's game, and told himself what it was and who had scored the winning goal. But something perplexed him. Then he remembered that he had fallen asleep before the end of the game. It dawned on him that he had just had a dream about the game before waking:

> *I'm watching the end of the hockey game. The game is tied two to two and goes into overtime. I'm glued to the set, straining to catch every fast whiz of the players on*

the ice. Suddenly the Canadien's Russ Courtnall swings his stick and deftly scores the winning goal, ending the game. The fans cheer wildly and it's the most exciting game I've seen in a long time.

Realizing it was only a dream, Bernard went out to the porch to pick up the morning paper and check the actual scores. To his amazement, his dream accurately depicted the final score and who had scored it.

IDENTIFYING FEATURES OF ESP DREAMS

1. They Foretell the Future

An ESP dream contains information about the future that is helpful to you in some way. It can be a preview of something good, bad, or neutral. Or it can be an assurance that something you are struggling with will work out. Or it can be a warning that helps you prepare for something and deal with it better than you otherwise would have.

2. ESP Dreams Can Be Completely Literal, or Can Be Partly Masked by Symbols

Some ESP dreams show a completely literal scene of what is to come, from beginning to end. Such one hundred percent literal ESP dreams are rare. More commonly, an ESP dream contains a mixture of literal and symbolic elements in the dream. In fact, dreams of all types often contain ESP features. If you pay attention to your dreams on a regular basis, this becomes obvious.

3. A Full ESP Dream Has Distinctive Features

There are partial ESP dreams, and ones that are one hundred percent ESP in content. The full-fledged, one hundred percent ESP dream tends to be somewhat rare. So if one does come to you, pay attention. Your unconscious has worked very hard to present details exactly, vividly, and intensely because something important will take place. It brings it to your attention with more emphasis because it will benefit you to be aware of what's about to take place. The one hundred percent dreams can be recognized by the following features:

VIVIDNESS. Full ESP dreams are more vivid than ordinary dreams. Colors are more intense, and you feel fully there rather than there just present as an observer.

INTENSITY. One hundred percent ESP dreams have an emotional intensity that leaves an impact on you. Some dreams can leave you feeling lukewarm. A full ESP dream makes such an impact that your feelings can be affected for the whole day by it, and sometimes longer. The emotional impact is a way of getting your attention.

PRESENCE OF EXACT DETAILS. In a full ESP dream, details are exact. People play themselves, scenes are real places, and objects are as they appear in reality. For example, a car will be the exact model and color of someone's actual car.

REACTIONS ARE CONSISTENT. The emotions you feel during the dream and upon waking are consistent with what is actually going on in the dream. If there is a wonderful event predicted, it feels wonderful during the dream and you wake up feeling wonderful. If it is a warning dream, you will feel afraid or disturbed in the dream and will feel the same way when you wake up.

4. Something About the Future Is Related to the Present

An ESP dream doesn't just appear out of the blue. Instead, your future is somehow related to the present. That is, the decisions you are making today and the actions you are carrying out now are building your future. So unless it is a catastrophe of some sort, the topic of the ESP dream should be familiar to you, because it is something you have been building over time, as, for example, a career goal. There are two ways you can consciously trigger or ask for a dream about your own future:

A QUESTION. A question that is on your mind may trigger an ESP dream. You may be wondering about a job, how a project will turn out, or how a loved one is doing. Pay attention to the questions on your mind as you are falling asleep, because these are often answered by ESP dreams. If you sincerely want to know something about your future, and you are ready for the truth, your dream psyche is very capable of taking a peek for you. In fact, if you want to, you can simply ask it as a direct question, and you will get a reply in dream form.

AN EMOTION THAT IS A QUESTION. Sometimes you are not actually asking a question. Instead, you are enveloped in a feeling or an emotion that "translates" into a question. For example, you might feel blue about your job because it doesn't fulfill you anymore. Your psyche will translate that feeling into a question such as: "What can I do to make my job or career more interesting?" or "Is there anything else for me career-wise, in my future?" Or, if you are a single person and feeling unhappy about it, your dream psyche may translate this into the question: "Will I ever meet Mr. Right?" You may well get an ESP dream, in reply, describing him.

CHAPTER 25

Dreams of Past Lives

Lead me from the unreal to the real.
Lead me from darkness to light.
Lead me from death to immortality.
— *THE UPANISHADS*

WHAT THEY DO

Two-thirds of the world's population, mainly in India and the Orient, believe in reincarnation. Recent surveys show that we in North America are rapidly catching up, with one-third to one-half of those in North America beginning to accept that we may walk this earth more than once.

Those who accept reincarnation look at it as a philosophy requiring you to reexamine your life and behavior with a new sense of responsibility, because you have yourself created whatever now happens to you in life. From this point of view, it suggests that you constantly re-meet yourself and the product of your actions, both positive and negative.

From the point of view of reincarnation, the crucial point of living is to understand how you create your own life, and how the present affects the future, in the hope that such an understanding enables a person to take control of their life. Only then can you begin to grow positively and happily in harmony with your destiny as a soul on an eternal journey. Let's call these causes and effects "rules of the game of life." For example, one rule that everyone has heard but few live by is: Do unto others as you would have them do unto you. When you believe in reincarnation, this isn't just a trite cliché, it's the first ground rule for survival!

The unconscious is said to be the storehouse of all your memories, including those of past lives. Perhaps the ninety percent of the brain that is rarely put to use holds memories not only of what's happening now, but of what happened in the past—the past of past lifetimes. And because dreams draw images from your unconscious, it would not be surprising if every now and then a dream accidentally touched a vivid memory from a past life and replayed it for you, just like the discovery of old photographs in an attic and glancing at them with nostalgia revives pungent memories.

Reincarnation dreams tend to appear spontaneously when something in the present jogs a memory. Full-fledged past-life dreams showing you in the costumes of the time are rare, but they do occur. Watch for reincarnation dreams during periods of change. When you are taking up new interests or activities, or changing jobs or your career, or when new people are coming into your life, past-life dreams are more likely to surface to explain how shades of past cycles are related to the new, emerging ones. We live in cycles, with past cycles overlapping onto present ones.

Sometimes the past peeks into the present with mere snatches, which become past-life glimpses interspersed in other dream types. Watch for background scenes such as the Old West, sailing on the high seas, and medieval castles; and watch for people unfamiliar to you such as ancient soldiers, medieval doctors or monks from past settings. These are often wisps from past lives weaving into dreams related to the present. I often see Chinese families in my dreams and they evoke tranquility and a sense of loyalty and closeness to loved ones. It wouldn't surprise me if I had lived a past life in China. Like children absorbing and imitating our parents' ways, our past-life heritage superimposes itself onto the present, though generally in totally unconscious ways. Talk about investigating your roots!

EXAMPLES OF PAST-LIFE DREAMS

1: A Past-Life Dream Helps Someone Understand a Present Relationship

Dawn was a sophomore in college taking a new psychology class at the beginning of the year. Too shy to speak to the strangers around her, she waited alone in the hall for her classroom to become free. Dawn noticed a fellow student waiting by the window whose kind and gentle yet strong and confident face drew her to him. She rarely went up to a stranger, but something drew her to him, so she approached him and said hello. He immediately responded in a warm and friendly manner. In the course of the year Dawn and Brian became good friends, enjoying camaraderie in classes, at concerts, and during long walks.

Brian's way of saying good night always struck Dawn as slightly odd. After normal good-byes and a good-night peck, Brian would lean forward as though making a slight bow, and then would back away ever so slightly as he left. This was not typical of youth in the modern generation. Amused, Dawn began to mull it over, wondering at his idiosyncracy. After an evening out on another occasion, she was again particularly struck by it so that it was still on her mind as she went to sleep. That night Dawn dreamed:

> I'm in the courtyard at the back of my childhood home. It's evening, around sunset. I'm standing at the bottom of an outdoor staircase, wearing a long gown in the style of the fifteenth or sixteenth century, elegant, but not too fancy. Suddenly I see Brian at the top of the staircase dressed in the clothing of a baron or a duke. He comes down the stairs, walking in a relaxed and dignified manner toward me. This is where we often meet to walk and chat, and as he approaches he gives me a sweeping bow. We feel natural and comfortable with each other, like brother and sister or very old friends.

Dawn's dream had all the characteristics of a full-fledged past-life dream. An opening scene often depicts "going back in time" to make the dreamer aware that they are touching something from the past. Dawn's dream begins by going back to her old neighborhood, while another dreamer saw himself flipping through his record albums until he came to Tchaikovsky's "1812 Overture." His dream then abruptly switched into the costumes and time period of the Old West, set around the 1800s. Look for such opening-scene cues taking you back in time.

In addition, in a full-fledged past-life dream the characters wear the costumes of the period, accurate in historical detail. You generally recognize at least one person with whom you are presently associated and the dream sheds light as to why this present relationship or situation is challenging or interesting to you. Or it explains some habit, talent, or inclination. A past-life dream may even provide insights regarding the history of a difficult problem with which you are struggling. Because dreams deal with whatever is on your mind, if an old refrain from the past catches your fancy, a past-life dream can pop up.

As a remnant of a past habit, Brian's odd good-night bow had plucked a string in Dawn's memory and unearthed a past-life dream that shed light on its origins. They had been good friends in some medieval setting, and at that time such bows by men were commonplace. Something different or odd often sparks a revealing past-life dream. Though life has taken them on separate pathways, Dawn and Brian are still the best of friends, exchanging support and understanding through adult years, and no doubt through many more lifetimes to come.

2: A Past-Life Dream Helps a Mother Understand Her Child

Pamela adored her two young sons and loved playing imaginative games with them. She encouraged them to act out exotic stories, contributing fancy costumes and assorted paraphernalia to childish productions in which all the neighborhood kids took part.

Danny, her five-year-old, had a unique game. While other children liked to play cowboys and Indians, Danny liked to play at just being an Indian. His mother would often join him in these pretend games, building a tent with an old blanket and sitting around a make-believe campfire telling intimate tales.

Danny was sensitive yet full of daring. He approached life with vigor, but had one persistent fear—a fear of the dark. He was an independent child, yet could not bear to have his mother out of his sight even for a moment. Pamela wondered at these contradictions in her son's behavior. How could he be so brave and outgoing in some ways and yet so fearful in others? The answer came in a dream in which she saw:

Danny is a young child, about the same age he is now. He and I are running through a field having fun and playing hide-and-seek. I see sunshine and blue skies and we're happy. Suddenly we hear shouting in the distance and see smoke and fire where our home is, at the edge of the field. I take Danny and run into a cave in a nearby hillside. Hearing voices, we run through the cave feeling very afraid. We run for a long, long time; it seems like we run forever, driven by terror. I look at my son and see that he is now an Indian boy and that I am his mother. We are caught. We become separated and I get killed. My son grieves terribly and is very frightened.

From this dream, Pamela understood Danny's love of playing at being an Indian as well as his fear of being separated from her. A believer in reincarnation, she took steps through storytelling to reassure Danny that both of them were now safe. Unusual behavior and interests such as Danny's can often be threads of past-life experiences.

3: A Past-Life Dream Explains an Unusual Talent That Was Acquired with Ease

Penelope was brought up in a traditional middle-class family, yet was always a touch sassy and a bit of a rebel. Her cheerful, open manner and intense enthusiasm endeared her to many, and her family adored her. But there was always something exotic and different about Penelope. Her high cheekbones, olive skin, daring eyes, and mass of curly black hair suggested a strong woman from the Andes instead of a lady from the suburbs of a large city.

When Penelope followed up her interest in dreams, metaphysics, and herbal medicine, her family took it in stride, knowing that her hobbies never hurt anyone and only made her happier and more interesting. Penelope became quite good at using herbs and natural products and even developed and distributed her own line of natural oils and creams. She sincerely wanted to help people heal their own bodies. This became a passion for her, one that persisted along with her interest in dreams. Why did Penelope become an expert on herbs and natural products for the body? In a striking dream that touched deep chords of recognition, Penelope saw:

> I'm on the banks of a river among reeds and rushes, picking herbs. I'm dressed in the clothing of some ancient civilization which could be Mayan or something similar. My hair is black and my cheekbones are high, with olive skin. I'm the local healing woman, gathering what I need.

This dream left a powerful impact, releasing streams of energies in Penelope from the wisdom of her forgotten past. Less dramatic dreams showed her as a North American Indian woman, mixing potions and lotions, and always cast in a healing role. Fact or fantasy? If you met Penelope and observed how naturally she takes to this subject, you might feel as I did, that these dreams mirror a profession that she has fulfilled in many past lifetimes.

4: A Past-Life Dream Explains a Businessman's Strange Experience During a Vacation

Jonathan is a very successful businessman with a strong spiritual side. He loves sports and adventurous pursuits and so it was no surprise that he decided to take up flying. Just before starting his lessons, it occurred to him that he sometimes dreamed of falling weightlessly into nothingness, much the same feeling as falling in a plane spinning out of control. He wondered if this was perhaps a warning and asked his psyche for a dream that would clarify the situation. The answer left him stunned:

I'm sitting around a table with a group of men. It's some sort of reunion. A young man sits next to me and shows me a yellowed newspaper clipping about the Glassman Railroad Company. He then tells me that he knows me—he took my picture once, and my name is Richard. I don't remember this, so he leads me to another room and shows me a photo of a group of men, obviously taken in the early 1800s. At the sight of myself—a big, strong man who is wearing glasses—I burst into tears.

Suddenly the scene shifts to that era. I see myself as the man in the photo. I'm a real outdoorsman, often gliding on snowshoes through the woods or on a mountain. I am part of a surveyors' team from the Glassman Railroad Company that is building a railroad between two mountains. I know that my coworkers are the same men at the reunion whom I saw earlier. We're working, crossing a footbridge that traverses a huge ravine. Unexpectedly, a train passes below us. Its rumbling vibration snaps the cables of the footbridge and we fall thousands of feet to our deaths into a huge empty space.

Jonathan awoke, certain that this was a glimpse of a former life, and he suddenly understood a recent event. He had been on a fishing trip with some friends in a remote section of the state. Bad weather had grounded the helicopter that was to bring them to the airport, and they were forced to walk along a stretch of railroad tracks. As they turned around a bend into a panoramic view, Jonathan had a déjà-vu experience that filled him with profound sadness. His emotional reactions had struck him as odd because the trip had been a very positive one. Now, walking along the railroad tracks, unexplained flashes of death—his own— had haunted him.

This past-life dream also explained his love of the outdoors and need for physical challenges, and a tendency to plan work projects on a grand scale and to want to see things from a full perspective, as a surveyor would. The dream and its aftermath left him in awe and with a much deeper understanding of himself.

Past-life dreams may point out your strengths and weaknesses from a past life that can now either help or challenge you. When I do public work related to mystical areas, Egyptian themes often appear, bringing qualities of insight and wisdom and hints of competition in relationships. When family matters come to the fore, I see Oriental themes which help me feel patient and thankful for the security of loving family ties. And when creative projects need my attention, I become a student of art in my dreams, letting myself just go with the flow as an artist does. Past-life overtones? Why not?

IDENTIFYING FEATURES OF PAST-LIFE DREAMS

1. Triggered by Something in the Present

Past-life dreams arise spontaneously, but they are triggered by something in the present that captures your attention in a new, deeper way. Like the string of a harp that begins to resonate, a present experience triggers a memory from the past, and your unconscious naturally reaches for it. The long-ago memory surfaces as a past-life dream.

2. The Opening Scene Shifts Your Attention to the Past

In a full-fledged past-life dream, there is usually an opening scene that shifts your attention, telling you that it's a clue to the past. You might see a date on a calendar of a hundred years ago, an old piece of music, or an old neighborhood that you grew up in. Then the scene will likely shift to the actual past lifetime, showing more or less accurate clothes and details of the time. Generally, at least one person in that scene from the past is someone you recognize from the present.

3. An Intense Impact

Past-life dreams have a very intense impact. You are not merely watching the dream; you are actually there and feel directly involved. And when you awaken, the impact continues, as though something very deep in you has been stirred.

4. Purposeful

Past-life dreams don't appear merely to entertain you. They respond to some sort of deep emotional feeling or unexpressed question that was triggered in you, and it explains a relationship, a question, or a situation in your present. It tends to have a healing and comforting effect because something falls into place for you.

5. Wisps or Snatches

Not all past-life dreams are full-fledged ones. Some appear
as snatches within regular dreams. For example, a motif of
a certain country may regularly appear in your dreams, like
China or the Mediterranean or the Old West. That's likely
a clue that you experienced a lifetime in that region or era.
Or you may see snatches of certain professions or events
such as medical motifs or cowboy scenes, or of being an
entertainer or an artist. You may not be one now, but if
such roles and scenes turn up regularly in your dreams, you
might have done something along those lines in a past life.
This may now carry over as an interest or a hobby.

6. They Appear During Periods of Change

Whenever your life goes through a significant change such
as a new job, a new location, or a new relationship, watch
for past-life dreams. One lifetime is said to reflect several
past lives at different stages of your life. So as your life
goes through dramatic times of change such as a wedding,
having a child, or getting a new job, glimpses into the past
are more easily triggered and well worth watching for. For
example, someone remarked at how many wedding gifts he
and his wife had received that had a Chinese theme, even
though they had not expressed such an interest to anyone.
He and his wife suspected that collectively, they and their
friends may well have known each other in a past lifetime
in the Orient.

CHAPTER 26

World-Event Dreams

In the one, there is the all,
In the all, there is the one.
—SENG TS'AN

WHAT THEY DO

World-event dreams are a variation of ESP dreams, but instead of telling you about a personal item that will cross your path, they tell you about a world situation, one to which you are not personally connected. Dreams of this kind have long been recorded in history and folklore. Joseph, the biblical character who owned a coat of many colors, intrepreted Pharaoh's dream of seven stalks of wheat eaten up ravenously by birds. Joseph correctly interpreted that the dream foretold seven years of plenty followed by seven years of famine, a forecast that won him a role as the Pharaoh's adviser. In more recent times, author and historian J. W. Dunne dreamed of Mt. Pelée's eruption on the island of Martinique in 1902, which killed 40,000.

Extraordinary as it sounds, ordinary people dream about world events. You are more tuned in to the world and to others than you may realize. You may dream correctly who will win an election, about the marriages and deaths of famous people, and about changes and disasters in the community and in the world. Even if you don't work with your dreams regularly, it is likely that you have such dreams but don't recognize or remember them.

World-event dreams are on the cutting edge of our ability to understand ourselves as human beings and as souls on an eternal journey. If any dream category reflects Gandhi's words that all men are brothers, world-event dreams do. World-event dreams take this great man's words one step further. Not only are all men brothers, but through our dreams we're capable of tuning in to all men and to the world, a thought that has enormous implications. This dream dynamic may tap into what Carl Jung called the collective unconscious; Jung thought that everyone has access to a collective unconscious, and that through dreams we interact with it. Examining world-event dreams gives you a sense of the wide and deep scope of this connection among all human beings. The following glimpses of world-event dreams explain why such dreams appear.

EXAMPLES OF WORLD-EVENT DREAMS

1: A School Child Dreams of a Disaster That Shocks the World and in Which She Dies

Tragedy struck a small town in Wales when a coal mine caved in, causing tons of coal to slide down a mountainside into a village. Hitting a school on the hillside, the victims, mostly children, were buried in this sudden landslide. A psychiatrist from England, Dr. J. C. Barker, arrived on the scene to help, and found that a large number of people claimed to have had warnings of this disaster in advance.* He collected their reports, including twenty-five dreams that had clear parallels to the actual event. One of the most notable dreams came from a young girl. For several days she had been trying to tell her mother about her strange dreams, but rushing to get her daughter off to school, her mother

* There are many accounts of this coal-mining tragedy and the work of Dr. Barker, one of which is described in the *Sun Dance Community Journal*, Vol. 2 (2).

brushed off her attempts and did not listen. Finally, one morning her mother listened to her dream, which was:

> *I'm on my way to school with my cousins Peter and June. We go to school, but there's no school there. Something black covers it all over.*

After relating the dream, the child told her mother, "I'm not afraid to die, Mommy. I'll be with Peter and June." All three children were among the 118 crushed beneath the black heap of coal. Because of these premonitions regarding this disaster, Dr. Barker began to collect "premonitions of world events." Over a two-year period, one hundred correctly foreshadowed events were reported, and no doubt a lot more are experienced than are ever shared or reported.

2: Members of a Dream Group All Dream of the Same Upcoming World Tragedy

I was in a dream group for a few years. When you share one another's dreams, you get to know people quite well and it becomes easy to recognize themes that fit each other. Yet for a few weeks all of us began to have dreams with drastic themes that we couldn't place. My dream was:

> *There's a murderer running rampant on* The Price Is Right *television show, but we don't know who he is. I'm getting involved in the game more and more deeply, wondering how and where the murderer will reveal himself.*
> *The host is a handsome, charming fellow. But then I see the host standing on the stage with a machine gun, which seems very odd. I'm sitting in the audience as he tells us to recite the "Our Father." He's a man I've trusted and respected, but what he's doing just doesn't make sense. I can't believe he's the bad guy, the murderer we are looking for, but I sense real danger. Up to now it all seemed harmless and fun, but now I realize something*

*is drastically wrong. I decide to stay calm and escape by
the door at the right.*

*The scene changes. Now I'm talking on the phone with
someone who lives thousands of miles away. I've always
made people welcome, but suddenly a friend is in my
home and has brought along a hundred others. We're all
getting ready to go to sleep, and it's chaotic. There's
hardly anyplace to sleep or even enough room to share
a blanket and pillow in a tiny corner, so everyone topples
over everyone else into a heap. There's loud talking in
the background, so loud and incessant that it's difficult to
sleep. I want to tell them to shut up.*

This dream's themes of feeling crowded, being coerced,
and being forced to say the "Our Father" at gunpoint made
no sense in terms of my own life. So, like many dreams I
can't immediately decipher, I put the dream aside for a
while. The other members of the group also had dreams
with strange themes that didn't have meaning in a personal
way. Henry dreamed:

*I see people drinking purple punch. Then there are re-
porters counting dead bodies. The scene is grotesque,
with twisted bodies all over, very vivid and painful.*

Kate saw shooting and mangled bodies; others saw scenes
of chaos and crowds. Never in our dream group's two-year
history did we have such collective themes of violence and
destruction. We found it distressing, yet could not reach any
satisfying conclusions about their meaning. That is, until a
news bulletin shocked the world a few weeks later. When
the media began to broadcast details of the Jonestown massacre, a shiver ran down our spines because of the horror of
the event, and also because of the inescapable parallel of
the tragedy to the themes and content of our recent dreams.
Without knowing it, we had all had world-event dreams
about the same event, the Jonestown massacre.

The Jonestown massacre was led by Jim Jones, a self-appointed religious fanatic who was as handsome and charismatic as any game show host. He created a cult in the United States, then led its hundreds of followers to a farm compound in Guyana, where loudspeakers blared brainwashing sermons all day long. His devotees, who had turned over all their worldly goods to Jones, worked in the fields. One afternoon he gathered the group outside the main building, pointed a rifle at the crowd (just as in my dream) and made them recite the "Our Father." Then, under threat of being shot by armed gunmen, members were forced to drink a grape drink (just as in Henry's dream) that contained cyanide. All but two people complied, and after drinking the poison, people fell into a dead sleep, bodies heaped upon each other (just as in my dream). Two men escaped and reported what happened (paralleled in my dream by my escaping), so the scene of terrible destruction was soon discovered. The world shuddered as the horrible event was broadcast by journalists all over the world.

This was my first experience with a world-event dream that came in such a dramatic way, where the whole group pre-dreamed it weeks in advance. How could a group of ordinary people, mostly newcomers to the use of their dreams, dream of an event thousands of miles away and weeks before it happened? Investigations later determined that the misguided demigod was likely contemplating the massacre for weeks. Mystics say that "thoughts are things, as real as bricks," which, it seems, enter some universal computer or collective unconscious to which we all have access. It appears that we were picking up on the destructive thought energies being created in advance by Jim Jones.

Why did we, as a group, have these dreams? It is likely that these world-event dreams came merely to cushion the shock for us, because every person in the group was a sensitive and spiritual-minded person. It does not surprise me anymore that we picked up on the event; instead, I wonder how many others, at that time, also had such disturbing world-event dreams about this tragedy. Such dreams do put you in touch, very clearly, with the fact that we are all connected in some mystical way.

3: A World-Event Dream Foretells the Assassination of a World Leader

I awoke from the following dream knowing clearly that it was about a world event. Foreboding filled me as I realized sabotage connected to something military was under way that would make headlines around the world. I've always followed politics and world events, and for the next few weeks I carefully watched the news to see if something similar to my dream would surface. I had dreamed:

> *I'm at a military camp or base where maneuvers or games and demonstrations of weapons are taking place. The most advanced weaponry is set up in an area of cubicles. Suddenly the enemy appears in the midst of the camp. It's shocking, but obviously the enemy has managed to get right into the heart of the action, sabotaging the event. It's too late to stop him. The enemy is aiming sophisticated weapons, about to destroy everyone. The key figure, who is the top commander, realizes with a shock what is happening. In reaction, he raises his hand dramatically and sincerely, saying, "No, no—don't do it!" Someone nearby takes a hose of water and aims it at the enemy's laser gun, but it is too weak a defense against his powerful weapons. It is too late. In seconds, people are killed, and all is blown up and destroyed. Later, newsmen are assessing the scene and saying, "Yes, all five were destroyed."*

It didn't take long for this event to show up in the news. Within a few weeks, the assassination of Egyptian President Anwar Sadat was announced to a shocked world. It was their national day in Egypt, celebrated by a parade. Sadat was seated in a box seat, like those in a grandstand, reminiscent of the cubicles of my dream. He was dressed in full military regalia as he officiated at Egypt's annual parade. As many will remember from the news accounts, two or three soldiers who were part of a group of rebels who wished to overthrow Sadat's regime, had infiltrated one of the regiments. As they passed directly in front of the reviewing stand in an open truck, posing as participants in the parade, they ambushed the president. They pulled out machine guns, killing and wounding a number of people, including Sadat. It all happened within seconds. Soldiers supportive of the president tried to prevent the carnage, but it was too late.

The similarities to my dream are unmistakable. I understood why I had this dream; it was due to the fact that Sadat was a political leader I admired. I had closely followed politics in the Middle East, and was impressed that his career began when he had a spiritual experience, a vision, which stimulated him to enter politics. I also admired Sadat for being a champion of women's rights in Egypt, a country that needed a lot of catching up in the area of women's rights. This sympathy and interest was reason enough for me to have this dream.

But one detail puzzled me. The vivid image of the general standing up and saying, "No, don't do it!" haunted me, for it had sounded so real and heart-wrenching in the dream, a dreadful and instant realization of impending death. I continued to collect news accounts of the assassination, and about three weeks later found an article that made my mouth drop wide open. It was an interview with Sadat's lovely, scholarly wife, Jehan, as she described her husband's final moments. Sitting beside him as the assassination occurred, Jehan saw her husband's face freeze in disbelief as he realized what was happening. Incredulous, Sadat stood up and raised his arm, saying, "No, don't do it . . ." just as I had seen in the dream. But even as he spoke, the bullets came. It was too late.

I still wonder how my dream was able to pick up that detail. Such a correspondence implies that world-event dreams place us in moments of "shared space," with two or more minds so attuned that they perceive as one. It suggests that we have a great deal to learn about mind and awareness. It hints of breathtaking vistas of telepathy, of consciousness and shared awareness that may one day be a topic of study for psychologists of the future.

IDENTIFYING FEATURES OF WORLD-EVENT DREAMS

1. Ordinary People

You don't have to have been working with your dreams for a long time in order to have a world-event dream. Ordinary people dream of world events. However, unless you monitor your dreams regularly, you won't notice them.

2. A Related Interest

There are always world events occurring. Why do you dream of a particular one? Generally, there is some connection between you and that event. A sports fanatic will dream of an event related to a sports celebrity or a sports event. If a particular world leader or country especially intrigues you, you are more likely to dream of a world event related to that leader or that country. In effect, you tune in to events that interest you, so that a world-event dream has at least an indirect connection to you.

3. Not to Shock or to Amuse

A world-event dream does come with a purpose, but that purpose is not to shock or amuse you. Instead, something in that event resonates with you in some way so that you will be particularly affected by it. Therefore, because you are affected by it, my hunch is that a world-event dream merely appears, first, in answer to your interest, and second, to ease the shock of it on you. Some people think that having a world-event dream indicates that they are special or especially psychic or intuitive. Instead, I think that such dreams are common and happen to many people. Some think that having such a dream makes them responsible for doing something to prevent the event. But in my experience the event is already in progress and whether it occurs or not is not connected to you, and is therefore not yours to change. Besides which, it is not likely that you could change it even if you tried, because there are lawful, universal processes going on that you may not know anything about. To my mind, having such a dream simply points out that we are truly all connected at some psychic or unconscious level, and that what affects others also affects us. It reminds us of that connection, which is a main feature of a world-event dream.

4. An Observer or As One of Those Involved

One of the amazing features of a world-event dream is that you actually experience it as though you are there, either on the sidelines as an observer or as one of the people actually present, as though you are in his or her shoes. That is why, if it is a future event of a tragedy, I believe one way you can help is to surround the event with prayer and light. This may not stop the event, but it may help someone.

5. It Includes Corroborating Details

A world-event dream tends to include corroborating details between the dream and the event; watch for them. We have much to learn about how dreams connect us. Your observations may help all of us understand how this unseen world of thought and psychic interactions actually take place. Such corroborating details may teach us about the mind's and soul's potentials.

CHAPTER 27

Lucid Dreams

Those who seek the transcendental Reality,
Unmanifested, without name or form,
Beyond the reach of feeling and thought,
With their senses subdued and mind serene,
... will verily come unto me.
— *THE BHAGAVAD GITA*

WHAT THEY DO

When you are asleep and dreaming and suddenly become aware that you are dreaming, you are having a lucid dream. Thus, in one sense a lucid dream is not about the content of the dream, but, rather, it is about your awareness level—the fact that you are aware that you are dreaming. On the other hand, the content portion of a lucid dream is important too, because at some unexplainable level your actions in the dream can lead to transformation. A transformation takes place because of a shift in consciousness that occurs due to your interaction in the dream.

Because the lucid dream is all about being conscious as you dream, it may be a good time to discuss the three ways in which "consciousness" affects your dreams. Your state of consciousness determines: (1) *Whether* or not you will dream at all (contact or no contact with the psyche) and (2) *What* you dream about (content). If you are anxious about a problem, the problem floods your awareness and becomes what you will dream about. And (3) *How* you experience a dream. For example, if you are in great conflict about some issue in your life, when you dream about it, its representation becomes masked with scary symbols. Your own fear or conflict interacts with the dream content so that you see the dream through tinted glass, in this case, through fear-tinted glass.

From these three ways that awareness interacts with the dream process, you can see that a lucid dream is all about the third way, the "how" of experiencing a dream. In the lucid dream the how is "with more awareness than usual." You experience most dreams in a passive way, as if watching a movie screen. But in the lucid dream you become an active participant. Why? What's the point of being conscious in a dream?

The importance of a lucid dream lies in what it enables you to do. A lucid dream is the unusual state of being able to observe yourself, that is, of self observing self, or, rather, the conscious part of you observing the unconscious part of you, or vice versa. You sometimes do that in your waking life. For example, a handsome man asks a pretty clerk in a department store the price of a pair of gloves and she tells him they cost "sex dollars" instead of "six dollars." Her slip of the tongue was unconscious, but it made her attraction to him conscious. A lucid dream is like that, except that you are asleep when it happens.

There are advantages to such interactions between the conscious and the unconscious mind, especially during sleep. For one thing, because you are more relaxed, you are reacting differently. Thus, if you become aware of a problem in a lucid dream state, you may make more progress in resolving the problem because you are relaxed and not as inclined to resist working with it. Or you may become aware of something very positive during a lucid dream, such as an awareness of the beauty of your own soul, and of the soul's inclination to reach out into the very universe itself to touch the Divine.

The Tibetans were the masters of the lucid dream. They believed it was a state of transition for the soul, a reality that links this life with eternity. They called lucid dreams the "dreamless sleep." In that sense, the Tibetans didn't consider the lucid dream as a dream; instead, they considered it an experience that prepares the soul for eternity. What Tibetans looked for in a lucid dream was the appearance of some bright light. They thought that if the dreamer interacted with this light without awakening, instant transformation would occur, because the light is an emissary of Divine grace or awareness. This can be a transformation of healing, whereby some spiritual grace makes you feel whole in an area of your life that has been troubling you. Or it may unleash your creativity so that you awaken with a sense of knowing how to proceed with something you have had trouble with. Or an experience of the light in a lucid dream may put you in touch with who "you" really are. This may sound simple, but remember, mystics believe the whole purpose of life is about discovering "who you really are" as in the expression "Know thyself." And it is only when you discover a new dimension of yourself by accident that you realize it feels great and that you didn't even know you had a part missing.

There are wonderful books written about lucid dreams as a completely separate topic in the dream field. If you want to know more about this most fascinating glimpse of eternity which the Tibetans call "The Dawning of the Clear Light," you can read all about it in depth elsewhere. Meanwhile, here are some examples. Keep in mind that like steps leading to an altar high on a mountaintop, there are stages of lucid dreaming that range from:

1. *Pre-lucid*
   Becoming aware that you are having a lucid dream but nothing major happens.
2. *Lucid Integration of Part of Self*
   In a lucid dream you may confront some part of yourself which represents a problem or a barrier to overcome. If you confront it and deal with it successfully, the dream creates an instant resolution of the problem, and lasting

growth in yourself. Or you may not be ready to deal with the problem, so that the dream is a practice session for noticing the problem exists. You will likely deal with it at a later time in some way.

3. *Partial Experience of the Light*
Encountering a light, approaching it but not yet interacting with it.

4. *The Dawning of the Clear Light*
A fully lucid dream in which you may encounter something frightening that you overcome and that leads to the appearance of light. Still remaining lucid, you interact with the light and it leaves you changed forever. There may be religious symbols or spiritual beings involved. These vary according to the beliefs of each individual.

EXAMPLES OF LUCID DREAMS

1: A Pre-lucid Dream

Michael was in a dream group. Having heard about lucid dreams, he wanted to experience one. To prime the pump, during the day he tried to note certain cues about his body, such as a ringing in his ears or a tingling in part of his hand. This is a technique lucid dreamers use—namely, to practice noting something about the body during the day, while awake, hoping it will help them notice the same perception in a dream. That perception in the dream then becomes the tip-off that they are in a lucid dream state. After about three weeks, his desire and sincere efforts paid off as Michael dreamed:

After waking up about five A.M., I fall back to sleep very rapidly, feeling as if I'm in a free fall. My body feels as if it is turning around and around, and I hear a buzzing sound. Then a picture begins to appear, piece by piece, like a jigsaw puzzle that is coming together. At first the picture is in fragments, then it is fully visible but still, and then the entire picture goes into motion, like a movie. At this point I realize I am dreaming. After watching the moving picture for a while, I say to myself, "Hey, as long as I know I am dreaming, I want to fly," and immediately I begin to do so. I soar through the trees and feel wonderful, telling myself out loud how good it feels and how beautiful the scenery is. There is immense pleasure during the experience. As I'm flying, I wonder if my wife, who is asleep beside me, can hear me talking. Somewhere along the way I become very absorbed and am no longer aware that I am dreaming and likely stop dreaming, as I continue to sleep.

This pre-lucid dream acted like a practice session, allowing Michael to experience what it is like to enter a lucid dream by choice. Though nothing dramatic happened in the dream, the experience of being lucid in itself brought him much joy and exhilaration. Because he reached for it, Michael went on to have other lucid dreams, at many levels.

2: A Lucid Dream Presents Something in Oneself to Change, But No Change Takes Place

Sharon is a very special woman. She is a dynamic aerobics teacher, a loyal friend, and a true spiritual seeker who wants to express her full talents in life, which are plentiful. At one point in her life Sharon had this lucid dream several times:

I'm sleeping, and become aware of a sensation of fear and the feeling that I am going to be harmed by a few people, three or four of them. I am aware of my surroundings, and see these people standing over me as I am sleeping, talking and watching me sleep. It makes me very uncomfortable. Then I realize I am sleeping and that this is just a dream and that I'll wake up and it will all go away. But it doesn't go away. The people remain and walk around the room. I feel they could hurt me, but I can't speak, even when I try to. I open my mouth to try to talk to them, but they laugh at me, and I am physically immobile. I tell myself to wake up, but I don't. I do not trust these people, or know them, and I hate being in that situation. It feels awkward, nightmarish, and disturbing.

This kind of lucid dream presents the dreamer with some information about herself. If you are aware that dreams present you with choices, you can fix a problem right there and then by reacting to troubling or annoying images with understanding and love. However, Sharon did not know that the dream represented an opportunity for growth. The images here of feeling trapped by others and not trusting others suggested that Sharon was trying to grow in the direction of letting go of fears, letting go of a need to control a situation, and trusting others more. You make choices while asleep just as you make choices while awake. If, in this dream, Sharon had decided to be friendly toward these people, or ask them in a nice way what they were doing in her room, the whole dream would likely have changed for the better. For example, the strangers might have turned into long-lost friends, or they might have told her they were there because they needed her and that she is the only person who can help them. However, because Sharon never gets past her fear and mistrust and awkward feelings, nothing changes. As a result, there is no integration. This is a lucid dream which is an opportunity the soul gives you to confront some part of yourself, look at it in a new and positive way, and thus let go of some fear or anger or anxiety. By doing so, it releases energy and a transformation occurs. We often lose such opportunities for instant, painless growth during a lucid dream simply because we do not understand it, as was the case for Sharon. Sharon learned from her experience and she went on to other dreams which did create transformation.

3: A Partial Experience of the Light

Wally is a health care professional who genuinely cares about people. His aim is to serve others with excellence, and he does. On a personal level Wally is someone who truly wants to live on a spiritual level and to understand life from a wide perspective. At a time of such inner seeking, he dreamed:

> *I am in a regular dream. Then, in the dream, I step on the edge of a building and dive off. As I descend, I think to myself, "This is quite a way to start to fly." This bit of self-reflection brings the world lucid into my mind, and I realize that I am dreaming and flying at the same time. I am thrilled, and think, "Wow, this is wonderful! I feel so alive." In the dream I turn over onto my back, and still flying but as if lying down, I look up to the sky, looking for the light. I see a light at the end of a curved path. The path is gold and silver, edged with jewels and diamonds, sparkling and looking so beautiful in the light. The pathway is warm and inviting. As I fly along it, it gives me the feeling of returning to a beloved home. But then, suddenly, it falls away beneath me and I lose sight of the path and of the light. Frantically, I look for both, trying so hard to see the path and the light that my eyes open, and I awaken.*

Notice that Wally does realize he is in a lucid dream, and does "look for the light," which is what the Tibetans suggest you do in a lucid dream. He manages to see it and to begin to interact with the light, which comes in the disguise of a shimmering pathway lined with gems. But therein lies the trick—to enjoy the journey and the interaction without becoming so carried away by it that you lose the experience. This time the full experience of interaction slipped from Wally. But thanks to practice from dreams like this one, he did achieve it fully in later lucid dreams.

Because it seems like a difficult thing to accomplish, you

may ask why anyone would want to reach for the light in a lucid dream and interact with it. The answer is like trying to describe the experience of eating Rocky Road ice cream to someone who has never eaten ice cream, or to describe how incredible hearing your favorite piece of music feels. It can't really be described; it's just one of those things you have to experience for yourself. But, once you do, you'll keep coming back for more . . . and more. . . . Such is the experience of the light in a lucid dream; it may be one of life's natural and ultimate highs, the high of a genuine spiritual awareness that brings an indescribable new sense of love into your waking life.

4: A Full Experience of the Light

Tara is a very intelligent and pretty young woman, and has a terrific way with people. However, as part of the normal growing pains people go through, she sometimes seesaws between being outgoing and feeling like a loner. But she looks at life as a spiritual journey, so she faces life with love. When she had this lucid dream that presented her with a choice toward growth, Tara took it. Of course, the fact that she was in a dream group and understood that dreams can present choices helped her do so.

I am in the old bedroom of my childhood home, look-ing out through the windows that are unusually large. Outside, I see that the trees are especially vivid and an incredibly beautiful shade of green. They look exciting and yet foreboding, swaying to and fro in the strong winds. It is evening, just at dusk, and the air is charged with electricity, just as before a storm. I watch the sky as the clouds form animated, colossal faces, like mytholog-ical Greek gods. Suddenly I realize I am dreaming. The cloud gods continue to blow large gusts of wind as I am summoned to approach a whirling, bright silvery light. I remind myself that this is a dream and want to use this opportunity for spiritual and psychological healing.

In a flash I see the silhouette of a wolf atop the hill across the street on the horizon. It turns, sees me, and immediately runs toward me in a direct line. The wolf stops in front of the window below my bedroom. I look down, fascinated at the opportunity to view this creature, and exhilarated at the connection we have as we stare eye to eye. At the same time, I am relieved that there is a window between us because I am afraid that this fierce wild animal could harm me. But as soon as this thought crosses my mind, the wolf leaps up and comes through the window without breaking it. The wolf sits in front of me, waiting, and just staring.

Now I am absolutely terrified, but I realize the wolf is a dream symbol representing a part of myself. Like a wolf, I can also seem unapproachable and give off a strong, cold exterior of one who needs no one. I am no longer afraid of this wolf, knowing we are both loners, and I lovingly put my arms around it. As I do so, the fearsome wolf turns into a perfect combination of a black Labrador and a poodle, so cuddly and loving that I rub my face in its fur and embrace it tightly. Nearby, its mate comes along, surrounded by cute, playful puppies, and I embrace the whole family all at once. Love flows through me as I realize we can all live together openly and without fear. I resolve to live openly from then on.

This lucid dream explains it all. Because she was aware that she was dreaming, Tara recognized that the wolf was really a part of herself, the loner part that could be distant with people. As she embraced that part of herself, it transformed into something positive, releasing a sense of love and openness that in the past had been barricaded within her. Now Tara could take this new sense of openness into her waking life, realizing that she had a lot of love to give to others, and needed to give it up without fear. In fact, all lucid dreams are a form of integration. Ultimately, the whole point is to integrate ourselves at all levels: to integrate the body and the physical with the mind, and to integrate our intellect with the spirit, until we are fully "whole." In the mystical sense, the point of growth is not to become perfect, but rather, to become whole.

IDENTIFYING FEATURES OF A LUCID DREAM

1. Aware You Are Dreaming

The main identifying feature of a lucid dream is that you become aware that you are dreaming as you dream. This awareness brings a feeling of exhilaration and freedom.

2. Some Obstacle or Difficulty

A lucid dream often comes as an invitation to grow in some way. It presents you with an obstacle to overcome. While this obstacle appears in the disguise of someone or something fearsome or troubling, what you fear is actually some part of yourself, or some reflection in yourself. Thus, if you interact with understanding or behave with love and kindness rather than with fear or anxiety, it transforms into the opposite—something loving and friendly. If such a transformation occurs, it releases an energy in you that you can permanently draw on, reflecting an integration that took place. If you were afraid of others, now you will feel comfortable with others. If you confronted your own fear of something, you will no longer fear it, and so on. Lucid dreams are about integration at all levels—body, mind, and spirit. So if you become lucid in a dream and meet something fearsome, react to it with love and understanding, and see what happens.

3. An Opportunity to Look for the Light

Ultimately, the major type of transformation you can have in a lucid dream is a spiritual one that comes as an interaction with grace from the Divine itself. The point is to keep your conscious awareness going without becoming distracted by doing fun things like flying or exploring the territory, and without getting bogged down by how good you feel. If you get that far, look for the light and begin to interact with it. Sometimes an interaction means staying calm and simply letting whatever happens happen. This is like befriending a butterfly by staying very still and letting it alight on you. If you get too excited, it is gone in a flash. What happens next is extraordinary—a true amazing grace that needs to be experienced in order to be believed. It is as though the Divine truly speaks to you in your dreams, especially in lucid dreams that are a full-fledged Dawning of the Clear Light.

Your Way Is Unique

Having read this far, you have a good idea of how a dream comes to you to achieve a specific purpose, one of twenty-seven specific purposes. A dream can keep you aware of your body's state of health, can put you in touch with how to interact with others and give you feedback on how decisions you've made are shaping up. A dream can show you whether you are feeling strong or vulnerable, whether you need to call on your sensitive feminine traits or stronger masculine ones in a situation, and can contribute to enhancing a romantic evening with a loved one.

When life's issues loom large, a dream can help you review where you stand, help unplug past pain and trauma, and give you a sense of new potentials on your horizon. Dreams can lend energy, stimulate creative thinking and approaches, and provide a tool to practice budding skills and traits as you seek to develop your potentials.

You have even seen how frightening dreams can actually help you understand a part of yourself to which you have been blind, and how dreams of death generally reflect themes of change. You have seen how dreams heal, how they put you in touch with your spiritual self, and how they put you in touch with others by allowing you to experience what the other is experiencing. And dreams lead us into unknown territory, that of exploring death and dying, ESP, other spiritual realms, and experiences with the Divine.

If there is a common theme among these twenty-seven strands of dream exploration, it is a theme of growth. From the time we attempt to walk as toddlers, we are constantly challenged to grow beyond the present moment. Dreams are one of the tools that give us solace, insight, and strength as we grapple with life's challenge to grow. In fact, dreams may be our most natural inner tool to help ourselves along the way. It is one of my favorite tools, one I find most useful.

And yet I can acknowledge that dreams are only one tool among many to give you insight and strength in life. You are responsible for choosing not just one tool, but a variety of tools that work best for you. Because I believe that all men are brothers who are all interconnected on this journey through life, I will briefly share with you other resources that you may find helpful and meaningful for the long and winding road of growth. They are specifically listed in the appendix.

I often use self-help seminars to overcome inner blocks—aspects of myself that would have kept me from achieving my vision in life. One powerful, effective seminar to get past oneself is the Three-Day Forum offered by Landmark Education. Other educationally oriented as well as experiential seminars related to inner sight, spirituality, and creativity are offered by fine institutes such as Omega, Common Boundary, and the Edgar Cayce Foundation. You can find correspondence courses, weekend or week-long seminars exploring almost any topic related to healing, dreams, art, spirituality, meditation, aging gracefully, and psychology, and many, many more topics, by writing for information to each resource listed. Having used each of the groups and resources listed in the appendix, I can vouch for the integrity and for the quality of what each offers.

Finally, I want to wish you love and strength on your personal journey of growth. I have shared my favorite tool with you in the hope that dreams can add insight and wonder to your life, as they have to mine. I look to my dreams for understanding, solace, and, occasionally, a kick in the seat to keep me from drifting into complacency. Because each journey is a unique work of art, you will uniquely derive what you need from your own dreams, in your own way, and at your own pace.

I wish you well on your own personal journey of growth. As we collectively enter the twenty-first century, may dreams aid each of us to use our talents to add light and love to the world. May dreams help each of us, as notes in a worldwide symphony, to create the music of harmony as we build a wonderful new world that is begging to be born. As God makes the rivers flow, may we hear the inner rhythm of ourselves—as glimpsed through dreams.

APPENDIX

Groups That Offer Growth Experiences

Do you want to discover who you really are, develop your talents, and nurture your own growth psychologically, intellectually, emotionally, and spiritually? Do you want to become the best you can be? To do so, investigate the activities, seminars, and books that one or all of these offer:

LANDMARK EDUCATION

Offers a basic three-day weekend seminar (Three-Day Forum) that puts you in touch with who you really are and allows you to remove inner blocks that prevent you from achieving what you want to. Offered in the United States and worldwide. To find one nearest you, contact the headquarters in San Francisco or in New York:

Landmark Education
450 Mission St., Suite 403
San Francisco, CA 94150
1-(415) 882-6300

425 Fifth Avenue
New York, NY 10016
1-(212) 447-2100

OMEGA INSTITUTE

Offers seminars with the most widely respected people in psychology, metaphysics, and the arts. For all age levels, presented in idyllic country settings.

For catalogue information, write to:

Omega Institute
260 Lake Drive
Rhinebeck, NY 12572-3212
1-(800) 944-1001 or 1-(914) 266-4444

COMMON BOUNDARY

A private, nonprofit educational organization founded to foster communication and support for those in mental health professions, helping and healing professions, and anyone interested in the interrelationships between psychotherapy, spirituality, and creativity. If you are in the health or psychology field and are interested in mind, body, and soul links, their yearly conference is for you. Mind you, register early. Their large yearly conference is usually booked to capacity very early in the process.

Common Boundary
4304 East-West Highway
Bethesda, MD 20814

THE EDGAR CAYCE FOUNDATION
& ATLANTIC UNIVERSITY

The Edgar Cayce Foundation, also known as the A.R.E.—the Association for Research and Enlightenment, is located on the shores of Virginia Beach, Virginia. Based on the work and preserved readings of famed psychic and mystic Edgar Cayce, it offers an extensive library for research on all topics of parapsychology, a bookstore, and year-round seminars on many topics, including dreams. All this takes place in an idyllic oceanside setting.

Atlantic University, which is an outgrowth of A.R.E., offers an accredited M.A. degree in transpersonal psychology as well as a wide range of at-home study courses or on-site courses in Virginia Beach. Inquire about both A.R.E. and A.U. offerings.

A.R.E.
P.O. Box 595
Virginia Beach, VA 23451
1-(804) 428-3588

Atlantic University
67th X Atlantic Avenue
P.O. Box 595
Virginia Beach, VA
23451-0595
1-(804) 428-1512